GERTRUDE, MABEL, MAY

GWENDOLYN LEICK

GERTRUDE, MABEL, MAY

An ABC of Gertrude Stein's love triangle

GREY SUIT EDITIONS | 2019

First published in 2019 by
Grey Suit Editions, an affiliate
of Phoenix Publishing House Ltd

British Library Cataloguing in Publication Data
A C.I.P. catalogue record for this book is available from the British Library
Paperback ISBN: 978-1-903006-14-6
E-Book ISBN: 978-1-903006-15-3

Designed and typeset by Peter Stickland (UK) and Kate Hargreaves (Canada)

Printed and bound in the United Kingdom
by Hobbs the Printers Ltd.

The frontispiece is an original drawing by Dilys Bidewell

Grey Suit Editions
33 Holcombe Road
London N17 9AS
https://greysuiteditions.org/

CONTENTS

This book is dedicated to Mabel Georgia Leick,
born 2018, great-great granddaughter of Mabel Haynes.

Alcohol

I have seen so many people drunk. I do not like to drink, I have no feeling about it but my stomach does not like it and I never do like to do what my stomach does not like to do. But I have seen so many people drunk.

I was amused with Carl Van Vechten one day, he never drinks now and one day we were together with a friend who was drunk. Carl did not like to see him, and I talked to him and Carl said how can you and I said well I have had to be with so many who were drunk that I have the habit of treating them as if they were sober. Oh, that's it said Carl, well I can't, and I said Oh Carl and he said yes I know but I can't.

Well anyway I am very fond of a number of people who are always more or less drunk. There is nothing to do about it if they are always more or less drunk.

Gertrude Stein could take drunkards and she could talk to them as if they were sober, which is a remarkable skill to have. When she wanted to talk to somebody it did not matter to her if the person was in a different frame of mind to hers – by being uneducated, very old, very young, black, Chinese, mad, or drunk. Indeed, such conversations, filled with non-sequiturs and misunderstandings amused her. Sometimes when I read her plays, I feel like a sober person surrounded by people in all stages of drunkenness and then I feel like Carl Van Vechten and can't stand it. Reading Gertrude Stein, who did not drink but was surrounded by people who did, can at times induce a state of intoxication. Her writing can exhilarate, confuse, and even give you a headache.

Gertrude Stein was pleased enough with herself to do without the disinhibiting effect of drink. Rather than get drunk herself she could allow the drunkenness of others to take the edge off her own sobriety. *No one in the family ever liked drinking*, she remarked, and therefore she did not have the experience of being a child surrounded by drunken adults.

Mabel Haynes and May Bookstaver liked their cocktails and it is odd that in Gertrude Stein's various re-telling of the times they spent together, they were always drinking tea. Many years later, when Mabel Haynes lived in Boston after the war, her doctor advised her to have a drink to help with her palpitations. *The cocktail for supper seems to do all right for me. Gorgeous drink when the ingredients are pure.*

The only letter by May Bookstaver that I have been able to find, is a brief note to Mabel Haynes, included in another letter to her daughter. She sent it so that her daughter would get an idea of her old friend's continuing high spirits. May Bookstaver, looking forward to a visit by Mabel Haynes, asks, rather rhetorically: *Shall I be prepared with tea, cocktails or a highball?*

It was to be their very last meeting as Mabel Haynes was on her way to England and May Bookstaver died later that year.

Analysis

…it is so rudimentary to be analysed and see a fine substance strangely, it is so earnest to have a green point not to red but to point again.

The young women studying at Bryn Mawr were not just offered the usual liberal arts courses but classics, mathematics and science. In the 1890s, Bryn Mawr was one the most important training centres for organic chemistry, and Mabel Haynes, who graduated in Chemistry and Biology in 1898, would have analysed her compounds and specimens in the newly built Dalton Hall. At the same time Gertrude Stein was at Radcliffe, where a fellow student summed up the attitude in the psychology department: *Metaphysics! Cells and stains, that is the real science.* Much of the work there took place in the laboratory.

Gertrude Stein, with her colleague Leon Solomons, experimented with the perception of colour saturation; they also worked together on automatic writing. Gertrude Stein published the results of their work in a paper entitled "Cultivated Motor Automatism: A Study of Character in relation to attention in 1898" where she found the difference between 'normal' and 'hysterical' subjects to lie in the latter's inability to retain attention. Gertrude Stein liked working in laboratories; she was attending classes in biology as well, and when she came to Johns Hopkins Medical School, she much preferred working on slides of brain tissue to attending patients. She discovered that she could apply the dissociated scrutiny of laboratory work to the study of character and type without having to submit to the male-dominated framework of formal academia. What she had acquired doing such work was patience and a great relish for observing and analysing minute variations and differences.

Transferred to the production of literature, this methodology accounts for the proliferation of repetitions with small variants observable only to those paying close attention. It also involved setting up pairs of opposites (such as the resistant/independent 'bottom nature' in *The Makings of Americans*) that lends itself to combinations and subsets, or in a more undifferentiated 'mixing up' of the various components. She made the attempt to account for 'everything', *describing every one, every one who could or would or had been living'*, a truly grand Enlightenment project, the classifying and observing and analysing and describing of all the traits that make human beings human beings.

When Gertrude Stein turned her attention to paintings, and especially to modern paintings, she did not analyse paintings. She made herself respond to paintings in a way that could not be verbalised. She liked a painting, or she found it interesting, or often, she found the painter of the painting interesting, but she was not interested in analysing paintings. In this respect she differed from her brother Leo Stein, who submitted the paintings he found interesting to close scrutiny so as to be able to say something about them. In their salon at 27, rue de Fleurus he talked about paintings a great deal. Gertrude Stein tried to apply what she found exciting in paintings to her writing. She analysed what made Picasso or Matisse such good painters in her eyes, but she did not offer descriptions or judgements of their work.

There is no doubt that Gertrude Stein knew about Sigmund Freud's psychoanalytical theories, given that her brother Leo Stein took such a passionate interest in them. Lisa Ruddick commented on the appearance of Freudian notions in certain passages of *The Making of Americans*, where Gertrude Stein writes on *repressed active being or repressed loving being.* However, she did not refer to Freud in her notebooks and refuted the idea that her writing allowed her unconscious to emerge: *there is no demarcation between my conscious and my unconscious self as I am my conscious self in other words there aint no such animal.*

Gertrude Stein was not interested in being analysed. She confided in her friends, especially Emma Lootz Erving and Mabel Weeks, and wrote them long letters that analysed her feelings. It has been suggested that much of her subsequent early writing, especially *The Makings of Americans,* could be seen as her own attempt creating an analytical manner in order to confront the traumas of her childhood and adolescence.

Leo Stein was fascinated with his own neuroses and he did seek the help of psychoanalysts while he stayed in New York during the First World War. However, he found *that they talked too much and had too many opinions* and he began to analyse himself, emulating Sigmund Freud. In 1927 he wrote a review of Trigant Burrows's book *The Social Basis of Consciousness,* entitled 'Psychoanalysis Psychoanalyzed,' and he began to write the story of his long years of self-analysis.

He diagnosed himself as suffering from 'serious neurosis' from his early youth that prevented him from ever finishing anything he set out to do. He never completed it.

Mabel Dodge, who had befriended Leo Stein and Gertrude Stein when they still lived together in 27, rue de Fleurus, and who entertained Gertrude Stein and Alice B. Toklas and Leo Stein at her magnificent Villa Curonia, turned to psychoanalyst Smith Ely Jeliffe, in an attempt to create within her a strong 'maternal self' and develop an ability for vaginal orgasms. However, she broke off therapy with Smith Ely Jeliffe and turned to A.A. Brill to help her overcome depression. He encouraged her to write, and she began at once to write her autobiography. *Intimate Memoirs* was published between 1933 to 1937. Even more voluminous than Gertrude Stein's 'fat book' *The Making of Americans*, it is written in a conventional, fluent style but startled contemporaries by the frank, almost clinical analysis of her sexual experiences. Mabel Haynes considered herself to be neither hysterical nor neurotic and like a good New Englander resisted probing her repressions. She may have wished her clearly neurotic daughters to get professional help but that was something her conservative second husband would never permit. They were to cope with their unexamined and un-analysed lives as best as they could. *Analysis is a womanly word.*

Appetite

And now then as to appetite. We have a very good appetite.

A person with a keen or good or even huge appetite, such as Gertrude Stein is said to have been, is called appetitive, which rhymes nicely with repetitive. There is repetition in appetite, which renews itself at intervals dependent on digestion, throughout the daily rhythms of appetite for breakfast, for a simple snack, for luncheon, tea and cakes, and supper. Gertrude Stein's appetite was up to the heavy Jewish cuisine of her parent's household in East Oakland or that of her relatives' in Baltimore. She liked lots of butter and lots of gravy. Her appetite could also do justice to what she was served in Spain or Italy and indeed France where a succession of cooks worked to satisfy the hearty appetite for food that Gertrude Stein had. Brillat-Savarin would say that this set her up well enough to do justice to her appetite for her work, her prodigious task of writing.

Being appetitive does not just mean having an appetite for food however appetising that might be, but having an appetite for living, for loving, for walking, for sleeping, for arguing, for looking, for listening, for talking, for just sitting quietly with a dog on the lap, for smelling, for touching, for tasting, for drinking, for anything one desires to do with one's body with a view of getting enjoyment. By all accounts Gertrude Stein was a woman with just such an appetite for living and this too fed her appetite for writing. She was as much a *gourmand* as a *gourmet* and her writing is a varied fare, from hearty to dainty, from salty to sweet, from homely to exotic and it needs a good appetite to do justice to what is served. It can happen that her writing does not feel appetising but indigestible and some people never recover from Steinian dyspepsia. Like all rich fare it takes getting used to and is safer in small portions, but she would not expect us to swallow all hook line and sinker.

Mabel Neathe, the fictionalised Mabel Haynes in *Q.E.D.* is described as having a peculiar face; *pale yellow brown in complexion and thin in the temples and forehead; heavy about the mouth, not with the weight of flesh but with the drag of un-idealised passion, continually sated and continually craving.*

The drag of un-idealised passion was irksome to the virtuous Adele who is taken unawares by the own appetite for the sort of passion Mabel Neathe indulges in. To be sated continually and to crave continually is the natural state of someone with an appetite, and Adele is resentful of the fact that Mabel Neathe is able to do this in respect to Helen, the object of desire for both characters.

Mabel Haynes' ability to work up an appetite seems to have been as prodigious as Gertrude Stein's and not just for May Bookstaver but for living and loving, for voracious reading and stimulating conversation. Mabel Haynes however, had more of an appetite for learning and acquiring knowledge than Gertrude Stein had, and less for food and none for cakes. She thus retained her long and angular New England body all her life while Gertrude Stein delighted in the bulk her appetite created. Alice B. Toklas was appetitive too and she made herself appetising for Gertrude Stein and she was careful to maintain her waist and slimness. James Mellow, the biographer of Gertrude Stein describes Alice B. Toklas in her dotage, still appetitive: *With the collection impounded and little means of support, Alice was in straitened circumstances. She was in her mid-80's suffering from arthritis and barely able to see. Nevertheless, she maintained a healthy appetite. Her tastes could often run to the exotic-- a yearning for fresh peaches in mid-November--and, with the true conviction of a gourmet, she insisted that the shopping be done at Fauchon, the most expensive green-grocer in Paris. When funds were at a particularly low ebb, friends would supply the maids with the distinctive black and white Fauchon bags and send them shopping around the corner.*

Arguments

Quarrelling to me is very interesting.

Gertrude Stein was always more interested in her own argument than the arguments made by others, and if they persisted too insistently to argue their case, she found them tiresome and stopped seeing them, as Georges Hugnet, Bravig Imbs, Virgil Thomson, Mabel Weeks, and many others, discovered.

What matters is that I am right, and you'll think so in time. Insisting on being right is one way of ending an argument and beginning a quarrel.

Mostly everyone is sometimes quarrelling with someone. Quarrelling as I am saying is to me very interesting. Beginning is interesting and ending is interesting to me as I have been saying…Quarrelling is not letting those having attacking be winning by attacking, those having resisting being the be winning by resisting, those having dependent being be winning by dependent being, this having engulfing being be winning by engulfing being. This is quarrelling in living. There is a great deal of quarrelling in living, that is reasonably certain and that is a very natural thing as certainly very many are not winning with the being in them.

Since there is, as she says, a great deal of quarrelling in living, an understanding of the 'bottom nature', one's own bottom nature and that of the one one might be quarrelling with, would be advantageous. There are a lot of quarrels in Gertrude Stein's early pieces of writing, in *Three Lives, Q.E.D.* and the *Making of Americans* and some of these quarrels were quarrels between Gertrude Stein and May Bookstaver and between Gertrude Stein and Mabel Haynes, who was not one to let sleeping dogs lie, as she says of herself in a letter: *I am too violent in my opinions to not blow up and express my opinions, which does no good and harms me.*

Aristocracy

In the American woman the aristocracy had become vulgarised and the power weakened. Having gained nothing moral, weakened by lack of adequate development of its strongest instincts, this nature expressed itself in a face no longer dangerous but only unillumined and unmoral, but yet with enough suggestion of the older aristocratic use to keep it from being merely contemptibly dishonest.

In this manner Gertrude Stein introduced the character of Mabel Neathe in her early novel *Q.E.D.,* a character based on Mabel Haynes, a Bostonian and fellow student at Johns Hopkins Medical School. Mabel Haynes' lineage on her father's side could be traced back eight hundred years, well beyond the ancestor who had come ashore on the Bay of Massachusetts on August 15th, 1635. This background, as much as her father's considerable wealth and her Bryn Mawr education, informed her demeanour and sense of self.

Gertrude Stein's *alter ego* in the novel 'Adele', whose origins and habits *suggested a land of laziness and sunshine*, embodied an American personage tempered by self-righteousness and puritanism strangely at odds with the land of laziness and sunshine. She challenges the prerogatives of an upper class she considers immured against moral scruples. Adele professes to defend the ideals of middle-class decency: *I simply contend that the middle-class ideal which demands that people be affectionate, respectable, honest and content, that they avoid excitements and cultivate serenity is the ideal that appeals to me, it is in short, the ideal of affectionate family life, of honourable business methods.* One might take this as an example of class antagonism played out within the privilege of a republican playing-field levelled by capitalism. Yet the argument is also one that resonates in much of the American fiction of the period, the question of what makes the uniquely American contribution to civilization and more specifically, what is it that American women, especially those privileged by breeding, education and wealth, can do to distinguish themselves. Gertrude Atherton's impulsive and original heroines, for instance, some sprung from the southern Spanish aristocracy, must learn to control their inclination to sensuality in order to be worthy of a Yankee male whose ideals are based on Puritan self-restraint; a theme equally important to the writer Constance Fenimore Woolson. Against the background of the Civil War, the question of what constituted real nobility as opposed to decadent reliance on traditional privilege and how this was translated into the domestic sphere to which women were still largely confined, had been portrayed as part of the struggle for the nation's soul. On a more superficial level, it could be reduced to matter of comportment and manners, in the mode of Mrs John Sherwood, whose *Manners and Social Usage* (1884) became a bestseller. Touching upon the *mischievous tendencies of our society*, such as *the vulgar worship of wealth*, impoliteness and fast manners in young men and women, she set out to mend these faults that impede an elegant society from forming in America: *With us, the manners of our people must proceed from their morals; and, as we have no queen, no court, no nobility, to set our fashions, we must set them ourselves.* So enthusiastic was the response to her advice and so assiduously it seems to have been taken on board that some years later Mrs Sherwood could assert an oxymoronic exhortation: *There is a native-born American aristocracy to which all should aspire to belong,* while adding that it is American women who constitute its finest creation, provided they have absorbed her admonitions: *The original and beautiful American women have a vivacity and wit that the older civilizations have lost. She should never lose her originality. But she should study to be low-voiced, sweet-voiced, calm, quiet, and thorough-bred.*

In Gertrude Stein's novel *Q.E.D.,* the object of Adele's passionate interest is Helen Thomas, *the American version of the English handsome girl (….) a woman of passions but not emotions, capable of long sustained action, incapable of regrets. In this American version it amounted at its best to no more than a brave bluff.* The real 'Helen Thomas', May Bookstaver, was a Colonial Dame of the seventh generation on her mother's side and had the credentials of an Old East pedigree. Her insouciance as to how her actions could be judged was both attractive and repellent to 'Adele' *alias* Gertrude Stein.

Mabel Haynes, herself a New Englander with a long pedigree, alone in Vienna, in 1904, sought introductions to as good a society as her standing and her wealth could procure, and she formed lifelong friendships with men and women from ancient Austrian lineages.

Gertrude Stein kept her sense of solid bourgeois respectability despite her friendships with some of the more dissolute artists and bohemians. *The Saturday evenings in those early days were frequented by many hungarians, quite a number of germans, quite a few mixed nationalities, a very thin sprinkling of americans and practically no english. These were to commence later, and with them came aristocracy of all countries and even some royalty.*

In the 1920s the social set of Gertrude Stein and Alice B. Toklas began to mix cautiously with the Left Bank feminists and Lesbians around Natalie Clifford Barney. Natalie Barney's companion and 'eternal mate', Élisabeth de Gramont, the Duchess of Clermont-Tonnerre, became, so the Autobiography suggests, a special friend. She inspired the short-haired look Gertrude Stein favoured thereafter: *We did give a great many parties in those days and the Duchess of Clermont-Tonnerre came very often. She and Gertrude Stein pleased one another. They were entirely different in life education and interests, but they delighted in each other's understanding. They were also the only two women whom they met who still had long hair. Gertrude Stein had always worn hers well on top of her head, an ancient fashion that she had never changed. Madame de Clermont-Tonnerre came in very late to one of the parties, almost everyone had gone, and her hair was cut. Do you like it, said Madame de Clermont-Tonnerre. I do, said Gertrude Stein. Well, said Madame de Clermont-Tonnerre, if you like it and my daughter likes it and she does like it I am satisfied. That night Gertrude Stein said to me, I guess I will have to too. Cut it off she said and I did.*

In the French Revolution aristocrats had their hair cut or shorn before they had their heads cut off by the guillotine.

Pardon the fretful autocrat who voices discontent. Pardon the colored water-color which is burnt. Pardon the intoning of the heavy way. Pardon the aristocrat who has not come to stay. Pardon the abuse which was begun. Pardon the yellow egg which has run. Pardon nothing yet, pardon what is wet, forget the opening now, and close the door again.

Aunts

...those cheerful pleasant little people, her uncles and aunts.

Gertrude Stein's mother did not get on with her sister-in-law Pauline, while they lived next to each other in Allegheny, Pittsburgh. The competitive tension between the brothers and their wives was such that they ended up living on opposite sides of the United States. Daniel Stein, Gertrude Stein's father, moving to East Oakland and Solomon Stein to New York. Gertrude Stein wrote of aunt Pauline as Mrs Henry Dehning in "The Making of Americans": *She was the quintessence of loud-voiced good-looking prosperity. She was a fair heavy woman, well-looking and firmly compacted and hitting the ground as she walked with the same hard jerk with which she rebuked her husband. Yes Mrs Dehning was a woman whose rasping insensibility to gentle courtesy deserved the prejudice one cherished against her, but she was a woman, to do her justice, generous and honest, one whom one might like better the more one saw her less.* This aunt was formidable, one to be reckoned with, and when Gertrude Stein had bought her first car during the First World War, in order to join the American Fund for the French Wounded, she called the Ford truck Auntie, *after Gertrude Stein's aunt Pauline who always behaved admirably in emergencies and behaved fairly well most times if she was properly flattered.*

The *cheerful pleasant little people* were the Baltimore siblings of Gertrude Stein's mother Amelia, especially Fanny Bachrach, who married well and was living the easy and rich life that Amelia Stein had always remembered as having lived herself. Gertrude Stein liked this aunt: *I was very fond of my aunts and uncles on my mother's side particularly the one named Fanny, Fanny is a nice name, I do not quite know why but it is a nice name.* Fanny Bachrach had told her how to save with dignity by counting *one one one* and keeping the separate ones in purses and in this way, *you could keep everybody well fed and prettily dressed and the furniture renewed whenever the covers grew shabby.*

This cheerful and pleasant aunt was also censorious of unconventionality and tried to find good Jewish husbands for her orphaned nieces who had come to live with her after their mother's death. Bertha Stein soon saw herself married; Gertrude Stein escaped to Radcliffe.

Mabel Haynes had four sisters who married and had children and she was aunt to five nephews and nine nieces. Mabel Haynes liked and admired the son of her eldest sister Alice, John Haynes Holmes, the Unitarian minister and pacifist, for his eloquence, intelligence and good looks. She did not think much of her sister's Cora's son, Kirkland, who *never made a steady go at anything… just a drunkard, always in debt, a real bum.* Her favourite niece was his sister Margaret, who looked after Mabel Haynes when she returned to Boston. As far as Mabel Haynes was concerned, her niece's unhappiness (and alcoholism) was the fault of her mother's selfish behaviour, as Mabel Haynes' explained in a letter to her daughter: *It would never occur to Aunt Cora that she alone is responsible for this. Margaret was always a weak character and fancy just being at the beck and call of your Mother for over 50 years. Aunt Cora said to me once that no mother could be more considerate. Meanwhile she has literally sucked out Margaret's life-blood like a vampire. It wasn't that she had any hard work to do but just be there. Perhaps you remember that I told you once I could be any servant rather than a maid hanging on the ringing of a bell. Well, she snapped up at last.* Mabel Haynes was also fond of Margaret's sister Marie, who was crippled, and who, she wrote, *bears her physical inabilities with great courage.* She was never given to sentimentality when it came to family and her forthrightness in pointing out flaws of character, weaknesses and self-indulgence made her a formidable and intimidating aunt to those nephews and nieces of whom she disapproved.

Gertrude Stein's brother Michael Stein had one son, Allan, who was born on March 27th 1896, while Gertrude Stein was at Radcliffe. Since Michael Stein moved his family to Paris in 1903, Allan saw quite a lot of his aunt Gertrude.

He was to get to know all the artists his father, mother and aunt knew then, and Matisse and Picasso painted his portraits. In several photographs Allan, the boy, stands or sits next to his parents and his aunt. She later considered him as her heir, writing in 1925: *It is best to support Allan Allan will Allan Allan is it best to support Allan Allan patriarchal poetry patriarchal poetry is it best to support Allan Allan will Allan best…Allan will patriarchal poetry Allan will.*

Gertrude Stein's sister Bertha Raffel had two children, Daniel, born in 1898 and Gertrude, born in 1900. They all lived in Baltimore. Gertrude Stein wrote one of her portrait poems about Daniel - "Dan Raffel. A Nephew". It is as opaque as any portrait and not likely that Gertrude Stein had ever met this nephew, as she had no interest in her sister or her offspring.

May Bookstaver had a paternal aunt, Catherine E. Bookstaver, who died in 1907. Her parents had no other surviving children. She may have known some of the nephews and nieces of her husband's eleven siblings, though his best-known brother, the playwright Edward Knoblock, never married and lived with his equally unmarried and childless sister, named Gertrude.

Automobiles and airplanes

Europe and America and railroad and water and stage coach and walking and horse back and in every there was no astonishment and that is the way war is.

When Gertrude Stein, May Bookstaver and Mabel Haynes were growing up they were driven about in horse-drawn vehicles, as their parents were affluent enough to keep horses and carriages.

This photograph taken in 1883 shows such a conveyance, a shiny black four-wheeled Rockaway Coupé, pulled by two horses. The seven-year-old Mabel Haynes, in a short dress and black stockings, sits proudly on the driver's bench next to her father, John C. Haynes. I do not know what type of carriage Daniel Stein, Gertrude Stein's father, kept while they were living in East Oakland. At any rate, children then were used to being pulled along by horses and used to seeing the swishing and flicking of their tails, to see the steam rising from their nostrils on cold days. They heard the clattering of hooves, the rattling of the wheels, and they were used to the smell of horse sweat and horse dung. Gertrude Stein wrote a children's book in 1940, when horse drawn carriages had all but disappeared from city streets. A horse called Active pulls a milk wagon and then a little cannon and then a plough. And this horse *just one day he would be an automobile not a new one an old old one and he was one, he was an automobile and an automobile never has a name and it never has a mane and it has rubber shoes not an*

iron one and finding rubber shoes does not mean anything like finding iron horse-shoes did and was the end of everything.

Gertrude Stein, Mabel Haynes and May Bookstaver were fourteen years old, in 1888, when Bertha Benz drove with her two children from one German town to another in a new kind of vehicle, the Benz Patent Motor car. This automobile had replaced the horse with a single wheel in front and a small combustion engine tucked under the seat of a two-wheeled wooden buggy with a high, upholstered seat. Bertha Benz had made a case for modern men and women to drive automobiles, and soon many modern and wealthy men and some modern and wealthy women began to own and drive automobiles, which looked less and less like carriages or buggies.

On August 15th 1906, the New York Times published an announcement that Mary Aletta Bookstaver was *quietly married at noon today to Charles Edward Knoblauch* and furthermore that *Mr and Mrs Knoblauch started this afternoon for Boston, and will soon set sail for Europe, on an extended automobile trip.* The very first thing this modern American couple did was to motor around Europe together. They had their car loaded onto the ocean liner, and rather than work out train timetables and organise luggage they could dash about Europe on whatever serviceable roads they could find and stop over wherever they wanted.

Before they did that Mabel Haynes had been driving her own automobile around Boston. Once she had become the wife of the Austrian officer, Captain Heissig, she had her American car shipped across the Atlantic. Mabel Haynes had written to Gertrude Stein on April 1st 1907 that now that car had arrived from Boston she could *skip about the country in summer.* It would have been an unusual sight in the villages of Austrian Galicia to see her skipping about the country-lanes. The story of grandmother Mabel causing quite a stir as she drove her American car, was often told when I was a child.

During the pioneering days age of motoring, before the First World War, there were few traffic rules, no driving tests had to be passed, no compulsory insurance needed to be purchased, no fines were issued for parking. When Mabel Haynes and May Bookstaver drove about, petrol stations were few and far between and so were garages to repair vehicles that broke down frequently. Mabel Haynes liked to say that she had spent more time under her car than in it. However, the modern women would drive themselves and would master the difficulties of the modern machine. Now they did not have to look at the tails of horses as they drove along, they did not have to breathe the sweat of the horses and fend off the flies their sweat attracted. Instead they could look straight ahead as they whizzed about at the speed of seventy miles an hour, smelling the petrol and oil and hearing the hum of engines instead of hooves trotting. They wore topcoats or leather dusters from Burberry's or Aquascutum, and donned goggles and motoring veils to protect their eyes and faces from oil smuts. The women able to skip about the country were few, and their cars and motoring clothes could be seen as just as conspicuous a manner of showing status as carriages and fine horses.

At the time when Mabel Haynes and May Bookstaver did their motoring excursions in Europe, Gertrude Stein did not have an automobile. She did not need a car to drive about in Paris since she liked walking for hours. But when during the First World War she decided to contribute to the efforts to help: *She was enthusiastic, she was always enthusiastic, and she said, get a car. But where, we asked. From America, she said. But how, we said. Ask somebody, she said, and Gertrude Stein did, and in a few months the ford car came.*

The car that Gertrude got by asking her brother-in-law in America was not the sort to skip about in the country with. It was a truck rather than an automobile and called 'Auntie Pauline' after a competent member of her family. She got this car to bring supplies to wounded American soldiers in various hospitals across the country. Her Ford model T truck had no automatic transmission or power steering. It took strength and skill to do the double-clutch gearshift. Gertrude Stein had strength and mechanical talent. She could fieldstrip her truck, and she loved driving it. After the war Gertrude Stein got another car, an automobile she called Godiva, *because of its nakedness of all amenities* and she drove that around Paris and around the French countryside. She was a reckless driver, as her friend W. G. Rodgers remembered: *She would regard corners as something to cut and another car as something to pass and she could scare the daylight out of all concerned.*

While Mabel Haynes bundled her children and nursemaids into her motorcar, Gertrude Stein's companion was Alice B. Toklas who could also drive but preferred to be driven. Sitting in the car and waiting for Alice B. Toklas to come back from an errand, Gertrude Stein *would pull out a pencil and a scrap of paper. She was inspired by the traffic on busy Parisian streets. Automobiles stopped and started with a rhythm that thrummed right into poetry and prose.* Gertrude Stein's automobile was a *little old Ford car.* It suited her to drive a simple car as it suited her to live a simple life. She liked it as an example of the American ingenuity. The car inspired her movie script, *Deux sœurs qui ne sont pas sœurs.* The scenario involves two women driving a car, clearly based on Gertrude Stein and Alice B. Toklas. When Gertrude Stein found herself flush with the money from *The Autobiography of*

Alice B. Toklas some of it was spent on getting a new car, an eight-cylinder version.

Automobiles were, as Gertrude said, *the end of progress on earth*. In fact, too many cars clogging the city road have reduced the speed once more to that of horse-drawn carriages. The stopping and starting of cars at rush hour inspires rage rather than abstract poetry. Too many rules restrict the freedom of movement. But that was not what Gertrude Stein meant. Having been taken up in an aeroplane when she and Alice B Toklas toured the United States with Gertrude Stein lecturing on modern art, she declared that that the earth seen from an aeroplane is more splendid than the earth seen from an automobile. Gertrude Stein went on an aeroplane in 1934 after the *Autobiography of Alice B. Toklas* had made her famous. They went from city to city and she talked about modern art at many universities and everywhere they went, Gertrude Stein was being photographed, waving from the steps of airplanes, as she called them, or getting into an automobile. In Chicago she rented a *self-drive car* for the first time and she found the whole procedure, from getting the car to having it fixed surprisingly simple and it confirmed her opinion that *everything in America is just as easy as that,* without bureaucracy and lengthy waits and all kinds of fuss she was used to in Europe. It made her realise too that the road signs in America relied on words rather than symbols and *mostly words of one syllable. No left turn, that took me some time so much so that I did one.* It made her think of words and language not of driving, but the policeman let her off with a warning. Automobiles, as the policeman in Chicago said, can get you killed. Gertrude Stein never had a serious accident. Naturally her cars broke down every now and then but she came to no harm. Nor did Mr and Mrs Wharton, Mr and Mrs Knoblauch or Mabel Haynes.

Gertrude Stein had enjoyed the experience of flying during her American tour and professed to have been sanguine about the dangers: *just now a great many are getting killed in the airplanes but when we were there they told us that major accidents never happened and certainly they did not happen to us, we liked wherever we went on an airplane.* Gertrude Stein never flew again, she did not go round the world and living in the countryside during the war she never experienced aerial bombardment, unlike Mabel Haynes, who stayed in Austria and lived in Graz when the city was being bombed, some 57 times, in 1945. In October 1946, some months after Gertrude Stein's death, Mabel Haynes, who had never flown before, boarded a Lockheed Constellation aircraft to fly from Vienna to New York City. She wrote about this experience in a letter from Boston from October 3rd to her daughter Gabrielle who had stayed behind in Austria: *That air journey was awful to me, uncomfortable and alarming. I discovered through Hector the cause of the delay. The machines of this "Constellation" type had all to be made over, as they discovered a construction error when one crashed here some months ago, just after starting the engine fell out! I really had to laugh and told Hector I should have been still more nervous had I realized that the bottom of the damned contraption might fall out.*

Alice Babette Toklas

(30th April 1877 to 7th March 1967)

Trembling was all living, living was all loving, some one was then the other one.

Alice B. Toklas, like Gertrude Stein, came from a family of Jewish immigrants, Polish in her case. In her own memoir she speaks of her maternal forebears, the Levinskys, who had come to California to mine gold before turning to more profitable ranching. She does not mention her father's ancestors who appear in Gertrude Stein's *The Autobiography of Alice B. Toklas* as coming *from polish patriotic stock*. Both accounts stress the genteel upbringing that the young Alice B. Toklas experienced and her progressive education. She learnt German and some Polish and was sent to good girls' school. Once the family, which included a younger brother, Clarence (born in 1870), had moved to Seattle in 1889, Alice B. Toklas attended the music conservatory. Then her mother, Emma Toklas, became ill; like Gertrude Stein's mother Amelia she was diagnosed with cancer. Alice B. Toklas, eighteen at the time, was to stay at home in order to look after her sick mother and her little brother. Her diversion from domestic responsibilities were friendships with young women, among them Annette Rosenshine, a cousin three years younger, who adored Alice B. Toklas. After her grandfather's death in 1904 the Toklas family moved to a smaller house, Clarence had grown up, and Alice B. Toklas began to think of a life of her own: *she did not like it all then as she did not like so much dying and she did not like any of the living she was doing then.* With her friend Harriet Levy she went to galleries, met artists and writers. She had all the accomplishments of a perfect housewife and gracious hostess and would have made a most eligible wife had she wished to be married. The great earthquake of 1906 helped her to get away. Gertrude Stein's brother Michael and his wife Sarah, who were then living in Paris, went to San Francisco in order to see if any of their properties had been damaged.

Harriet Levy knew Sarah Stein and hoped to persuade her to take Alice B. Toklas and herself with her back to Paris, but neither of them had enough money and Annette Rosenshine went instead. Through Annette Rosenshine's letters from Paris Alice B. Toklas first heard about Gertrude Stein, of her *dynamic magnetism…the beauty of her splendid head…[the] intellectual luminous quality [that] shone on her face.* And it was through the letters that Alice B. Toklas sent to Annette Rosenshine, which Gertrude Stein had persuaded her to let her read, that Gertrude Stein first became aware of Alice B. Toklas. She used these letters as material for her investigation into people's characters, which she worked out in her 'Book of Diagrams'. Her first impressions of Alice B. Toklas, partly informed by having read her letters to Annette Rosenshine, when she had, rather timidly, called at 27, rue de Fleurus, having made it to Paris in August 1907, were harsh: *A liar of the most sordid, unillumined, undramatic, unimaginative prostitute type, coward, ungenerous, conscienceless, mean, vulgarly triumphant and remorseless, caddish, in short just plain rotten low.*

Alice B. Toklas however, quietly, and with her genteel discretion, knew how to make herself agreeable. Gertrude Stein was looking for someone to type her manuscripts; Etta Cone from Baltimore had done some of it, not very well. Alice B. Toklas set to work, making a daily trip to the rue de Fleurus. Her comments about what she was typing pleased Gertrude Stein but they were both still wary of each other. In the summer of 1909, Alice B. Toklas and Harriet Levy joined the Steins who were holidaying in Fiesole, staying with Gertrude Stein at the Villa Ricci. It was there, during the hot summer weeks in Tuscany, that Alice B. Toklas, not desisting in following Gertrude Stein's arduous rambling across the Tuscan countryside, not weakening, always present and perceptive, and once, discreetly relieving herself of her *silk combinations and stockings,* won the profession of undying love from Gertrude Stein and agreed to be her ever loving wife. Alice B. Toklas was dissolved with happiness: *Day after day she wept because of the new love that come into her life.*

On their return to Paris, having moved into an apartment with Harriet Levy in the rue Notre Dame des Champs, she set out to make herself ever more useful to Gertrude Stein. *Three Lives* had just been published and Alice B. Toklas took out a subscription to Romeike's press-clipping service, so as not to miss any reviews. Every morning she was typing the *Making of Americans.* Instead of hitting the ivory keys of a piano she now hit the keys of the newly purchased Smith Premier typewriter. Her skill on it was to serve only Gertrude Stein; her own letters had to be typed by someone else, and she gave the machine away after Gertrude Stein died: *I got a Gertrude Stein technique, like playing Bach. My fingers were adapted only to Gertrude Stein's work.* She spent more and more time at the studio. She moved into a small room at 27, rue de Fleurus, where she spent the winter of 1909 and 1910 - *not too uncomfortably.* When Mabel Dodge visited the

Steins in 1911, she found Alice B. Toklas well installed and described her first impression: *She was slight and dark, with beautiful gray eyes hung with black lashes – she had a drooping, Jewish nose, and her eyelids drooped, and the corners of her red mouth and the lobes of her ears drooped under the black, folded Hebraic hair, weighted down, as they were, with long, heavy Oriental earrings.*

The small room given over to the use of Alice B. Toklas may not have been uncomfortable but living in the atmosphere of growing tension between Leo and Gertrude Stein was tiresome. Leo Stein was not able to see any merit in his sister's work, finding it too hermetic. Alice B. Toklas did see the merit of Gertrude Stein's work, and her praise and intelligent comments on the writing made her steadily more dear to Gertrude Stein.

She became as much as fixture of 27, rue de Fleurus, in her quietly observant way and polished manners, as Leo Stein's looming presence and flows of rhetoric had been before. Thus Alice B. Toklas made herself an indispensable part of Gertrude Stein's world; the ever-varying company of artists, expatriates, the sundry visitors curious to see the paintings displayed on the walls. She contributed her own discrete and vigilant presence. Alice B. Toklas was to guard her place at the centre of Gertrude Stein's loving devotion as fiercely as she thought necessary by eliminating all those who might make a claim to Gertrude Stein's affection in such a way as to jeopardise her prerogatives. Leo Stein had to leave, which he did, for good, in 1913. It was a pattern that continued throughout their lives together. She would not discourage visitors at first, but when they failed to meet her requirements or expectations, she would quietly cancel further visits. Mabel Haynes saw Gertrude Stein on a few occasions in the 1920s, but as she failed to get the name right, leaving greetings simply to 'Miss Thekla', she was among those who were not asked again.

The two women settled into a rhythm of living that was equitably divided in order to serve the genius of Gertrude Stein, which Alice B. Toklas claims to have recognized immediately. They delighted in each other's love and they delighted in the delight they took in their bodies, and the intensity of their intimacy permeates much of Gertrude Stein's writing of the time, especially *Lifting Belly.*

Alice B. Toklas preferred, in public, to be self-effacing; to be seen as 'the secretary'; the one who served. Alone with Gertrude Stein, she was *wifey,* but by no means submissive or dominated, as so many wives are; in a little Christmas message Alice B. Toklas wrote to Gertrude Stein, she affirms the mutuality and reciprocity of their intimacy:

> *Baby boy*
> *You're no toy*
> *But a strong-strong husband*
> *I don't obey*
> *Do this you say*
> *Well do it together and*
> *That's the way we obey*

People who saw them together, such as W.R. Rogers, who first knew them during the Great War, and later visited them in Bilignin, could observe a rather less delicately balanced system of power in their daily lives, and the battles that were fought between them; with Alice B. Toklas, always practical, being *always right* and Gertrude Stein being *naughty.*

When historical contingencies, such as the outbreak of the Great War, threatened to disrupt this happy quotidian existence, Alice B. Toklas summoned all resourcefulness to meet the challenge; subtly encouraging Gertrude Stein's impulses so as to direct them along the most propitious course – such as leaving Paris for Spain, and living in Palma de Mallorca, in an idyll fragrant with tuberoses, where Gertrude Stein would write her most lyrical *florilèges* in her honour. Once the reality of the war intruded upon their retreat in such a way as to spoil their contentment, she did not withhold her support in doing something useful, like many other women of means did at the time. And so Alice B. Toklas sat next to Gertrude Stein in the Ford truck while they delivered supplies to wounded soldiers in the south of France. Alice B. Toklas could, when required, buckle up.

She was also ready to take on further responsibilities in order to ensure that the 'babies' that had been made: the many manuscripts that had been written, typed and stored in a cupboard, would no longer languish in obscurity but become available to the world of readers. The solution, to start their own press and to oversee the whole production and distribution, would not have been possible without the full collaboration of Alice B. Toklas.

This entailed considerable labour and effort, as well as money, which could only come from the sale of some of the paintings. In only three years, between 1930 and 1933, Plain Editions brought out five books *Lucy Church Amiably* (1930), *Before the Flowers of Friendship Faded Friendship Faded* (1931), *How to Write* (1931), *Operas and Plays* (1932), and *Matisse, Picasso & Gertrude Stein* (1933). The books could be sent to friends, critics; they could be displayed in some bookshops; they did not sell well. Entertaining and feeding guests, especially at the country-house in Bilignin, where people stayed for days, was expensive. She began to nudge Gertrude Stein into trying out a new way of writing, to broaden her appeal so as to make her writing as popular as their *young friends'* – Hemingway, Fitzgerald. Gertrude Stein was not interested; *it does not bother me to delight them*, she declared. Alice B. Toklas got her way eventually, not least because she had been deeply upset by the discovery of Gertrude Stein's manuscript from 1903, of *Q.E.D.*, which traced her unhappy love for May Bookstaver. Gertrude Stein had been keeping silent about this affair and about the manuscript that had been buried underneath many others. *When Alice B. Toklas read the novel and then the letters, she became enraged. She destroyed the correspondence and forbade Gertrude to publish the book.* Alice B. Toklas had to be pacified. Gertrude Stein relented and wrote *The Autobiography of Alice B. Toklas* as a peace offering, written in *money-making* mode. Alice B. Toklas does not mention any of this in her own memoir; in fact she hardly mentions the *Autobiography*. It was a great success and it also served link Gertrude Stein and Alice B. Toklas forever in public consciousness; with Alice B. Toklas' judicious and sometimes malicious gossip given free rein so to frame her essential goodness, as well as the genius of Gertrude Stein. Alice B. Toklas, placated, joined Gertrude Stein on her triumphant American tour, where she made sure that none of the crowd who had been around Gertrude Stein between 1900 and 1903 would come anywhere near them.

During the Second World War they left their belongings in the flat in rue Christine, to which they had moved once the lease on 27, rue de Fleurus expired, and stayed in the relative safety of the countryside, in their rented manor house in Bilignin. It was an anxious time, and they had to cope with Germans being quartered in the house, with money being short, with worries about friends and relatives, and not least their own safety in Nazi-occupied France. When the war was over and they returned to Paris, their flat became a popular haunt of American soldiers.

They resumed their life in Paris, surrounded by the familiar objects and paintings, which had also survived. Gertrude Stein died a year later, on July 27th 1946. Alice B. Toklas was now a widow. She had their old friend Francis Rose design a simple headstone for Gertrude Stein's grave at the cemetery of Père Lachaise.

Gertrude Stein had appointed Carl van Vechten to be her literary executor, willing him to publish all her unpublished writings. Alice B. Toklas encouraged writers interested in Gertrude Stein, supplied materials and gave interviews to Elizabeth Sprigge, Donald Sutherland, and John Malcolm Brinnin, whose biographies of Gertrude Stein failed to please her. The last scholar to interview her at length was Leon Katz, who eventually published Gertrude Stein's early writings, including *Q.E.D.* Increasingly crippled with arthritis, Alice B. Toklas forced herself to walk the dog Basket (he died in 1952). She occasionally received visitors and kept up a voluminous correspondence: *Alice in her widowhood, had taken on a regal air, stooped though she was and weighing less than one hundred pounds. Enthroned in her armchair, smoking her inevitable cigarettes, she had the presence and an authority that only intimates had known before.*

Once *Vogue* had published an article of hers on cookery, she hit upon the idea of writing *The Alice B. Toklas Cookbook* (1950). She wrote it in the hoping of making money, dwelling on her life with Gertrude Stein, a memoir with recipes gleaned from former servants, friends and neighbours; some of them were her own. The book did well but her economic situation remained difficult. In her will Gertrude Stein had left her money and her art collection to Alice B. Toklas *for her use for life,* but she made Allan Stein, her only nephew, the executor of her estate, and the estate was to revert to the family. Alice B. Toklas did not get on well with Allan Stein or his widow Roubina. She lived frugally, drawing $400 a month from the Stein estate. In the winter she only heated one room and huddled close to the radiator. In 1957, during a stay in the French countryside, *conversion came over me almost completely.* A Catholic priest in Paris accepted her affirmation that she had been baptised as a small child, took her confession, and gave her communion. Bernard Faÿ, their old friend, had often told her that Gertrude was in Heaven and that Gertrude was waiting there.

At the age of nearly eighty, in 1958, she began to write her own memoir although she wanted this to be essentially her own tribute to Gertrude Stein, with only a brief glimpse of her own life before she met Gertrude Stein, and nothing but silence about the time after Gertrude Stein's death. It took her two years to write, after she had given up on collaboration with other writers. It was finally published as *What is Remembered* in 1963. She spent increasing periods of time away from her flat in rue Christine, sheltering with friends, or in monasteries. When she returned after a prolonged stay with an order of Canadian nuns in Rome, in 1961, she discovered that all the paintings were gone: *The walls were bare – not one Picasso left – the children of Allan Stein want them loaned to a museum where they would be adequately insured which of course I could not do.* Three years later, at the age of eighty-six she was evicted from her flat on the pretext that she spent too much of the year away from it. Friends found her a new, modern, well-heated flat, where she stayed, increasingly bed-ridden and nearly blind. Lucid until the end she died, a few months before her ninetieth birthday, on March 7th1967. She was buried next to Gertrude Stein, and her name and dates are engraved at the back of the marble headstone.

Baby

Babiest preciousest sweetest adorest

It is usually the first child whose every exploit is a source of wonder but Gertrude Stein, the last-born child, received the most attention in her family. *Baby Gertrude…such a darling, so plump, and round,* her aunt wrote approvingly. Gertrude and Leo, the last born of her family, discovered that they had been born because two other babies of their parents had died in their infancy, a boy and girl each. Their parents said that early on they had decided just to have five children: *If two little ones had not died there would be no Gertrude Stein of course not…Two died in babyhood or else I would not have come nor my brother just two years older and we never talked about this after we had heard of it that they never intended to have more than five children it made us feel funny.*

Gertrude Stein, having enjoyed being the baby of the family, always liked the word 'baby'. Dear friends, such as Carl van Vechten, would be called Baby and they could call her Baby too. The dearest of friends was Alice B. Toklas whom Gertrude Stein called Baby Precious. Alice B. Toklas called Gertrude Baby Boy. They would leave little notes for each other and Gertrude would be writing that

> *Baby precious Hubby worked and*
> *Loved his wifey, sweet sleepy wifey, baby precious sleep*
> *Sweetly and long is hubby's song,*
> *All mine and sweet is hubby's*
> *Treat and precious and true and all*
> *For you is hubby.*

Alice B. Toklas could be 'wifey' and 'baby' at the same time and Gertrude Stein could be 'hubby' and 'baby' at the same time and being together 'always' they brought forth what Gertrude Stein was writing and Alice B. Toklas was typing up; they wrote for each other and they read to each other.

Gertrude Stein loved the sight of the word Baby and she liked the sound of it too, as she liked the sound of many words, which she liked to write and to hear in her mind over and over, like the blues and the "Coon songs" she had heard in Baltimore:

> *Baby might baby might baby baby baby baby baby baby baby baby*
> *Might baby might baby baby baby might*
> *Very near to tears.*

That Mabel Haynes' first baby was *as healthy as could be*, was about all she could tell Gertrude Stein about her, and that *she was all father too so far*. Everything else was anticipation and a mother's long observation of incremental changes which in hindsight would become a blurred forgetting, like that of the act of childbirth itself. The baby Itha, so healthy, so promising, turned out to disappoint as a daughter. Itha had been the long-awaited first child of two aging parents - an Austrian captain who had not been wealthy enough to marry and the wealthy American doctor who had been too independently-minded for any usual suitor of her class. Exquisitely educated and expected to emulate her mother's ambitions, Itha fell pregnant by a much older man and went on to produce four babies.

Mabel Haynes herself went on to produce four more babies. She kept a Baby Book for each of them, recording weights and heights and gifts and genealogy, first words, first outings, illnesses and anecdotes. Mabel Haynes was present when I was born to her last child, my father, and I was the last of the babies in her family that Mabel Haynes would observe with her critical, medical eye.

Thomas Bernhardt once remarked that we never give birth to just babies, but to people who are already old, weak and leaky and doomed to die. The babies Mabel Haynes had, her five Austrian babies, turned out to disappoint, or to die, or at times delight and they are all dead. The babies that Gertrude Baby made in her being Baby with her Baby Precious can be a source of delight or confusion, of hope and disappointment. They are not dead.

Baltimore, Maryland

Baltimore is famous for the delicate sensibilities and conscientiousness of its inhabitants.

In the late 1890s, when Gertrude Stein, Emma Lootz, and Mabel Haynes were students at Johns Hopkins Medical School, Baltimore had grown to a city of nearly half a million people, roughly the same as Boston. It was the most southern of the northern cities or one could say it was the most northern of the southern ones. At the eve of the Civil War, Baltimore had the largest concentration of Black Americans of any city. At the same time, immigration from Germany and then also Eastern Europe brought Jewish settlers to Baltimore. The medical students did much of their practical work in the more deprived parts of town, attending births and manning dispensaries and they came to know the way that poor black people lived.

Gertrude Stein had family in Baltimore. It was the home of her mother, Amelia Keyser, who had experienced there *the good rich living that was natural to her.* Amelia's sister Fanny had married David Bachrach and their home in Linden Avenue became the social centre of the family. It was David's Bachrach family that Gertrude, Leo and Bertha Stein went to live with in 1892. She was eighteen years old at the time and although she relished at first *the cheerful life of all her aunts and uncles*, as well as the comfort of the good rich living, she found the idle confinement of the women not to her liking. Leo Stein went to Harvard in the autumn of 1892, the year they had come to Baltimore. Gertrude Stein, missing her brother, and weary of her relatives' efforts to find a suitable match for her, followed him north the following autumn to enrol at the Harvard Annex, the women's college which became Radcliffe in 1894. She returned with Leo Stein to Baltimore three years later, but they did not to continue to live with the Bachrachs. Instead they rented a three-storey terraced house, 215 Biddle Street, not far from the mansions around Vernon Hill, but in a decidedly poorer neighbourhood. In 1898 Gertrude passed with *magna cum laude* from Radcliffe College. Leo Stein, who had also graduated from Harvard, decided to study science at Johns Hopkins University and Gertrude opted for medicine. The medical school had only recently begun to admit female students through the intervention of the Baltimore Women's Fund committee, led by Mary Elizabeth Garrett, who had made a very handsome endowment of $500,000 to the School, contingent on the admission of women.

Mabel Haynes also arrived in Baltimore in 1898. She had completed her studies of Chemistry, Biology and Physics at Bryn Mawr and had passed the preliminary entrance for the medical school. She took lodgings in the large new apartment house 'The Severn' on Vernon Hill. The building, with its columned portico and red stone cladding, still exists. It was the first high-rise apartment building in Baltimore and had modern amenities such as bathrooms. The flats had no kitchens at the time Mabel Haynes lived there, and meals were being taken in a café room or the hotel upstairs. During the summer of 1898 Mabel Haynes went to Europe with Grace Lounsbery, a fellow graduate from Bryn Mawr, who had also completed the preliminary medical course. I don't know why Grace Lounsbery did not enrol at Johns Hopkins Medical School, perhaps she did not pass their strict exam, but she continued to stay in Baltimore with Mabel Haynes. The Bryn Mawr Alumni Yearbook from 1898 to 1901 lists Haynes and

Lounsbery first as living at an apartment house 'St. Paul', on the corner of St. Paul and Mount Royal Avenue and then further south, at Mount Vernon, at 611 St. Paul Street. Both buildings from that period no longer exist. The two women had the habit of inviting interesting people to come for tea and discuss the sort of matters that were interesting to them, to these very well educated and wealthy college women. Gertrude and Leo Stein were among the interesting people they invited. Grace Lounsbery would later tell Elizabeth Sprigge, Gertrude Stein's early biographer, that they thought the Stein siblings *not at all well brought up, coming from a pretty rough background. They rather exaggerated their roughness too – as people do if they have any kind of inferiority complex.*

Gertrude Stein for her part did as she pleased and enjoyed being provocative while holding forth on moral questions. Another interesting person was Dr Claribel Cone, who lived with her sister Etta, people whose *delicate sensibilities and conscientiousness* impressed Gertrude Stein. Claribel Cone was ten years older than Gertrude Stein and Mabel Haynes; she had graduated from the Baltimore Woman's Medical College in 1891 and worked on some research in the Pathology laboratory at Johns Hopkins Medical School, not having the taste for the practical side of being a doctor. She took an interest in some of the younger women who were now studying alongside men and were being taught by men who did not think much of having to teach women.

The first two years at Baltimore were happy years for Gertrude Stein. She enjoyed the research and laboratory work and the 'cheerful aunts and uncles' she could visit at will, as well as intellectual debates with her fellow students. Gertrude Stein went to live in a house in Eager Street, sharing it with another Bostonian medical student, Emma Lootz. Lena Lebender, the model for 'The Good Lena' in *Three Lives*, was keeping house. At some point Gertrude Stein no longer enjoyed studying at Johns Hopkins Medical School. She longer wanted to become a doctor. Like Dr Claribel Cone, she did not like the physical contact with patients and she did not like diseases. She worried that she had diseases inside her and took lessons in boxing to strengthen her body. It was during that final period of Gertrude Stein's life in Baltimore, after she had lost interest in medicine that she became particularly interested in Mary, known as 'May' Bookstaver. May Bookstaver was not a medical student, she was interested in politics and the problem of women, or rather the problem of women's inferior position in society, which she hoped to could improve through activism. She had studied Politics at Bryn Mawr College and graduated the same year as Mabel Haynes. She did not continue her studies, perhaps because her father, Judge Bookstaver, would not provide her with the means to do so. She did come to Baltimore however, and worked as a tutor. It was been suggested that Mabel Haynes 'threw over' Grace Lounsbery and became intimate with May Bookstaver instead.

Mabel Haynes, Emma Lootz, Marion Walker, and all the other female students, except for Gertrude Stein, persevered in their clinical and practical work, endured the sneers and contempt of their male colleagues and teachers, and completed their degree in 1902. Mabel Haynes left Baltimore and went to live in Boston and so did Emma Lootz. By that time Gertrude Stein had joined her brother in Europe and like him she never came back to Johns Hopkins. In her will she described herself as *legally domiciled in Baltimore, Maryland, but residing in Paris.*

In 1928 Gertrude Stein wrote a text called 'Business in Baltimore', a hymn-like text, with long crescendos and the word 'Baltimore' beating out the rhythm: *This can be Baltimore and or and Baltimore and for and Baltimore and Baltimore and Baltimore and or.* Then there is the matter of the business: *Business in Baltimore need never be finished here when it is there when it is commenced there when it is completed here when it is added to here when it is established there. It is this they mean he means to too and two.*

This passage seems like a very straightforward summary of what was to happen to Gertrude Stein; the business in Baltimore that ultimately mattered to her more than any other business she may have had in Baltimore, such as financial business that concerned her family's fortunes. Her own business, that of being a writer, had its beginning there. The whole last page of this text is an ecstatic accumulation of the most affirmative affirmations: *and yes and yes and better and yes and more and yes and better and yes and yes.* A whole beautiful page full of beautiful yeses and ands and more.

What a way to resolve the business of Baltimore.

Bilignin

Lucy Church rented a valuable house for what it was worth. She was prepared to indulge herself in this pleasure and did so. She was not able to take possession at once as it was at that time occupied by a lieutenant in the French navy who was not able to make other arrangements and as the owner of the house was unwilling to disturb one who in his way had been able to be devoted to the land which had given birth and pleasure to them both there inevitably was and would be delay in the enjoyment of the very pleasant situation which occupying the house so well adapted to the pleasures of agreeableness and delicacy would undoubtedly continue. And so it was.

Gertrude Stein and Alice B. Toklas, like all Parisians, preferred to spend their summers away from the city. They first tried the Mediterranean coast but found the climate and the landscape of the Rhône valley more congenial. They had come across the house of their dreams by accident, a charming 17th century manor house of Bilignin near Belley, set in a little park and surrounded by stone walls, and in 1929 they had secured its lease with cunning and persistence.

Gertrude Stein installed modern conveniences, such as an electric cooker, a bath, a telephone; they were also *enjoying using the furniture from the Brillat-Savarin which house belongs to the owner of this house.* Alice B. Toklas set to work on the garden and the parkland and over the years they planted roses, fruit trees and shrubs. They began to keep dogs, first of all the little Byron, later the large white poodles, Basket I and Basket II. Gertrude Stein found the countryside inspirational: *The landscape at Bilignin so completely made a play that I wrote quantities of plays.*

Between 1929 and 1939 Gertrude Stein and Alice B. Toklas spent the months between April and October in Bilignin and then returned to spend the winter in Paris. When Paris was occupied in June 1940 they decided that it would be safer to stay in the country. Gertrude Stein drove with Alice B. Toklas to Paris to pack their winter clothes and their passports. They left all of their paintings on the walls of their apartment at rue Christine, except for two Picassos and a Cézanne landscape that could be wrapped up easily. In 1943 the lease of their house in Bilignin ran out and Gertrude Stein and Alice B. Toklas moved to a more modern house of similar size and aspect in nearby Culoz. They were never to return to the house of their dreams, and they stayed in Culoz until the war ended.

I wanted to see Bilignin myself and drove with a friend from Lyon on a hot day in July. It is still *a one-street, four-or-five house community,* as William Rogers saw it in 1934, although the one street is now called Rue Gertrude Stein. The four-five houses are old, stone walled village houses, with orchards and gardens behind stone walled fences. Gertrude Stein's house is privately owned and sports a bronze plaque commemorating her presence, with a relief that shows her writing at a table opposite a knitting Alice B. Toklas, with a dog stretched out at their feet. We walked down a path that skirts the property to lead to a walnut grove and some fields, a path Gertrude Stein and her dogs would have walked many times. It was very pleasant to walk beneath the fragrant lime trees on a quiet afternoon. We came to a grotto dug into the hillside beneath the house and found a fountain placed between two thigh-shaped boulders, soft and green with moss, forming a generous vulva, trickling water from a slender spout wrapped in willow bark. The water was fresh and could well work miracles springing forth from such an auspicious site and just below the house *so well adapted to the pleasures of agreeableness and delicacy.*

Books

Book was there, it was there. Book was there. Stop it, stop it, it was a cleaner, a wet cleaner and it was not where it was wet, it was not high, it was directly placed back, not back again, back it was returned, it was needless, it put a bank, a bank when, a bank care.

I like book people vastly better than world people.

When I was a child, Mabel Haynes' glass fronted bookcases took up a whole wall in the living room. Whenever the doors were opened a peculiar smell was released, a dry, old smell of wood and fine leather. The books behind glass had well-tooled bindings of soft leather – the softest and smoothest was a small edition of Lamb's *Tales from Shakespeare,* which Mabel Haynes was given in 1887 when she was thirteen years old. The pages were lined with gold and this made the head and tail of books gleam like treasure. Some of the poetry volumes, those of Lord Byron for instance, printed on soft and yet strong paper, were small enough to fit into a pocket. The collected works of Emerson, of Stevenson, Thackeray, of Poe, were larger and the thicker paper had serrated edges, left by the action of the pen-knife that had slit them open. The books in our flat were only a small part of Mabel Haynes' library. Most had been put into a storage facility that was looted in the war. Her own copies of Gertrude Stein's books are lost, as well as the New York edition of Henry James and much else that I wish had survived.

Gertrude Stein, May Bookstaver and Mabel Haynes grew up in houses that had bookcases filled with the collected works of recognized Masters of Literature, with philosophical and spiritual tracts, tomes on natural history, on law or art, according to the inclination of the household. The books that the fathers bought, handsomely bound and seldom read, were hardly the sort of books their bookish children would like to read. Gertrude Stein remembers in *Everybody's Autobiography* that on one occasion the children were given money to buy books to read on the journey they were to take with their mother, and though they eventually never did go, they could keep the books. They were about nine and eleven then: *We bought Jules Verne lots of them …there was the Cryptogram and Twenty Thousand Miles Under the Sea and The Children of Captain Grant…the English at the North Pole and the Mysterious Island we had bought all these for travelling and Around the World in Eighty Days.*

Some years later, after their mother had died, Gertrude Stein and her brother Leo found solace again in buying books for themselves: *We had by that time been given an allowance for spending but naturally we bought books with it, we always bought books with it, I bought a Shelley in green and Morocco binding and we bought an illustrated set of Thackeray and we had a simple book plate made.*

While spending some months in London in 1902, feeling lonely and missing May Bookstaver, Gertrude Stein read a great deal in the libraries. She also bought editions of the Victorian English writers, published by the German editor Bernhard Tauschitz.

After Gertrude Stein and Leo Stein had settled in Paris in 1903, they began to spend most of their money on buying paintings and works of art, and some antiques on their travels to Spain and Italy. Their allowance was not ample enough to continue buying handsome and expensive books as well. Later, when she lived with Alice B. Toklas, they frequented bookshops together that doubled as lending libraries, such as Shakespeare and Co., also the American Library, and, once they had begun to make friends with writers, French writers as well as American writers, they were given first editions of their books, inscribed with dedications. By then Gertrude Stein had become indifferent to the physical quality of books: *She reads books but she is not fussy about them, she cares about neither editions nor make-up as long as the print is not too bad and she is not even very much bothered about that.* She also liked to show that she was not in the least high-minded about the sort of books she would buy when hard up: *I am still like that only now I buy only the cheapest detective and adventure stories and then I bought the most expensive history and poetry and literature. As I say incomes are incomes and counting is counting and reading is reading. Why not.*

After the death of Alice B. Toklas, the Yale University Library received the books that had been on her shelves when Gertrude Stein died. It still contained the set of Thackeray in twelve volumes that she had bought when she was seventeen. Donald Gallup, the librarian at Yale, wrote that *Her library, like herself, was comprehensive and enveloping; it was clearly a library to be read and lent, not of rare editions but of serviceable books printed in good legible type – a friendly collection.*

Gertrude Stein died with her books still on the shelves and the paintings she had collected on the walls. It had been such a relief to her that the Germans had not ransacked her apartment in 5, rue Christine during that war; they had rifled through their possessions and taken some linen and household utensils but left all else intact.

May Bookstaver's interests in history and politics would have informed her choice of books although, like her friends, she had a love of literature and contributed volumes to the library at Bryn Mawr. As she remained in her apartment until she died in 1950, she would have had her books around her.

When Mabel Haynes had to sell up her house in Graz and passed on her possessions to her children or put them into storage, she had to live without her own books around her and she came to rely on public libraries. She often deplored the lack of decent reading material. She was most grateful to May Bookstaver, who spent much of her meagre income to supply her old friend with books.

May Bookstaver and Mabel Haynes were readers, not writers. Gertrude Stein had to exercise much patience to see her writing become books. She wrote in longhand in exercise books (*cahiers*) aimed for children, with colourful covers and wide margins. She kept all her notebooks (*carnets*), her first and second manuscripts, as well as the typescripts that Alice B. Toklas made. After trying for years to get *Three Lives* into print, she financed it herself. *The Making of Americans* was completed in 1911 and rejected again and again until a first edition was made in France in 1925, before the first American one from 1926. Her exasperation over the seeming impossibility of her books becoming books can be seen in 'Descriptions of Literature', probably written in 1924 before *The Making of Americans* had come off. The text consists of 65 sentences, all but one beginning with the words *A Book:*

> *A book which shows that the next and best is to be found out when there is pleasure in the reason.*
> *For this reason.*
> *A book in which nearly all of it finally and an obstruction is planned as unified and nearly a distinction, To be distinguished is what is desired.*

Alice B. Toklas and Gertrude Stein set up their own publishing venture, Plain Editions. They sold some Picasso paintings and between 1930 and 1933 published five books with money raised from the sale. The printer Maurice Darantière, who had done the typesetting for *The Making of Americans,* knew how they could get cheap but good-looking books made: *We will have your book set by monotype which is comparatively cheap, I will see to that, then I will handpull your books on good but not too expensive paper and they will be beautifully printed and instead of any covers I will have them bound in heavy paper like The Making of Americans, paper just like that, and I will have made little boxes in which they will fit perfectly, well made little boxes and there you are. And I will be able to sell them at a reasonable price.*

The text, however, was not always set well or in accordance with the manuscripts, as is especially evident in *Operas and Plays.* When the books finally appeared in some Parisian bookshops Gertrude Stein was happy: *It was easy to get the book put in the window of all the booksellers in Paris that sold english books. This event gave Gertrude Stein a childish delight amounting almost to ecstasy. She had never seen a book of hers in a bookstore window before, except a french translation of The Ten Portraits, and she spent all her time in her wanderings about Paris looking at the copies of Lucy Church Amiably in the windows and coming back and telling me about it.*

The Autobiography of Alice B. Toklas did sell well. It remained her only commercial success. When she died her unpublished works by far exceeded those that had become books.

Boston Marriages

There were, in my parent's circle of friends in Boston, several households consisting of two ladies, living sweetly and devotedly together. Such an alliance I was brought up to hear called a "Boston marriage".

Lifelong cohabitation was not uncommon in the second half of the nineteenth century among women who had attended the then newly established boarding schools and who belonged to the upper-middle classes. Since many of these women believed marriage and motherhood to be obstacles to the attainment of women's ultimate goal of self-realization, they embraced spinsterhood as the mode of being best suited to a fulfilling life. They could afford not to marry men because they either had a private income or because they could earn sufficiently by exercising a profession. In order to forestall loneliness and isolation they would turn to another woman who shared these aspirations and outlook and with whom a companionable life could be led. These alliances were most common in the progressive North East, with Boston as its centre. One of the most respected and generally accepted of such alliances was the union between the two writers, Annie Fields and Sarah Orne Jewett, who lived for some twenty years in Annie Field's house in Charles Street. When Henry James decided, in 1883, while searching for a peculiarly 'American' subject, to write about women, *the agitation on their behalf* and the *failure of the sentiment of sex*, what he had in mind were *those friendships between women which are so common in New England* in his novel *The Bostonians*, serialized in 1885-86. The novel that takes aim at the absurdity of the Boston Marriage ends up suggesting that it might, on occasion, to be preferable to the narrow confines of patriarchal marriage.

The Bostonians is set in the milieu of reformist and women's emancipation movements and quite a few suffrage leaders and social reformers, such as Susan B. Anthony, Carrie Chapman Catt, Frances Witherspoon, had long-time attachments with women with whom they lived, and worked for the common cause. Academic women who considered themselves to be New Women, and in particular those with that heightened sense of exclusivity and privilege their cultural status afforded, would insist that their professional careers could not withstand marriage to men and they would seek out kindred female spirits to make a life with. So common were these domestic arrangements among female professors that they would be known also as 'Wellesley marriages' after Wellesley College, where only one of fifty-three female faculty members married conventionally. Mary Wolley of Mount Holyoake and Dr Martha Carey Thomas of Bryn Mawr, some of the most prominent examples, relied on the female companions for emotional and practical support, some escaped into conventional marriages, notably Mamie Gwinn, who left M. Carey Thomas for the dashing English professor, Alfred Hodder. Gertrude Stein gave a slightly fictionalised account of this story in 'Fernhurst'. Interestingly, in her version the male intruder disappears, leaving the dean and her friend *in their very same place.*

Taking up the literary theme of a Boston marriage threatened by Southern (here New Orleans) masculinity, Florence Converse wrote what could be seen as a riposte to Henry James' novel. *Diana Victrix: A Novel* was published in 1897 and here the Boston marriage of the female protagonists, Enid Spenser and Sylvia Bennett, endures and is strengthened by the exposure of the two women to the languid and backwards milieu of the South. Here the progressive spirit of New England is embodied in the marriage-like union of two educated women committed to public good, while all the French-influenced, backwards and languid South has to offer is conventional marriage. As Enid Spenser explains her reasons for preferring her female friend to her male suitor: *I share with her thoughts that I have no wish to share with you, I give her a love surpassing any affection I could teach myself to have for you. She comes first. She is my friend as you can never be, and I could not marry you unless you were a nearer friends than she. You would have to come first. And you could not, for she is first." "And this is all that separates us?" said Jacques, in a tone of amazement. "Only a woman?" "The reason the woman separates us," said Enid, "is because the woman and I understand each other, sympathise with each other, are necessary to each other. And you and I are not. It is not simply her womanliness, it is her friendship. There might be a man who would give me the inspiration, the equalness of sympathy, I find in her, - there might be, - some women find such men. But there are not yet enough for all of us.*

The novel is an impassioned vindication of a social solution to the problem of men's inability to offer these progressive and active women the sort of companionship they need. It draws on Florence Converse's own experience and convictions. Hailing herself from New Orleans, she made the transition from a conservative South to a radical North. She was educated at Wellesely, where she met Vida Dutton Scudder, ten years her senior, who taught in the English department. Together they led the sort of socially useful and progressive life that she describes her heroines leading in the novel. Vida Scudder not only taught, but organized one of the first Federal Labor Unions, founded the Denison House in Boston, which offered education and social services to the poor, and wrote a number of theological books. Florence Converse became a novelist and journalist. Vida Scudder and Florence Converse, both writing and both working as activists, lived together thirty-five years until Vida Scudder died, at the age of ninety-one in 1954. When Florence Converse followed, in 1967, at the even more venerable age of 96, she was buried close to her best friend in Newton Cemetery, Massachusetts. Some years ago, the Episcopal Church added Vida Scudder to its lists of saints.

Could the relationships of Mabel Haynes, Bostonian, with Grace Lounsbery, with whom she lived for some years in Baltimore and with whom she travelled to Europe be seen as a Boston Marriage? Could her relationship with May Bookstaver, who replaced Grace Lounsbery, be seen as one? Mabel Haynes was a woman with a generous allowance, who studied and worked as a doctor after obtaining her degree, and while it is clear that she shared an apartment with Grace Lounsbery, who had literary aspirations and later did become a writer, it is not clear that they meant to devote themselves to each other. Grace Lounsbery was to share much of her later life with Esther Swainson at a time when such relationships were no longer referred to as Boston Marriages. Mabel Haynes and May Bookstaver did not make a life with each other. Gertrude Stein found Alice B. Toklas and, when she proposed to Alice B. Toklas, Alice B.

Toklas said yes and they lived together, productively and happily, in what she certainly never called a Boston Marriage, loathing Boston the way she did, for as long as she lived. When Alice B. Toklas died after Gertrude Stein, she was put into the same grave, and their names are on either side of the same the tombstone.

Bryn Mawr

Is there any place in the world where the evening light lies so long and so delicate as at Bryn Mawr?

On a sunny late September day in 2014, I went to see the college where my grandmother, Mabel Haynes, had studied hundred and twenty years ago. I had an appointment at the library to see what the archive held on her and her friend May Bookstaver. The archivists handed me boxes with a few letters written by M. Carey Thomas to Mabel Haynes, some clippings, notebooks; no photographs survive from the class of 1898.

When Mabel Haynes and May Bookstaver were students there, between 1894-1898, the college was new and only some of the buildings that can be seen now on the beautiful campus grounds, designed by Frederick Law Olmstead, had been built. Mabel Haynes and Mary Bookstaver lived in 'Pembroke', one of the students' houses that had been finished in 1984. When I mentioned this to a student, she let me come in and I touched the wooden handrail on the stairway, which their hands, as well as those of innumerable students since, had worn to a smooth surface. It is always surprising for someone from England to see these American universities in their expansiveness and their mock-Gothic romanticism. The trees have had time to mature and to mask some of the ungainliness of the architecture. Bryn Mawr was a Quaker foundation, funded by the wealthy bachelor Dr Joseph Wright Taylor, who left all his money for this purpose. The name Bryn Mawr is Welsh and means 'high hill' and all the halls were given Welsh names to honour the Welsh ancestry of Dr Taylor. The founders of the College hoped to communicate their Quaker aesthetic through the architecture, wishing to convey an impression like that produced by some Quaker lady with her simple grey silk dress, satin bonnet and kid gloves, *which are made to harmonize with the expression on her face which is both intellectual and holy.*

It was to be a college for young women, such as the already existing Vassar, Wellseley, or Smith College. When the college opened in 1885, Dr Martha Carey Thomas was appointed to be Dean with control over all academic affairs, as well as the appointment of teaching staff. M. Carey Thomas had very clear view of the ideal Bryn Mawr woman, and she thought it was her task to mould the various 'types' into a highly-tuned and perfected human being: *if the Bryn Mawr woman could add to scholarship and character gentle breeding and could join high standards of behavior and usages of culture and gentle observances to high standards of scholarship we should have the type we are seeking to create.'*

Mabel Haynes, Mary Bookstaver and Grace Lounsbery, along with their contemporaries, experienced a Bryn Mawr that bore the imprint of the Quaker founders and the personality of M. Carey Thomas. The student body consisted mainly of the daughters of wealthy, protestant, upper-middle class families mainly from the East Coast. For most of them 'gentle' breeding had already been instilled. The all-female environment was to allow the young women to pursue subjects that were generally considered as uncongenial to the 'fair sex' without fear of censure. A curriculum that included ancient and modern languages, science, and sports, as well as the spirit of competition for various prizes, was to instil in the students the ability for hard work and persistence, a habit of scholarship, a liking for decadent poetry, scientific theories and athletic pursuits. It refined manners, promoted self-assurance based on having a well-trained mind, and gave them a sense of superiority as being part of a new breed of women. They were also used to having crushes on some of the female professors and to forming passionate attachments with each other. Gertrude Stein, who was to fashion her genius from a lack of this sense of superiority, felt her antipathy keenly when first confronted with the Bryn Mawr women at Baltimore. Her dislike of their being the way they appeared to her was also born from her own sense of uncertainty and roughness, and her inability to see things through. She would have made an impact on Bryn Mawr, but she would have resented Bryn Mawr leaving its imprint on her the way it did on Mabel Haynes, Mary Bookstaver and Grace Lounsbery. In 1934 Gertrude Stein came to lecture at Bryn Mawr and she talked about her writing to a packed audience of young women students. She stayed with Alice B. Toklas in M. Carey Thomas' old room in the Deanery and was thrilled to notice that it had not been changed at all, *they even had the photographs of the same works of art that we used to have in our rooms in college in ninety-seven. It was exciting.*

Busts

Some women have a prominent bust and some women are prominent enough to have a bust made of their likeness. Gertrude Stein had both. Her cousin, Helen Bachrach described the young Gertrude *as an exceedingly attractive buxom young woman;* others noted that while her brother Leo was very tall and slim, she *was very short and buxom… Gertrude was a dark, buxom young woman with flashing eyes.* The corsets women wore at the time would be laced tightly in the middle and supported the bust from below. In a photograph taken while Gertrude Stein was at Radcliffe, she has the ideal hourglass figure so much admired at the time. It is a demure and well-tailored outfit with its row of little button down the front, leg-of-mutton sleeves, and a scallop edged white collar.

Gertrude Stein found such clothes irksome and she shocked her bourgeois relatives by discarding restrictive underwear and restrictive footwear during her student years at Baltimore. She also balked at some of the contraptions, such as the cage-back crinolines and pads, that had to be worn in order to achieve the best effect of the Edwardian S-silhouette. Later, in Paris, Gertrude Stein adopted a square silhouette; she wore straight-cut kaftan-like dresses or skirts with waistcoats, which did not draw attention to bust or bottom. In the same way as she tried to free her writing from the constrictions of the nineteenth century, she tried to liberate her body from the constraints of fashion. When she sat for Jacques Lipchitz in 1921 to have her likeness modelled to be cast in bronze, he was only interested in her head not her clothes. She appears as serene as a Buddha, an impression strengthened by her hair that sits like the Enlightened One's topknot on the crown of her skull. Gertrude Stein did not buy the bust and it is now privately owned, but she did a written portrait of the sculptor in return some years later: *Like and like and likely likely and likely like and like.*

Man Ray captured a moment when Gertrude Stein sat for Jo Davidson as he worked on the clay model for the sculpture, he made of her in 1928. He made her sit on a low stool, with her legs spread wide, covered in an ample skirt, in pose like a peasant grandmother's; everything is large and comfortable about her: her bosom, her hips, her forehead, her hands. One of the ten copies made of this statue was put outdoors, in Bryant Park near the New York Public Library. Gertrude Stein once said that he had made her look *like a goddess of pregnancy.*

Lipchitz made more than one bust of Gertrude Stein. In 1938, when she met her after a long absence, he asked to sit for another. This sculpted head shows a tired and careworn face and is roughly modelled rather than polished to sheen. Jacques Lipschitz said that *she looked now like a shrivelled old rabbi, with a rabbi's cap on her head.*

Cancer

Gertrude Stein spent four years at one of the best medical schools of the time, studying medicine, without wanting to become a doctor. She later said that examinations bored her. She did not become a doctor like her friends Emma Lootz, Mabel Haynes and Marion Walker.

So far, I have not found the words 'cancer', 'tumour' or 'carcinoma' in any of her literary works. She wrote in one of her plays that William Erving, Emma Lootz' husband, died of tuberculosis; she had Melanctha in *Three Lives* die of consumption. In *The Making of Americans* she wrote about her mother being ill and how she became a mother wasting away: *She was lost among them, sometimes they would be good to her, oftener she would not be existing for them, mostly she was scared then and the important feeling was dead in her then, she had lost them, they were not of her any more then and she lost her body with them. Sometimes then they would be good to her, mostly they forgot about her, slowly she dies away from all of them.* She remembered her adolescent ambivalence about her mother's slow dying which nobody was ready to see as dying. She does not say what her mother's illness was; it was perhaps not discussed in her household, or not in front of the children. Amelia Stein knew that she had stomach cancer. Their physician, Dr Fine, had diagnosed her persistent abdominal pains, diarrhoea, and tiredness as such in 1885. His treatment was palliative; surgery did not seem to have been suggested. Amelia Stein tersely chronicled the course of her illness in her diary. Too weakened to keep holding a fractious family together, she took to her bed and withdrew into herself. She died at home, surrounded by her family in 1888. She was forty-six years old. The experience of watching her mother become but a shadow of her former self, despite the ministrations of Dr Fine, may account for some of Gertrude Stein's ambivalence towards practicing medicine. In her novella *Melanctha*, the heroine's lover is Dr Jeff Campbell, who goes to the sick and stays up with them sometimes all night. He can at times alleviate pain, but he is never said to have healed any one.

When Gertrude Stein was writing *Melanctha,* in the early 1900s, the most common causes of death in the United States of America and in Western Europe were infectious diseases (such as pneumonia, tuberculosis and gastro-intestinal infections, diphtheria). The populations of the densely inhabited slums of the great cities were particularly, but far from exclusively, at risk from contagion. Advances in epidemiology and the discovery of penicillin (in 1928) greatly reduced mortality from infections and increased average life expectancy. During the Second World War, the director of the School Service of the American Cancer Society could state that *several times as many people on the home front have died of cancer as have been killed on all battle fronts.*

Gertrude Stein, who, like her brother Simon, was a glutton and prone to overeating, frequently suffered from indigestion and colitis. In the early 1920s was told that she did have an abdominal tumour, which she refused to have operated though she remained fearful of cancer. The knowledge of having a tumour and her wish to change her lifestyle so as to improve her health, provided motivation for their annual stays in the country and the acquisition of their summer house in Bilignin. Gertrude Stein's health did improve; she ate less, and Alice B. Toklas increased her vigilance. Both women survived living in Nazi occupied France, but the worry and uncertainty had taken its toll on Gertrude Stein's resilience. She did not survive the operation for a stomach cancer that had been diagnosed as such in 1946. She had insisted on surgery despite the risks. She did not wish to die in the slow and agonizing way her mother had suffered. She wanted her own kind of dying. She demanded that the doctors of the American hospital use the modern and more radical form of treatment despite the fact that she might be too weak to see it through surgery. Finally, in the afternoon of 27th of July 1946, one of the younger doctors agreed to operate. Failing to recover consciousness *after the anaesthetic was administered, she died (…) holding in each hand a copy of her latest book, 'Brewsie and Willie'.*

Gertrude Stein's sister Bertha, the dutiful daughter who had nursed her bedridden mother for the last two years before her death, had died of diabetes, in 1924. The eldest Stein sibling, Michael, succumbed to cancer too, in 1938. Leo Stein was diagnosed with colon cancer half a year after Gertrude Stein's death. He paid for the then new treatment of radiotherapy *with the last of his Picasso drawings* and he died, of peritonitis after surgery, almost a year after Gertrude Stein, on July 29th, 1947.

Mabel Haynes, Gertrude Stein's erstwhile fellow student at medical school, did not die of cancer since she was alert to early warnings. Noticing blood on her underwear she went straight to the clinic in Graz, where she lived at the time, and demanded an immediate cauterization of her cervix, as she knew this to be a possible sign of cancer given that she had long passed menopause.

When I was born with a scarlet birthmark near my right ear, my father consulted his mother, Mabel Haynes, whose medical speciality had been dermatology, as well as colleagues at the university of Graz. They recommended a new preventive treatment that was supposed to stop the birthmark from spreading – radiation therapy. From the age of one to four I received yearly doses of radiation. The birthmark did not spread. Sixty years later, a few months after the death of Mabel Haynes' last child, Gabrielle, I was diagnosed with a malignant tumour below my right ear. Given the history of radiation on this part of the body, the only treatment available is surgery. Fortunately, the consultant who treats me is no Dr Fine. He does fine by me. The statistics of mortality have not changed since 1945; cancer remains the prime cause of death in the rich world, even though a greater number of people diagnosed with it manage to die from something else now.

Catholicism

Avec Gertrude, j'ai raté.

Catholic to be turned is to venture on youth and a section of debate, it even means that no class where each one over fifty is regular is so stationary that there are invitations.

Gertrude Stein described herself as Jewish but not religious and said that she had read the Old Testament for its poetry. In Catholic Spain and Italy, which she began to visit with Leo Stein in 1900, she saw a great many churches with paintings and statues; she noticed the wayside shrines, the church bells and processions. In Fiesole, near Florence, where Leo Stein had gone to study painting, they rented a house called the Casa Ricci, in which they were to pass several summers and in *The Autobiography of Alice B. Toklas* she described their eccentric landlady who had converted to Catholicism: *It had been made liveable by a Scotch woman who born Presbyterian became an ardent Catholic and took her old Presbyterian mother from one convent to another. Finally they came to rest in Casa Ricci and there she made for herself a chapel and there her mother died. She then abandoned this for a larger villa which she turned into a retreat for retired priests and Gertrude Stein and her brother rented the Casa Ricci from her. Gertrude Stein delighted in her landlady who looked exactly like a lady-in-waiting to Mary Stuart and with all her trailing black robes genuflected before every Catholic symbol and would then climb up a precipitous ladder and open a little window in the roof to look at the stars. A strange mingling of Catholic and Protestant exaltation.*

Alice B. Toklas came to stay at the Casa Ricci the summer of 1907, not long after she had met Gertrude Stein in Paris. They visited many churches together and made a pilgrimage to Assisi on foot. By that time Gertrude Stein had already started to be interested in some of the Catholic saints, such as Saint Francis,

Saint Theresa of Avila, and Saint Ignatius of Loyola. She read their writings and she liked their images and she was thinking about what being a saint amounted to. She also liked to buy objects and works of art that had originally served devotional uses. After Gertrude Stein and Alice B. Toklas began to spend their summers in France, in their country-house in Bilignin, they could observe the lives of the country people, their church going and their ways of life. She wrote *Lucy Church Amiably*, which was inspired by Lucey Church on a hill near Bugey:

> *Lucy Church heard them say that they liked continuity.*
> *It is more continuous to have clouds than rain snow than rain mist*
> *Than rain hail rain rain than rain.*

Gertrude Stein's writing at that time, in the late 1920s and early 1930s, takes the form of abstract, lyrical evocations of being alive. The happy domesticity with Alice B. Toklas and their shared interest in some Counter-Reformation saints given to mystical visions, were conducive to a state of mind that allowed such exultation by writing. She wrote *Four Saints in Three Acts* at that time (1927-8) and in her autobiography she explains that what excited her was their simple being: *A saint a real saint never does anything. A martyr does something, but a really good saint does nothing, and so I wanted to have Four Saints who did nothing and I wrote the Four Saints in Three Acts and they did nothing and that was everything.*

The saints talk of course but not with each other, nor do they describe anything, they intone words in a way that remind me of litanies, such as the Laurentian Litany, in its cadences:

> *Saint Ignatius. Withdrew with with withdrew.*
> *Saint Ignatius. Occurred.*
> *Saint Ignatius. Occurred withdrew.*
> *Saint Ignatius. Withdrew Occurred.*

Saint Ignatius. Withdrew Occurred.
Saint Ignatius. Withdrew Occurred.
Saint Ignatius occurred Saint Ignatius withdrew occurred withdrew.

The American critic and composer Virgil Thompson set her text to music and in 1933 it was performed with great success by a cast of black singers. The score is essentially a pastiche of 19th century American popular music and obscures the incantatory rhythm of the writing. Linda Watts suggested that Gertrude Stein, *by recasting traditional religious imagery created an alternative spirituality and an alternative literature.* However, Catholicism was but one element of its literary landscape, just as the peculiar shape of the steeple of Lucey Church was one peculiar element of the landscape. Later, during the war, Gertrude Stein took comfort from reading the prophecies of the medieval Saint Odile, who had seen a calamity befall the people of France, from which they would be saved.

To what extent Bernard Faÿ, fervent Catholic and Vichy administration officer, who had protected Gertrude Stein and Alice B. Toklas during the war, had tried to convert the two women to become Catholics cannot be determined. He admitted having *failed with Gertrude Stein* and this seems to suggest that he thought it had worked with Alice B. Toklas who did indeed convert after Gertrude Stein's death in the hope of being re-united with her beloved in another world. So great did she rate her companion's particular saintliness that it did was not necessary for Gertrude Stein to have become a Catholic in any conventional way. *When Toklas later asked Pablo Picasso what Gertrude Stein might have thought of her conversion to the Catholic Church, he is said to have replied, "Oh, she was there long before you".* A religion one is born into is a religion one can reject. This was my father's argument when the question arose as to whether his children should be baptised. He said that it was like an immunisation, that knowing a religion from childhood allowed one to outgrow it. His own baptism into the Roman Catholic faith had been a condition stipulated in the marriage contract between his father, the Austrian officer Rudolf Leick, and his mother, the American Mabel Haynes, who in order to marry her first husband, also an Austrian officer, had to be baptised herself, having been born into a long line of Christian non-conformists who did not practice baptisms and confirmation. She drew the line when it came to Catholicism and chose the Lutheran option as more congenial to her upbringing.

Jews living in Austria-Hungary were encouraged to convert to Catholicism to raise their civic status; some of the wealthier ones were ennobled for it, some, across Europe, converted for spiritual reasons. Gertrude Stein's namesake, the German Edith Stein, who had studied Phenomenology with Edmund Husserl, became a Carmelite, having read Saint Theresa of Avila, Gertrude Stein's favourite saint. Like many other Jews who had converted to Catholicism she perished in Auschwitz. She was canonized and beatified by Pope John Paul II in May 1987.

Character

Then there will be realised the complete history of every one, the fundamental character of every one, the bottom nature in them, the mixtures in them, the strength and weakness of everything they have inside them, the flavor of them, the meaning in them, the being in them, and then you have a whole history then of each one.

Gertrude Stein, so her brother Leo Stein wrote after she had died, had always been very different from himself: *The differences between Gertrude's character and mine were profound. My interest was critical interest in science and art. Gertrude had no interest whatever in science or philosophy and no critical interest in art or literature 'til the Paris period and, apart from college texts, never, in my time at least, read a book on these subjects. Her critical interest was entirely in character, in people's personalities. She was practically inaccessible to ideas and I was accessible to nothing else. She was much influenced by people and I was not influenced by them at all but only by ideas.*

She often expressed, especially in her early work, her ardent wish to understand other people, to understand the differences between people and to find some means of discovering the essential components that in various combinations, make up what could be taken as character. In one of her American Lectures she summarised this process: *While I was at college and doing philosophy and psychology I became more and more interested in my own mental and physical processes and less in that of others and all I then was learning of what made people what they were came to me by experience and not by talking and listening. Then as I say I became more interested in psychology, and one of the things I did was testing reactions of the average college student in a state of normal activity and in the state of fatigue induced by their examinations. I was supposed to be interested in their reactions but soon I found that I was not but instead that I was enormously interested in the types of their characters that is what I even then thought of as the bottom nature of them, and when in May 1898 I wrote my half of the report of these experiments I expressed these results as follows : In these descriptions it will be readily observed that habits of attention are reflexes of the complete character of the individual.*

In this report, that tested various people's reaction to 'automatic writing', she assigned different 'types', - characters, to the subjects of her experiments, such as:

TYPE II., CASE I. Female subject. No automatic sleep habit, good natured, phlegmatic. She has premonitory conversations that come true. Falls readily under personal influences, not a determined character nor imaginative. Strongly dominated by impressions of childhood and superstitions. She does not concentrate her attention easily and finds it very fatiguing when she does. When tired she relaxes by giggling. She says she keeps on working long after she has ceased to work vigorously.

When she left Radcliffe for Johns Hopkins, she wished to find a more scientifically grounded means to study character from a medical, psychiatric avenue. Confronted with the insane she recoiled; later she would put her reaction into Alice B. Toklas' mouth: *She always says she dislikes the abnormal, it is so obvious. She says the normal is so much more simply complicated and interesting.*

The normal could be much more simply complicated or simply more complicated than her experimental subjects or the lunatics in their asylum, as she was to discover when she became puzzled and confused about her own conflicting emotions and powerful erotic responses to May Bookstaver. Gertrude Stein was so derailed by this experience that she abandoned the hope of getting to the bottom of understanding character through medical science. Instead, she turned to working it out through writing. All her early writing, in different modes, influenced by different sorts of books, show her grappling with character and the dynamics between characters. There is a passage in *Everybody's Autobiography*, where she remarks how when she had returned to America after an absence of some thirty years, *so little of my past came up. I went to school with lots of them and to college at Radcliffe and Medical School and know lots in Paris, but not a great many turned up. However, Edstrom did... he used to complain so that I liked everybody in character. In those comparatively young days I did. I thought everybody had a character and I knew it and I liked them to be in character. Now, well they are in character I suppose so but I would like it just as well if they were not anyway if they are or if they are not is not exciting to me now. Anything that is quite enough as it is.*

In the late 1930s when she wrote this, she had indeed become less interested in the subject, it had stopped to be exciting to her, and she even goes on to fudge the issue by pretending that she had simply liked people to be in character, as if they were had been characters in a book or a play. Perhaps having made some of her objects and subjects into characters in her own books they could be more or less in character, but at the time she was writing them she was still very much excited by trying to understand the underlying system of characteristics. When she was writing *The Making of Americans*, between 1905 and 1908, she drew on her experiences of growing up in East Oakland, as much as on the stories of various family members, friends and people who interested her; with *the idea of describing really describing every individual that could exist.* It was to be as much a description as a history: *Then there will be realised the complete history of every one, the fundamental character of every one, the bottom nature in them, the mixtures in them, the strength and weakness of everything they have inside them, the flavor of them, the meaning in them, the being in them, and then you have a whole history then of each one.*

Yet while there are some narrative and (auto) biographical strands in the book, this was not a primary interest but rather an example for the mechanism of characterological typology in a given person; most clearly realised in 'David Hershland'. While Gertrude Stein subsequently explained what she had attempted to do in this book, as well as in a number of other ones that ploughed the same furrow (*The Long Gay Book, Many Many Women, Two*), she never acknowledged one source she had absorbed, that had excited both her and Leo Stein when they had come across the first English translation in 1908. It was Leon Katz, who discovered in her note books and letters from the period that she read the English translation of the Austrian philosopher Otto Weininger's book *Sex and Character* with particular interest. Weininger produced an introduction to characterology by tackling the relationship between the sexes and by reducing the differences based on sex to a universal dichotomy between 'male' and 'female'. Making use of psychological, medical material, and anthropological texts, as much as of philosophical writings and his own prejudices and attitudes, he investigated topics such as sexual morphology (positing a 'uni-or bi-sexuality' as fundamental), pederasty, emancipated women, and how male and female characteristics play out in sexuality, consciousness, intellectual faculties, the potential for genius, memory, etc. Weininger's binary system envisages an abstract, 'absolute male' as opposed to an 'absolute female'; the former is all ego, the later without any ego, the former completely moral, the latter amoral, the former attaining genius, the latter unable to attain genius.

Gertrude Stein had also been trying to situate a person's 'bottom nature' between extremes and she could take from Weininger, disregarding his misogyny, at least the encouragement to proceed in her endeavour. As Leon Katz argues, *Gertrude's whole interest in character was centered in its dynamic - and for her it was dynamic in two senses. She "saw" character in the thrust and withdrawal, the attack and resistance, the fight and surrender, the campaigning skill or ineptitude of human beings; from the days of her earliest writing, and her first analyses of May Bookstaver and Mabel Haynes, characters became clarified for her, became "themselves" in fact, when they were in motion, struggling, winning, and losing in their endless war for power over one another.... two aspects that were of primary interest to her. The first was that each one had a constant of some kind that guaranteed the uniqueness and consistency of character throughout one's life...The second was that, from the point of view of the observer, there was some sort of order - an "arrangement" of facets of character - through which order the whole character was gradually to be seen and ultimately to be understood.*

By the time she concluded "The Diagram Book" and the notebooks written concurrently, "attack" and "resistance," not Weininger's "maleness" and "femaleness," are used as the alpha and omega of her classification. ... Alternatively, her two basic types are also those who need to love and those who need to be loved. These two complementary needs - reflecting the complementary roles of maleness and femaleness in Weininger, but no longer intending the same distinction - overlap but do not everywhere coalesce with the notions of attack and resistance. They overlap because the two "needs" are thought of simply as the controlling factors in the choice of weapons in human relations: always, Stein thought of human relations, with cold consistence, in terms of battle.

Gertrude Stein, so her friend Mabel Weeks thought, *had successfully integrated her character around her limitations.* Given her dependent-independent nature, one attacking rather than resisting; one of geniality, a lover rather than a beloved, and as far on the side characterized according to Weininger's scheme as 'male' without becoming a travesty, she strove to realise her destiny to become a genius. According to Leon Katz, *The whole incrustation of Stein's ideas and feelings in her writings from 1908 to the end of her life derives from Weininger's envisioning of the highest "type" of human being - the only true individuality - in terms of his achieving the promise of immortality by escaping from the contingency of time.*

Mabel Haynes, with her own dependent-independent character and impetuous nature, saw character in terms of an ability to resist weakness in the moral constitution. Her niece Margaret, having taken to drink as the result of being bullied by a demanding mother, she deemed as having a weak character; that of her daughter Gabrielle, able to retain selfless devotion to those around her, as a strong character, that of her daughter Itha as a simple bad character: *Stick to daily facts and character that is the only way to master fate.*

Charles E. Knoblauch
(7th April 1870 - 12th October 1934)

Charles E. Knoblauch, also known as 'Chas' or 'Charlie', was the husband of May Bookstaver. His father, of German origin, had settled in New York City and joined the Stock Exchange in 1869 *where he had the reputation of being an excellent broker, wide-awake, alert and active.* Charles Edward, one of eleven children, was born in a brownstone house in New York City, 60 West 17th Street in the Flatiron District. Later the family moved to a prestigious and modern development, the Dakota Apartment building on West 72nd Street. The mother

Gertrude, a musician, died suddenly in 1880. In 1885 the father married again but died himself two years later at the early age of forty. The stepmother took all the children to Germany, where she pursued her musical career until a large bequest left by an uncle allowed the family's return to New York.

Nothing is known about Charles E. Knoblauch's education, but on October 4th, 1893, at the age of twenty-three he obtained a seat in the New York Stock Exchange where he was an independent broker. He was also a keen sportsman and felt fit and adventurous enough to sign up for volunteer regiments that were assembled for an assault on Spanish held Cuba. The idea was to create a crack troop of non-professional soldiers who would be well armed and who could, with minimal preparation, assist the regular army in a swift campaign to oust the Spanish from the island. He could fit the bill: *Knoblauch [is] a giant who boxes, wrestles, swims and rides expertly*. He joined the 1st United States Voluntary Cavalry, later known as the Rough Riders, commanded by Theodore Roosevelt, who later became president of the United States. The Rough Riders were an extraordinary assembly of characters, drawn as much from frontiersmen, cowboys, Indians, trappers as college educated sporty types from the East Coast, such as C. E. Knoblauch. Charles E. Knoblauch took part in the skirmish at Las Guasimas on June 24th, 1898 and his conduct at San Juan Hill won him promotion to corporal. He had a highly successful war and returned to Wall Street. The Wall Street atmosphere of high risk, excitement and money quickly made and lost appealed to Charles E. Knoblauch's combative and high-spirited nature.

It is not known when and where May Bookstaver made the acquaintance of the notorious broker. He was fighting in Cuba when she finished her degree at Bryn Mawr and she may read about his exploits in the newspaper. By 1906, May Bookstaver was still living with her parents, the censorious Judge Bookstaver and her less than sympathetic mother in New York. Her relationship with Mabel Haynes had suffered from her affair with Gertrude Stein. Mabel Haynes had returned to Boston, where she was working at the General Hospital and she had gone to spend some months studying medicine in Vienna. It is quite likely that any financial support Mabel Haynes may have offered had come to an end. Marriage to a wealthy and energetic banker would have solved May Bookstaver's financial dependence on her tight-fisted father. Furthermore, Mabel Haynes had met a dashing Austrian officer in Vienna and had invited him to Boston to meet the parents, with a view to getting married. May Bookstaver may have cast her eye on a similarly valiant candidate in New York City. Like Charles E. Knoblauch, she was clubbable, - she was a member of Women's Cosmopolitan Club for instance, she was a keen horsewoman, she liked to dazzle with witty conversation, having no qualms about ridiculing those in hopeless love with her, like Gertrude Stein, whose letters she read aloud at dinner parties. They may well have simply fallen in love.

In August 1906, as the *New York Times* reported, *Miss Mary Aletta Bookstaver, daughter of Judge and Mrs Henry W. Bookstaver of New York, was quietly married at noon today to Charles Edward Knoblauch, also of New York. The ceremony was performed at the Judge Bookstaver's summer residence, Wyn Wye, on Purgatory Road [Rhode Island], in the presence of a small company of intimate friends of the families by Rev. R.B Pomeroy of Emanuel Church. There were no attendants.* They went off straight away, for a motoring holiday in Europe. Charles E. Knoblauch also secured a suitable domicile, a large apartment in 'The Wyoming' – newly rebuilt on the corner of 55th Street and Seventh Avenue. In its luxuriously appointed rooms, with all modern amenities and several bathrooms, Mrs and Mrs Knoblauch lived all their lives.

Mrs Charles Knoblauch, as she now preferred be known, continued to be active in the Suffrage Movement and she also worked with Margaret Sanger on the Birth Control magazine. Mr and Mrs Knoblauch had no children.

Charles E. Knoblauch is never mentioned in print by any of the artistic friends of Mrs Knoblauch. Judging from the social notices in the *New York Times,* the couple were part of New York society, attending numerous functions, such as dinners and balls and receptions throughout their life together. Charles E. Knoblauch was a progressive man and he supported his wife's activities on behalf of Suffrage. On the one photograph I found, where they appear together, on the occasion of their dog's moment of fame in 1915, they look pleased with themselves, with the dog, and, why not, with each other.

The company Schuyler, Chadwick & Burnham, of which Charles E. Knoblauch was a 'floor partner', was placed in receivership and suspended from trading, one of the many casualties of the stock market crash of 1929. This also made

Charles E. Knoblauch bankrupt; he retired from the Stock Exchange in 1932 at the age of sixty-two. Two years later, on October 12th, 1934, he died of heart disease, after a week's illness, at his home, the Wyoming, leaving his wife the apartment but little money to live on.

Childhood

About an unhappy childhood well I never had an unhappy anything. What is the use of having an unhappy anything.

My brother and I had everything. Gradually he was remembering that his childhood had not been a happy one. My eldest brother and I had not had that impression, certainly not however my brother led in everything. He had always been my brother two years older and a brother. I had always been following.

I led in my childhood and youth the gently bred existence of my class and kind.

Gertrude Stein and May Bookstaver and Mabel Haynes were children in the decade that followed the American Civil War. They grew up in families that employed nursemaids and governesses to look after the children who spent most of their time in nurseries or in the parks they were taken to. They had 'everything', as Gertrude Stein and her brother had everything. They had what their parents thought they needed – clothing, suitable nourishment, regular exercise, educational toys, the attention of their parents at certain times, especially Sundays. *I am the youngest of the family,* wrote Gertrude Stein, *it is nice being the youngest or the oldest, and I am the youngest.* Since she was also a good looking and clever child, she had more attention and praise than the middle siblings and she never grew out of expecting attention and praise. May Bookstaver had the misfortune of being the only one of her siblings to survive, and she seems not to have been more loved for it. Mabel Haynes was the penultimate of six, born some eight years after the first and two years before the last.

There are those who remember the intensity of delight they felt as children. Sometimes watching a shiny beetle in a patch of summer grass or catching sweetness on a breeze can bring that back to me for an instant – and there are those who remember the intensity of dread they felt as children. Gertrude Stein remembered that *when I was young the most awful moment of my life was when I really realised that the stars are worlds and when I really realised that there were civilizations that had completely disappeared from this earth (…) Then I was frightened badly frightened, now well now being frightened is something less frightening than it was.*

She would come back to that when the war of 1939 had begun, and always she felt that that first fright had been worse.

Gertrude Stein wrote several books for children, some of them inspired by children born to friends of hers: *To Do: The Book of Alphabets and Birthdays* (1940), which she wrote for Picasso's son Pablo, *The World is Round* (1939) dedicated to Rose Lucie Renée Anne d'Aiguey, grand-daughter of the Baroness Lucy Pierlot, *The Gertrude Stein First Reader* and *Three Plays* (1941).

The characters in these books are children and these children wander off and nearly drown, they cry quite a lot and sometimes for joy, they sing when they are sad and when they are frightened, and they are frightened, as Rose is, in *The World is Round,* not by being all alone on a mountain at night but by not knowing what and where and when they are who they are in a world that is forever round and spinning and where the sense of self is elusive:

> *I am a little girl and my name is Rose, Rose is my name.*
> *Why am I a little girl*
> *And why is my name Rose*

And when am I a little girl
And when is my name Rose
And where am I a little girl
And where is my name Rose
And which little girl am I am I the little girl named Rose
Which little girl named Rose.

Gertrude Stein never stopped worrying about the ontological implications of identity and the one phrase which she consoled herself time again is quite a childish phrase, *I am I because my little dog knows me.*

Gertrude Stein and May Bookstaver did not have children themselves and so they were not responsible for the childhood of their own children.

Mabel Haynes, with her five Austrian children - she always wanted a large family as she thought *how sad it is to be an only child* - also had nursemaids and governesses to take care of the daily needs of infants but it was a struggle to provide for them during and immediately after the Great War. Her husband's head injuries that made him behave cruelly towards his children blighted their childhood and her loving care could not undo that.

I had no wars to contend with, nor mad husbands; none of the children was gravely ill and none of them died. Drawing on what was for me a source of delight, forests, cows, and country living, I could bring up my own children in rural surroundings and take them to spend summer holidays by the sea though I doubt that they considered they had led a gently bred existence.

Cigars and cigarettes

Left open, to be left pounded, to be left closed, to be circulating in summer and winter, and sick color that is grey that is not dusty and red shows, to be sure cigarettes do measure an empty length sooner than a choice in color.

Winged, to be winged means that white is yellow and pieces pieces that are brown are dust color if dust is washed off, then it is choice that is to say it is fitting cigarettes sooner than paper.

Jacques Derrida once spoke of tobacco as *symbolizing the symbolic.* When Gertrude Stein was a student at the Johns Hopkins University Medical School, still a bastion of male privilege that had been bribed with substantial donations to allow women to study alongside men, she knew something about symbolizing the symbolic: *Fellow students described her as charismatic and confident. She learned to box. She smoked cigars. She tried to break through society's restrictions on women.*

She did not just smoke cigarettes she smoked cigars. She smoked cigars while her college women friends, such as Mabel Haynes and May Bookstaver, smoked cigarettes. At Bryn Mawr they had learnt *the pleasures of conversation over cigarettes.* The stimulating effect of tobacco, which had long contributed whatever lift was needed to the conversations of men, was becoming abrogated by educated women, eager to prove that they were not just equal but superior to men. Gertrude Stein took it a step further, showing off the superiority of her more original intellect in the context of women who smoked subversively themselves. After World War One and with the growing movement for female suffrage and for women's rights, *the cigarette became a symbol of new roles and expectations of women's behaviour.* Gertrude Stein's second car stripped so bare that she named it 'Lady

Godiva', was fitted with headlights and a cigarette lighter. At that time *Gertrude smoked continuously* as Sylvia Beach remembered. In the 1920s marketing campaigns by tobacco companies eager to increase consumption targeted women by capitalizing on the appetite suppressant qualities of tobacco. Marketing managers went further; in order to make women smoking in public socially acceptable and hence more visible, they organised a stunt for which purpose Great General Tobacco had hired good looking young women to march in New York's Easter Parade of 1929, apparently protesting women's equality while lighting up and smoking their *torches of freedom*. By that time Gertrude Stein had given up a habit that was no longer subversive. Though no longer a prerogative of New Women, women in general took to cigarettes; working women as much as intellectuals like Mabel Haynes.

Alice B. Toklas, though never a cigar smoker and as a good American disdainful of French tobacco, kept smoking her *Pall Mall* until well into old age (she died at ninety). Clutching a rosary in one hand, her cigarette in the other, it allowed her to do what she desired most, to commune with the spirit of Gertrude Stein. *....to be sure cigarettes do measure an empty length sooner than a choice in color.*

Clothes

There was nothing to distinguish Mabel Neathe and Helen Thomas from the average American tourist as they walked down the Via Nazionale. Their shirt-waists trimly pinned down, their veils depending in graceless folds from their hats, the little bags with the steel chain firmly grasped in the left hand, the straightness of their backs and the determination of their observation all marked them an integral part of that national sisterhood which shows a more uncompromising family likeness than a continental group of sisters with all their dresses made exactly alike.

A LONG DRESS

What is the current that makes machinery, that makes it crackle, what is the current that presents a long line and a necessary waist. What is this current.

Mabel Haynes, Gertrude Stein and May Bookstaver came of age in the gilded age and they were of a class that expected them to display themselves with decorum, with the right cut of their garments, the right sort of bearing to carry it off. However, being college women and New Women, they preferred clothes that were not only less cumbersome than those worn by women of fashion, but less designed to flaunt wealth and its possibilities for conspicuous consumption. Instead of tapering dresses with bustles college women wore the 'shirtwaist', a combination of long flared skirts that allowed a wide stride, and long-sleeved blouses, sometimes with detachable collars. They also adopted neckties rather than lace ruffles, and close-fitting three-quarter length jackets similar to those worn by men. Gertrude Stein as a student at Radcliffe *refused to be bound by the dictates of style, though she then dressed conventionally.* One photograph, taken in the Bachrach Studio, shows her wearing an elaborately pleated black blouse with tightly fitted shoulder of mutton sleeves, while Mabel Haynes, in a snapshot taken after her marriage in 1907, looks at ease in her sporty woollen suit, the sort of outfit she would wear for motoring excursions in the Polish countryside.

Clothes worn during the day could be more or less comfortable, simply cut, blouse and skirt combinations, but evening wear, suitable to appear in for dinner, were made of finer material, low cut and worn with jewellery. By that time, in 1904, Gertrude Stein had moved to Paris and refashioned herself to suit the Bohemian world of Montparnasse. She began wearing loose brown velvet and corduroy wraps, teamed with a blouse fastened with one of her brooches, woollen socks and Greek sandals with upturned toes.

Addressing the velvet robe Gertrude Stein donned in one of the photographs by Alvin Langdon Coburn in 1913, C. E. Mitranto made the following observation:

What she wears becomes a studied costume that cuts across genders, cultures, and historical periods. This costume connotes simultaneously public consequence, authority, and exoticism. Draped in its folds, her body is abstracted from time and cultural divides.

In later periods, after the First World War, Gertrude Stein wore wide skirts made of heavy fabric of mid-calf length, with cotton shirts and embroidered waistcoats. Once Gertrude Stein and Alice B. Toklas had settled into the routine of spending summers in Bilignin they decided to have all their clothes made in

Belley: *That is one of the nice things in France if you are anywhere near Lyon you can get very good clothes made… so we had all our clothes made in Belley.*

The clothes that Gertrude Stein adopted ostensibly for the ease of movement and comfort made an impression she wished to convey of the sort of person she was, homely rather than fashionable, sensible rather than extravagant, straight-forward rather than fussy. She did not go for clothes that could be seen as cross-dressing; she might don homburgs, but she never wore trousers. Gertrude Stein's clothes were also suitable for the sort of husband she was to Alice B. Toklas, suggesting solidity, loyalty, undemonstrative strength and a comfortable ruggedness. Alice B. Toklas, always a self-conscious dresser, could flutter in her batik draperies or appear trim and elegant in her tailored suits, wearing exquisite hats, silk stockings and heeled shoes. She could be as fashionable, extravagant and fussy as she wished to be. Pierre Balmain remembered that during the Second World War, when civilians were advised to make themselves inconspicuous, the two women, who had reasons enough not to draw attention to themselves, sported clothes sawn together from bright yellow and red cloth and alarmed by such untoward visibility he made them more discrete suits of tweed. He was also amused by the way Gertrude Stein tried the skirts he made for her by first sitting down in them; they had to be commodious enough for her to sit with her legs apart, her preferred mode of being seated.

Mabel Haynes bought her evening dresses in Paris, mainly from Worth, while her daywear was made to measure by local dressmakers. She dressed in accordance to prevailing fashions, discarding long skirts in the 1920s – she had shapely and long legs and did not mind showing them – although drop-waist frocks and cloche-hats were hardly flattering for her face or figure. In the late 1940s, when she had temporarily returned to the United States, she spent much of her income on keeping her family and friends in Austria supplied with food, as well as clothes. She particularly enjoyed selecting clothes for her daughter Gabrielle, whose sense of style she much admired. This daughter admired her own sense of style just as much and she was a merciless critic of the sort of clothes I was wearing, never as ladylike as she would have wished. I remember one time, at the age of six, when I was completely delighted wearing a white smocked seersucker dress printed all over with tiny violets, the sort of dress with a current that *could make the machinery crackle...*

Clubs

Our Modern celebrated Clubs are founded upon Eating and Drinking, which are Points wherein most Men agree, and in which the Learned and Illiterate, the Dull and the Airy, the philosopher and the Buffoon, can all of them bear a Part.

So according to an article from 1720, published in *The Spectator*. The dull, the airy, and the buffoons congregated in exclusive gentlemen's clubs, where grandees entered their male children's name upon their birth, safe in the knowledge that all members had been carefully vetted to ensure their clubbability. Gentlemen's clubs excluded not only all those not deemed to be gentlemen but also ladies. Part of the very appeal of the gentlemen's club was the fact that they excluded women, and the most exclusive ones still persist in not allowing women to become members.

Since there were some women who perceived the advantages of being able to congregate with those who shared the same ideas, prejudices, level of education and income, they found means to establish their own clubs. May Bookstaver, once she had become Mrs Charles E. Knoblauch, joined The Women's Cosmopolitan Club in New York, in addition to her membership at various political and women's suffrage organisations.

May Bookstaver was an enthusiastic committee woman and helped to organize all sorts of receptions and events to raise funds for causes worthy of her support. May Bookstaver's husband, the gregarious banker Charles 'Chas' Knoblauch, was also a club man, although he favoured smart clubs that catered for sporty types like himself.

Mabel Haynes' father, John C. Haynes, came from New English Puritan stock who did not think that his own comfort or amusement were worth spending money on. *Mr. Haynes was never a club man in the ordinary sense of the term. If he was a member of certain associations, it was on account of something beside mere social intercourse that they stood for. For example, he was a member of the Unitarian Club, the Home Market Club, the Massachusetts Club, the Boston Merchants' Association, and the Music Publishers Association of the United States, but in every case he had at heart, not his own amusement, but the promotion of some great interest which he regarded as vital.*

In such clubs, public minded and philanthropic Men of Substance sought congenial company to deliberate how best to spend their money on causes worthy of support.

Mabel Haynes did not live in New York, where she might have joined the Bryn Mawr Alumnae Club, as May Bookstaver had done. She went to live in Austria-Hungary in remote garrison towns or provincial cities where there either were no clubs or none she would have wished to join.

Gertrude Stein was never a member of any club and I wonder what she would have thought of a club in Washington DC that bears her name. Gertrude Stein was a Republican and whether she would have accepted membership in the Gertrude Stein Democratic Club or whether she would have reacted in the manner of Groucho Marx is something that the members of this club might well have deliberated.

Communism and fascism

Gertrude Stein, May Bookstaver, and Mabel Haynes were born into a world where the notion of communism had just been invented but the word fascism had no currency. By the time Gertrude Stein, May Bookstaver, and Mabel Haynes ended their lives (between 1946 and 1955) fascism was thought to have been defeated. However, while the fascist regimes of Germany and Italy had been defeated, those of Spain and Portugal had not. Communism had yet to be defeated, and the Cold War that was meant to bring this defeat about had only just started by the time Gertrude Stein died.

Gertrude Stein and Mabel Haynes were both life-long Republicans who deplored any measures undertaken by the American government to chip away at the idea that everybody had to fend for themselves without handouts from the government. In 1936 Gertrude Stein wrote a series of articles about money where she was critical of Roosevelt's New Deal. She did not like his attempts *to do away with money,* to get rid of the rich and help the unemployed. She feared that such policies would provoke in the Americans *a passion to be enslaved.* She repeated these ideas about money, paternalistic governments, human nature and the human mind in several texts she worked on in the 1930s, not least in "Everybody's Autobiography": *Roosevelt tries to spend so much that perhaps money will not exist, communists try to live without money but it never lasts because if you live without money you have to do as the animals do live on what you find each day to eat and that is just the difference the minute you do not do that you have to have money and so everybody has to make up their mind if money is money or if money isn't money and sooner or later they always decide that money is money.*

Mabel Haynes had similar views: *I am delighted that it was Eisenhower; Stevenson is highly intellectual but I fear the welfare state idea that he might have felt he had to take over from Truman. Eisenhower will let capital have free play. It is un-American to want to be cared for at the state's expense from the cradle to the grave or in drastic American 'from the womb to the town'.*

Gertrude Stein's pronouncements on economics and politics, especially those she wrote for the popular press during the 1930s, did not go unchallenged. Michael Gold wrote article entitled *Gertrude Stein, A Literary Idiot*, in the *New Masses*, the radical socialist American magazine: *For Gertrude Stein and the other artists like her, art exists in the vacuum of a private income. In order to pursue the kind of art, in order to be the kind of artist Gertrude Stein is, it is necessary to live in that kind of society which will permit one to have a private income from wealthy parents or sound investments. With this as a basis, you can write as you please. You can destroy language, mutilate grammar, rave or rant in the name of the higher knowledge. Nobody will disturb you. And in time perhaps you can impress or intimidate a certain number of critics and win a kind of reputation. …Which seems to me to be proof that with enough money and enough persistence a madman can convince a world of his sanity. Gertrude Stein appears to have convinced America that she is a genius. But Marxists refuse to be impressed with her own opinion of herself. They see in the work of Gertrude Stein extreme symptoms of the decay of capitalist culture. They view her work as the complete attempt to annihilate all relations between the artist and the society in which he lives. They see in her work the same kind of orgy and spiritual abandon that marks the life of the whole leisure class.*

Gertrude Stein had indeed succeeded to connect to American society by that time, despite the fact that her work was hardly read. As a public intellectual she responded to questions about money and politics, sometimes talking straight, and sometimes tongue in cheek. Perhaps stung by criticism about her sometimes simply reactionary and sometimes highly provocative remarks, she said in an interview in 1938: *Writers only think they are interested in politics, they are not really, it gives them a chance to talk and writers like to talk but really no real writer is really interested in politics.* This could be seen as disingenuous as Gertrude Stein liked to have her views on politics widely known and a good many people read her articles in the American press and heard her interviews as they were broadcast, especially during the Second World War, when she lived in occupied France. She was too much an American Republican to have anything but distrust and instinctual dislike for communism and she made her views of that very clear. Gertrude Stein's instinctual sympathies were with the fascists in those places where fascists and communists confronted each other, as in in Spain or Italy, even in Germany. She could at times think about why intellectuals, and she certainly included herself in that category, were drawn to authoritarian forms of government: *It could be a puzzle why the intellectuals in every country are always wanting a form of government which would inevitably treat them badly, purge them so to speak before anybody else is purged. It has always happened from the French revolution to today. It would be a puzzle this if it were not that it is true that the world is round and that space is illimitable unlimited. I suppose it is that that makes the intellectual so anxious for a regimenting government which they could so ill endure.*

During the first three years Second World War Gertrude Stein and Alice B. Toklas lived in the part of France that was not under German occupation. This changed in 1942. The fact that both women survived unscathed has been taken as proof of their collaborationist attitude, and the fact that Gertrude Stein openly admired Marshal Pétain was seen as further evidence for continuing fascist sympathies. This has led to her being posthumously vilified after an exhibition of the Metropolitan Museum in New York brought this to public attention. Gertrude Stein, by not becoming a victim of fascist Germany's race laws and by never having been a person with sympathies for the Left, could thus become, in the eyes of some, as despicable as the fascists themselves, while in the eyes of others she was an individualist who espoused an essentially a-political '*rugged individualism*' or an artist who resisted being taken in by any ideology.

Mabel Haynes lived during the 1930s and during the whole of the Second World War in Austria, no longer Austria-Hungary but simply Austria, reduced to the German speaking part of the former empire. Her husband, a retired officer, retained nostalgic memories of the old Austria and sympathised with militaristic though not pan-German *Heimwehr*. Mabel Haynes did not communicate her thoughts on Austrian politics to her American friends, though she did express regret over the break-up of the empire. In 1924 she wrote a message to the Bryn Mawr Alumnae Bulletin: *Many of you know how beautiful Vienna is and how delightful are the people. They are keeping up their music at the cost of other things and are getting bravely on their feet. But there is very bitter political rivalry, and still much sad poverty.* Sad poverty and political rivalry continued to be a fact of life in post-war Austria and it has been argued that these conditions, made increasingly intolerable in the years following the Depression, made fascism attractive to so many Austrians. To what extent the American Mabel Haynes thought Austro-Fascism attractive, or indeed National-Socialism, remains unclear. The descendants of her daughter Itha maintain that she had been a fervent Nazi, something her third daughter always denied. One letter does give an impression of her views, written on July 31st 1951: *The "big four" have allowed 2 million people to be displaced, taking nothing with them, and with no home anywhere. That spirit of revenge began with the unjust Nuremberg trial, and one vengeance leads to another. It can never be forgiven that generals were hanged. Fancy keeping Petain in prison with 94 years. By his so-called collaboration, he saved half of France. Hitler could have overrun it all. Just as in Belgium. By trying to pacify Hitler Belgium was saved all destruction. And how have they thanked him? The Dutch royal family sailed off to a place of safety and left its people to take the bombs. History's verdict will straighten out much of this...*

This view was broadly similar to Gertrude Stein's. Both women, like the majority of the population, favoured appeasement over resistance and burying the past over retribution. Gertrude Stein toured Germany with Alice B. Toklas after the war and had herself photographed at Hitler's house in Berchtesgaden, her arms raised in mock Nazi salute.

Mabel Haynes and Gertrude Stein lived part of their lives under a totalitarian system, in their case a fascist one, and they had survived. A great many had not. A great many were not to survive the totalitarian communist systems either. Which ideological system one has sympathies with, and which ideological system one may have to survive, can make one a hero, another a collaborator.

Cooking

Alas, alas the pull alas the bell alas the coach in china, alas the little put in leaf alas the wedding butter meat, alas the receptacle, alas the back shape of mussle, mussle and soda.

I do inevitably take my comparisons from the kitchen because I like food and cooking and know something about it.

One might measure a culture's sophistication by the complexity of its *battérie de cuisine* and the number of successive procedures applied to a single dish. The greater the distance between social classes the more elaborate the cooking for the elite and the more dependent that is on the services of professional cooks. When May Bookstaver, Gertrude Stein and Mabel Haynes were growing up in their upper middle-class households, the cooking, as much as any other household tasks, was not the responsibility of their mothers, but of their cooks or housekeepers, and these cooks and housekeepers did not take kindly to interference. While other women's colleges encouraged students to do some share of domestic work, M. Carey Thomas insisted that her students at Bryn Mawr would be better employed studying. A Bryn Mawr alumna of these years was educated to despise doing anything that would detract from pursuing intellectual endeavours. Mabel Haynes never set foot into the kitchen and never cooked anything in her life but tea or perhaps a slice of toast. When she no longer had her own household, she would go to eat in restaurants. When May Bookstaver married Charles E. Knoblauch they moved into a large modern apartment in the recently completed 'Wyoming', an upmarket apartment block on 55th Street Seven in Midtown Manhattan. One of the advantages of living in these stylish new blocks was the catering service offered by the restaurant situated on the ground floor. This made cooking at home unnecessary and entertaining in the suite of the apartments' receptions rooms effortless in terms of providing food. This modern lifestyle of the wealthy inhabitants of New York City would have suited Mrs Charles E. Knoblauch perfectly well.

Gertrude Stein also never cooked, though she did set foot into the kitchen, as she liked to see what was cooking. When she rented a house in Baltimore with Emma Lootz they had a German housekeeper, and later, sharing the studio with Leo Stein in the rue de Fleurus, they employed Hélène to do the cooking and Hélène cooked French food. It was one of the many strong points of Alice B. Toklas that she had not been brought up to despise cooking, that she professed to enjoy cooking and that she could cook for Gertrude Stein the sort of things her French cook would not. Alice B. Toklas cooked American food and she was also adept at making the cakes and sweets that Gertrude Stein was inordinately fond of. In their later years together, they employed a great many different cooks, Austrian cooks, French cooks, Chinese cooks and Vietnamese, but Alice B. Toklas would continue to cook for Gertrude Stein the dishes she wanted to eat that and which these cooks would or could not do. She was a connoisseur of food and enjoyed the preparation and the critique better than its consumption.

When Gertrude Stein says on Alice B. Toklas' behalf that she takes her comparisons from the kitchen because she likes cooking and knows something about it that is equally true of herself. It is true, not just because she enjoyed eating, but because she was interested in the different ways of cooking. She noticed, for instance, how the cooking she had known in her childhood and youth in America had all but disappeared there, to be replaced with new forms of cooking. She was interested in the process of cooking, from the growing of the vegetables and fruit and the shopping to the cooking itself, and one might say that much of her writing is a form of cooking, in the sense of a good cook who sees what there is at hand and puts it together in such a way that it suits the occasion and the time or the year and the particular mood of the day and then presents it so that appeals to all the senses. A lot of vegetables and fruits and meat and dishes and implements appear in Gertrude Stein's writing, not just in *Tender Buttons*. At her texts are like an elaborate dinner with many courses and sometimes it's more like a dish of freshly pulled radishes with a bit of earth still clinging to the roots to be eaten with sweet butter. There is also the texture of things being chopped finely or coarsely, mashed or strained, or being velvety or rough, soft and wet or dry and crusty. Of course, she did not cook in a kitchen and handle vegetables and meat. She used words instead, and while Alice B. Toklas or her other cooks cooked up a storm in the kitchen, she cooked up her sentences and paragraphs, concoctions that delighted her to make and which she wished to share with everyone who likes to partake of such fare.

Corsets

Mabel Haynes, Gertrude Stein and Mary Bookstaver would all have worn corsets when they were young women. *The Encyclopaedia Britannica* of 1951 has an entry *corselet*, which signifies *ancient and medieval body armour which covered the whole body though it later was restricted to that which covered the body between the neck and thighs*. The etymology of the term clearly derives from Latin *corpus*. Such a military connotation provides a useful perspective on the 19th century corset, which encased women's bodies like an armour that was be worn underneath.

However, while the metal plated corselet worn by medieval warriors offered protection against the slashing and cutting instruments of war current at the time and was later useless against fire weapons, the female corset was to strengthen the upright posture of a woman and at the same time emphasize fragility by the cinched waist, a breaking point between the upper and the lower regions of the body. Much has been said about the moulding of female bodies by 19th century dress, which restrained independence and agency. Female dress and male dress complemented each other: the woman's corset worked from within the publicly seen figure, the man's stiff suits, waistcoats, stiffened shirt-front and collars, the tight-fitting rock-coats encased them too in layers of enforcement, complemented by stiff, tall hats. The materials favoured for men's clothing were tightly woven wool or serge or linen. Clearly these layers of close-fitted, sturdy materials encased men's bodies like bourgeois armour to enable their engagement in the thrust and parry of capitalist competition. Women's street garments, their cashmere shawls and velvet cloaks, on the other hand, offered inadequate protection from the elements, the better to keep them safely at home, but there they were fortified by the ever-present stricture of the corset, which allowed but shallow breathing and decorous movement. Thorsten Veblen argued that the whole point of the apparel of women belonging to the Leisure Class was to demonstrate the *wearer's abstinence from productive employment.* In addition to unsuitable footwear, hobbling skirts and excessively long hair, he identifies the corset as a contrivance most successful in differentiating women from men: *The corset is, in economic theory, a mutilation, undergone for the purpose of lowering the subject's vitality and rendering her permanently and obviously unfit for work. It is true, the corset permanently impairs the personal attraction of the wearer, but the loss suffered on the score is offset by the gain in reputability which comes of her visibly increased expensiveness and infirmity.*

The discipline that made women not just to submit to the corset, but to identify with its aims to differentiate the wearer in term of class and gender, came at a high price. Bodies that from childhood on (by means of training corsets) were severely constricted could no longer support themselves without pain, necessitating the wearing of stays even at night.

Not all women did put their four-year old daughters in a training corset, force teenagers into tight-laced bodices that made them faint or adopt it for themselves. As Veblen pointed out, such practices were restricted to the upper class that could afford their womenfolk not to engage in productive work.

When women colleges encouraged athleticism and fostered a sense of female professional competence, young girls were permitted to lay aside their corsets or use those specifically made for the purpose of greater movement by the insertion of elasticated panels. When Mabel Haynes and May Bookstaver were students at Bryn Mawr College, they would take part in the many forms of exercise, since their principal, Dr M. Carey Thomas thought vigorous exercise to be conductive to serious study.

Gertrude Stein loved to go for long hikes and to move freely. Although her family would want her to look the part of a member of a well-off bourgeois family used to 'good rich living', and that meant wearing suitably fashionable clothes, made by seamstresses and dressmakers, she felt free to divest herself of the restraining garments when she saw fit. Already at Baltimore, in the later 1890s, her relative recalls *Gertie flopping around the place – big and floppy and sandaled and not caring a damn.* On the other hand, a photograph of Gertrude Stein at Radcliffe, shows her in a very tightly fitted wool dress, with a white scalloped collar and another, from 1903, the time she left for Paris, in a shirt waist with a black, close fitting blouse. She did not jettison the corset altogether, until a few years later, once she had settled in with Alice B. Toklas. From about 1908 onwards, she never ever squeezed herself into a restrictive undergarment again and adopted loose fitting robes and skirts. Gertrude Stein was never a thin woman but Alice B. Toklas was a thin woman who never put on much flesh. Even so, she wore corsets and in her own autobiography she relates, with some delight, how she jettisoned that garment: *Because of the heat I got rid on my cerise ribbon girdle in the dressing room of the train, throwing it out of the window. When I returned to our compartment Harriet said, What a strange coincidence, I just saw your cherry-coloured corset pass by the window.*

Alice B. Toklas had journeyed to Italy with her friend Harriet Levy, but she returned secretly married to Gertrude Stein, and by throwing her cherry corset out of the window, instead of just taking it off while she was hot, she threw out her whole previous life and freed herself to be unencumbered for Gertrude Stein.

Countenance

If can in countenance to countenance a countenance as in as
seen.
Change it.
Not nearly so much.
He had.
She had.
Had she.
He had nearly very nearly as much.
She had very nearly as much as had had.
Had she.
She had.

Well-bred New England women, such as Mabel Haynes, knew how to dissimulate their feelings and how to maintain their composure, even in the most trying of circumstances. They considered the vivacious expressions of southern folk an example of their generally indolent nature, one unwilling to exert self-control and too easily given to tantrums and childish displays of emotion. Mabel Haynes' Yankee cool composure facilitated her access to European society, where her wealth and her learning alone would not have been sufficient. Emma Lootz always admired her equanimity in the face of adversity, not only during May Bookstaver's affair with Gertrude Stein, which had thrown Gertrude Stein off her course enough to lose her sense of self-control.

Well-bred Victorian women who were taught to keep the countenance under control were often those to lose their countenance in spectacular ways by having fits of paralysis where they would not be able to move at all, the whole body made rigid with a surfeit of repression. Such women, generally well-bred women with amiable countenances, would become hysterical, psychotic, neurotic, or paranoid, and some of their more or less successful attempts at being cured made them exemplary case studies.

Gertrude Stein was not a New England woman and not one constantly reminded to keep her face and gestures under control. She laughed loudly and heartily, she would glare and glower and purse her lips, and she may have rolled her eyes, not unlike the emotional southerners or blacks. When she transposed the theme of her pursuit of May Bookstaver into the negro world evoked in *Melanctha,* she transposed the habitus of her protagonists into a southern mode, loosened their stays one might say.

Hysteria all but disappeared from the case studies of psychoanalysts after the Great War, when it had become clear to well-bred women that they had other avenues to pursue than repression. The hugely magnified and back-lit faces of silent movie stars that filled the screen were perhaps the last apotheosis of the cool northern composure and the perfectly kept countenance.

My father, Mabel Haynes' son, not one of whom it could be said that he had a stiff upper lip, always worried about the possibility of his daughters ending up hysterics, not surprising given that some of his sisters had clearly shown a predisposition to this. His method was to administer a good thrashing, which had to be borne with equanimity and the exhortation to weep quietly. Since he did not present this a means to become a well-bred young lady but a stoical Indian brave or a Spartan warrior, I could accept it as necessary training to be able to endure grief and pain without losing face.

Dance

Dance a clean dream and an extravagant turn up, secure the steady rights and translate more than translate the authority, show the choice and make no more mistakes than yesterday.

This could be read as good advice given to young people on the eve of their first ball, though scrambled by excitement. Girls from very wealthy families, like Mabel Haynes and her sisters, even girls from not quite as wealthy families, such as May Bookstaver and Gertrude Stein, would have been expected to comport themselves with circumspection and confidence, showing their bared shoulders and *décolletage*, their jewellery and coiffed hair, in a more or less *extravagant turn up,* to perform a *Valse Boston* or a *cotillion.* Gertrude Stein was orphaned at the age of seventeen and when she joined her well-to-do relatives in Baltimore they were prepared to launch her into the world of well-to-do Jewish society. She chose to follow her brother Leo to Cambridge, Massachusetts, instead, and to begin a life of study. Mabel Haynes and May Bookstaver also preferred to attend college rather than balls. At Bryn Mawr, living primarily in the company of women who formed passionate attachments to each other, they would have danced with other girls at college functions. Whether the young women of their class enjoyed balls or tea dances or not, they would all have been taught how to perform them. Years later, in 1932, when Gertrude Stein was writing *Four in America,* she was remembering the movement of the dances they learned, and she made a connection between forward and back movement and warfare: *And the minuet as we were taught to dance the waltz a little but the minuet made me feel that. (….) That is war is and dancing it is forward and back, when one out walking one wants not to go back the way they came but in dancing and in war it is forward and back.*

The waltz, so we were told at home, the Viennese waltz in particular, with its reverse turns and changes of tempo, was the undoing of Mabel Haynes' resolve to keep her independence. Perhaps this is a myth that her daughters liked to perpetuate, given that they were both enthusiastic dancers and enthusiastic lovers of men. However, the possibility remains that once Mabel Haynes allowed her body to be moved backwards and forwards, while continuously whirling, she learned something about her body that surprised her. At any rate, she herself would say, when she was no longer of an age where she cared to dance, that dancing at the balls in *Fin de Siècle* Vienna had been indescribably delightful. Was the pleasure of dancing also the pleasure of submitting to be led, to step backwards and sideways, following the pressure of a man's hand on her back? Did these steps backwards means a backwards movement of Mabel Haynes' emancipation? In a minuet the advance and retreat is much clearer than in a waltz, as Gertrude Stein noticed. Perhaps it could only have happened in Vienna that Mabel Haynes lost her head and became a woman who married men.

While Gertrude Stein did not dance herself, she enjoyed watching other people dance. *The Autobiography of Alice B. Toklas* has quite a few references to people dancing, professional performers or friends at parties. The descriptions 'Alice B. Toklas' gives of these dances convey as much her sense of humour as her judgement as a self-confessed expert: *Dancing excites me tremendously and it is a thing I know a great deal about. I have seen three very great dancers. My geniuses seem to run in threes, but that is not my fault, it happens to be a fact. The three really great dancers I have seen are the Argentina, Isadora Duncan and Nijinsky. Like the three geniuses I have known they are each one of a different nationality.*

Gertrude Stein, on her first journey to Spain with Alice B. Toklas, saw performances of Flamenco that impressed her enough to compose one of her 'portraits':

Susie Asado

        Sweet sweet sweet sweet sweet tea.

        Susie Asado.

    Sweet sweet sweet sweet sweet tea.

        Susie Asado.

   Susie Asado which is a told tray sure.

   A lean on the shoe this means slips slips hers.

The dancer they had watched was Antonia Mercé, known as La Argentina, one of the three dance geniuses in Alice B. Toklas' trio, a modernist dancer, said to have used gypsy traditions in the way Picasso used Iberian masks. Gertrude Stein later said that her experiments resulted in things with *extraordinary melody of words and a melody of excitement in trying that I had done this thing.* Was she excited that she had turned the excitement of watching a woman dancing the Flamenco into a pattern of words on the page, which when read loud conveys the stamping of feet and swishing of skirts and clicking of fingers and castanets? And she could do it while observing her rule, the absolute refusal of never using a word that was not an exact word.

The other dancing genius Gertrude Stein responded to in her writing was Isadora Duncan. Her text 'Orta or One Dancing' (from 1911-12) did not respond to the physical qualities of Isadora Duncan's dancing – her fluidity, her natural movements – but her identity as a modern artist who does not just dance but thinks as well as dances:

This one is one being dancing. This one is the one thinking in believing in dancing having meaning. This one is believing in thinking. This one is one thinking in dancing having meaning. This one is one believing in dance having meaning. His one is one dancing. This one is one being that one. This one is one being one being dancing. This one is one being in being one who is dancing. This one is one being. This one is one being in being one.

Although Gertrude Stein went to the *Ballets Russes* and saw Vaslav Nijinsky, the third genius of dance, he did not seem to have inspired her to write about the way he danced or on the way that his dancing made her think. Perhaps his tremendous leaps were too uncongenial, or his genius too alien to her own. On the evening of his last performance, the 19th of January 1919, Nijinsky began to write, almost non-stop, for 45 days, not caring *what my hand writes*. He filled 381 pages and then stopped never to take up a pen again. The text, with its simplified language and frequent repetitions, has some superficial resemblance to Gertrude Stein's writing. Unlike her though, he could not accomplish the feat of dancing and writing at the same time.

Depressions and the Great Depression

They believed the depression was a depression, before that booms had busted but a busted boom is not a depression.

Was Gertrude Stein a melancholic genius? The art critic of the *New York Times* thought he detected some signs of that: *There is evidence that Stein had a history of depression. Being brainy, bulky and gay must have made her feel like a misfit pretty much everywhere she went. And writing, which she had begun to do, can be a lonely occupation, particularly if you're inventing a mode that gives you little hope of readers. "I write for myself and strangers" is a repeated refrain in "The Making of Americans," which was composed in part before Stein and Toklas met.* There is however little evidence that she had a truly atrabilious temperament, and certainly, once she and Alice B. Toklas established their union, she was said to have been even-tempered and generally cheerful. She had, by that time, finished her mourning for the loss of her first love object, May Bookstaver. Her second book, the one she had not put away in a cupboard, *Three Lives* contains stories about deeply depressed protagonists who each come to a sorry end.

The one that most closely takes up the May Bookstaver - Mabel Haynes - Gertrude Stein drama, transposed into a Negro milieu, is the aptly named 'Melanctha'. One medical critic suggested that *from a clinical perspective, Melanctha suffers from neurotic depression or, in DSM IV terms, dysthymia. She is chronically unhappy, ruminates a lot, and is never clear about what she really wants to do. Toward the end of the story, she probably has an episode of major depression and considers suicide but goes on to die (anticlimactically) of tuberculosis.*

The second time Gertrude Stein was to experience symptoms of depression occurred during the period known as the Great Depression, in 1933. Having been worried about the financial difficulties brought about by the bank crash in America and the fact that none of her books had been a success in terms of sales, she had written *The Autobiography of Alice B. Toklas* with a view of writing a commercially successful book. Although the dollars that flowed from the publication pleased her well enough, Gertrude Stein experienced a loss of identity and this time the melancholia was such that she could not write: *All this time I did no writing. I had written and was writing nothing. Nothing needed any word and there was no word inside me that could not be spoken and so there was no word inside me. And I was not writing. I began to worry about identity. I had always been I because I had words that had to be written inside me and now any word I had inside me could be spoken it it did not to be written. I am I because my little dog knows me. But was I I when I had no written word inside me. It was very bothersome. I sometimes thought that I would try but to try is to die and so I did not really try. I was not doing any writing.*

Having success and money at a time when this was in such dreadfully short supply, with millions of people out of work and destitute, did not trouble Gertrude Stein. She could surely feel sorry for those made homeless and destitute, but these effects of the Great Depression did not depress her. Her success depressed her: *When the success began, and it was a success I got completely lost...I did not know myself, I lost my personality. It has always been completely included in myself my personality as any personality naturally is. And here all of a sudden, I was not just I because so many people did know me. It was just the opposite of I am I because my little dog knows me. So many people knowing me I was I no longer and for the first time since I began to write I could not write and that was worse.*

However, the summer of 1933, she called it *that funny summer,* proved to be so full of strange events - unexplained deaths in the vicinity, problems with servants, falling outs with friends, her opera *Three Saints in Four Acts* being produced in America - that she was too distracted to give herself up to melancholia and the following years she was to face being a celebrity who is known to a great many people straight on. She had a shock on seeing herself in a newsreel, but after the lecture tour the writer's block lifted never to re-occur. She could henceforth continue to be a genius, of that she was quite sure, without being a melancholic genius.

By 1933 the shock waves of the great crash of the New York stock exchange two years earlier had reached around the world. May Bookstaver's husband, Charles E. Knoblauch, who had traded on the Wall Street since 1893, was made bankrupt. He managed to hold on to his seat at the Stock Exchange and could sell it 1932 for $85,000.

His wife, contributing to the Bryn Mawr Alumnae Bulletin of 1931, writes rather wryly that every the good Socialist was aware others were much worse off: *I wish I could tell you that we were about to start for a try at Everest, or a trip to Mars or even to the Moon, but alas! we must stay right here and endeavor to absorb the iceman, the coal man, the orchestra men, and all the others thrown out of employment by the machines to the disturbing if not permanent distress of all of us.*

Charles Knoblauch seems to have managed the remainder of his money in such a way that his wife had a small income after he died in 1934 of a heart attack.

Even so, May Bookstaver found herself a widow in rather reduced circumstance at the time when Gertrude Stein's name was spelled in neon letters in Times Square at the beginning of her lecture tour. May Bookstaver had a generous nature by all accounts and she may therefore have been pleased for her old friend's success, perhaps this was even a consolation during her time of mourning. They did not meet in person.

In Germany Adolf Hitler had managed to capitalize on the fears and despair caused by the Great Depression, which was not called *Grosse Depression* but simply *Wirtschaftskrise* or at best, *Weltwirtschaftskrise* (world economic crisis), and he got himself elected, with 44% of the population voting for his National Socialist Party. Gertrude Stein did not find this depressing. In fact, she told a reporter from *New York Times Magazine*, who interviewed her at her Parisian flat that Hitler deserved the Nobel Peace prize *because he is removing all elements of contest and of struggle from Germany. By driving out the Jews and the democratic and Left elements, he is driving out everything that conduces to activity. That means peace.*

Gertrude Stein's political views can make depressing reading unless one allows that she may have been joking.

Mabel Haynes, divorced from her second husband, saw her income dwindle in the course of the Depression and had to sell the house in Graz that she had loved. Austria in the 1930's also experienced high unemployment, social unrest and an increasingly violent political climate. Mabel Haynes wrote to her daughter Gabrielle, then living in Berlin, on August 5th 1936, from a Carinthian lakeside resort: *It is beastly being so hard up. I met some Americans who claimed that prosperity was returning in America but we don't feel it as yet. I hope you have managed to see Hitler.* After the war, Mabel Haynes returned to Boston. She felt lonely and out of touch with an American society she found greatly changed for the worse. At times, the cheerful and optimistic tone she adopts in her letters, slips: *I have been too miserable to buckle down to writing; one of my fiercest colds. I had no fever just daily more weakness, wracking cough, complete insomnia. I just couldn't get hold of myself. I crawled (in the car) to my meals, as it is best to run no risk of pneumonia by lying flat too much, Well I am better – I got this time a big dose of mental depression. Emma Erving turned up 2 days ago and that boosted me along.*

Doctors

In 1934 Bernard Faÿ, *knowing what such an honorary degree would mean to her,* tried to use his American academic contacts to get an honorary doctorate for his friend Gertrude Stein. He approached both the University of Chicago and Harvard, but nothing came of it. Like Samuel Johnson Gertrude Stein had not completed her doctorate, although not, as in his case, for lack of funds. Gertrude Stein, only a few examinations away from graduating, had lost interest. This is the way she tells the story in *the Autobiography of Alice B. Toklas:*

There was great excitement in the medical school. Her very close friend Marion Walker pleaded with her, she said, but Gertrude Gertrude remember the cause of women, and Gertrude Stein said, you don't know what it is to be bored. The professor who had flunked her asked her to come to see him. She did. He said, of course Miss Stein all you have to do is to take a summer course here and in the fall naturally you will take your degree. But not at all, said Gertrude Stein, you have no idea how grateful I am to you. I have so much inertia and so little initiative that very possibly if you had not kept me from taking my degree I would have, well, not taken to the practice of medicine, but at any rate to pathological psychology and you don't know how little I like pathological psychology, and how all medicine bores me.

Bernard Faÿ did not succeed in his concerted efforts to get her the MD she was too bored to obtain: it would have been a doctorate in the Humanities. Her friends and fellow-students, Marion Walker, Emma Lootz and Mabel Haynes, took all their exams, obtained their medical doctorate, and became doctors who worked in hospitals, dispensaries and private practice. Mabel Haynes gave up her practice of medicine, but she was always known as Dr Haynes and eventually, married for the second time, Dr Leick. When she needed medical treatment herself, she knew at least what the doctor was talking about: *Of course, I told him that I was a doctor, so that he would speak up in the King's English.* Mabel Haynes did not get bored with medicine after she stopped treating patients, once she had married and had children, she continued to read medical journals, talk to doctors about their interesting cases, and she became the sort of patient doctors like to treat. She also made sure that her children were the sort of patient's doctors get on with. The most important quality is the willingness to get better and to do all one can to bring this about so that the treatment the doctor proscribes actually works. It also helps to like doctors in general and the doctor in charge in particular. In Mabel Haynes' case she followed her mother's predilection: *I am just like my mother - Crazy about doctors and should be glad to have a call a day as she did for years.*

A call a day was also made by Dr Fine to the mother of Gertrude Stein, as she lay slowly dying of cancer. He treated her as well as he could though it is not known to what extent she looked forward to his visits or dreaded them. Mabel Haynes' mother lived almost twice as long as Amelia Stein, to eighty-eight. Mabel Haynes herself knew to find the sort of doctor to make pleasure a vehicle of health: *For your comfort I have found a doctor who can be phoned to at night I liked him, and he is young enough to be up to date (40 or so). Said, as all do, that cigarettes are poison (I haven't even tried a puff at one) but that alcohol is good for me.* Mabel Haynes being a doctor also knew the limitations of their art, as when she realised there was no cure for her first husband's paresis or her young son's leukaemia. Jubilant when her youngest son obtained his doctorate in medicine, she watched his struggles to set up practice in post-war Austria with anxiety and pride. He turned out to be the sort of doctor in general practice whom some of his patients desired to see very day, *a serious, earnest, good young joyous doctor,* like Jeff Campbell, described as such by Gertrude Stein in her story *Melanctha.* In his manner of treating us children he could be experimental, making use of traditional remedies some of his patients brought to him, such as resin poultices for coughs, crushed garlic for worms, syrup made of fermented dandelion flowers for catarrh. He taught me not to be afraid of injections and to submit cheerfully to any medical procedure. Gertrude Stein's father, who was not a doctor, also made them submit to his experiments with doctoring: *They had some troubles with him then in their early living, sometimes in ways of doctoring, sometimes when he thought it was good for them to have castor oil given to them, sometimes when he thought a Chinese doctor would be good for them, sometimes when he had a queer blind man to examine one of them; but all this, and the ways of eating, ways of cooking, he thought good for them, will come out in the history of each one of the three of them, for in each one of them it had a different effect on them in their later living, these new beginnings in all their younger living, beginnings and new ways in doctoring and in ways of eating.*

For Leo Stein, the effect of such fathering and doctoring was a serious neurosis, which he diagnosed and eventually cured himself of. For Daniel Stein it led to obesity, and for Gertrude Stein a robust constitution and a delicate digestion.

When Gertrude Stein was very ill she was taken to the American hospital where the doctors thought she was too ill to be operated on. She insisted that they try. Alice B. Toklas was with her: *Then, however, the surgeons refused to perform the operation, saying she was not in a fit condition any more. But amongst the surgeons was one who said, I have told Miss Stein that I would perform the operation and you don't give your word of honour to a woman of her character and not keep it. So, I shall operate. .... The whole afternoon was troubled, confused and very uncertain, and later in the afternoon they took her away on a wheeled stretcher to the operating room and I never saw her again.* Almost a year later her brother Leo Stein died from an infected wound after his last cancer operation in Italy.

Dogs

Qu'est ce que c'est cette comedie d'un chien.

Gertrude Stein always says that she has only two real distractions, pictures and automobiles. Perhaps she might now add dogs.

I am I because my little dog knows me.

In January 1915, Kuroki, a Boston bulldog belonging to Mrs Charles E. Knoblauch, became the most talked about dog in American newspapers. The Texan daily, *El Paso Morning Times*, gives a flavour of the reporting: *Kuroki is the devoted subject of Mrs Charles E. Knoblauch, wife of a member of the stock exchange, who was one of Roosevelt's Rough Riders in Cuba. She, too, is fashioned of heroic stuff. She suffered imprisonment for Kuroki in her effort to show that he was being made a victim of an unconstitutional law. It was only an hour in the district prison, but a city gaol is a city gaol, whether it is spelled with g or a j, and it is usually a place in which no one other than a person fired by principles would be content to stay, even for an hour. Mrs. Knoblauch refused to give bail, and Miss Bertha Rembaugh, her lawyer, at once brought the case before the Supreme Court on a writ of habeas corpus.*

Then the American Kennel Club, which rightly believes that a dog is more than a mere dog, threw its influence with Kuroki's mistress. It had a brief prepared, in which it was indicated what a hardship the muzzle law would work on dogs, already under leash. For the point – and one that will interest every dog owner in cities and towns – is that those who are opposed to muzzling believe that the general public is sufficiently safeguarded by the leash.

But what makes this test case unusual is the contention that the ordinary muzzle will not stay on Kuroki – Kuroki, who never so much as growled at a person in all his life. In the beginning

Mrs. Knoblauch, much as she disliked to, endeavoured to obey the law, but the architecture of Kuroki was a barrier that really caused her revolt.

Mrs C. Knoblauch, previously known as May Bookstaver, received a huge amount of mail and Kuroki numerous presents. At the final hearing Justice Lehman of the Supreme Court decided *that the Board of Health did have jurisdiction and that its rules, made for the preservation of public health, would have to be obeyed.* (…) *if Kuroki could not be fitted to any ordinary ready-made muzzle, being a dog of fashion, one should be specially fitted to one by some artist in the business – whether he – the dog – be noseless or bigger of neck than the head made not the slightest difference to the eyes of the law.* I could not find out whether Kuroki was subsequently led about Central Park wearing an artist-made muzzle but as the Texan reporter summarized: *However further the case may develop, Kuroki is not worrying himself. In public attention, in the space he has occupied in the newspapers, in the legal expenses and high court processes he has caused to be put in motion, he certainly has been shown the consideration due even the two-legged animal who stands on his inalienable right to life and the pursuit of happiness. Yes, this dog is having his day!*

No doubt Mrs C. Knoblauch was also having her day.

A few years before she achieved notoriety on behalf of Kuroki, she had made an impression on the photographer Alfred Stieglitz when she paid him a visit at his gallery 291. He later told his lover and biographer, Dorothy Norman, that *In December 1911, or perhaps it was January 1912, a huge woman leading a huge Boston bulldog entered 291. She had a portfolio filled with manuscripts under her arm. It was a funny sight to see the woman with her bulldog and bursting portfolio in that tiny room.* Gertrude Stein had sent May Bookstaver (Mrs Knoblauch) some examples of her recent writing, which she took to Alfred Stieglitz as a person suitable to be shown such works, given that he had been the first to show Picasso in New York and that she had been advised that he was the *one man in this country… crazy enough to be interested in anything like them".* Alfred Stieglitz accepted two of the texts *as soon as he saw them, principally because he did not understand them.* 'Picasso' and 'Matisse' were published in the next issue of *Camera Works* and Gertrude Stein was *genuinely pleased that he had liked her things.* Alfred Stieglitz had visited Gertrude and Leo Stein in 1909, and he remembered her as *dark and bulksome* and as not saying much as she sat on her high chair in the corner while the men held forth. The size of the women, the dog, and the portfolio made an impression on Alfred Stieglitz, which may have more to do with the relative size of the gallery space and his own predilection of thin women than mere bulkiness of volume. Kuroki would not have weighed much more than 11kg, judging from a photograph that shows his proudly smiling owners, Mr and Mrs C. Knoblauch. However, there is no doubt that this indomitable dog would have liked to appear as a huge bulldog to people and to other dogs and to the excitable Alfred Stieglitz.

In February 1915, while in New York City, Mrs Charles Knoblauch championed the cause of all muzzled dogs on behalf of Kuroki, German zeppelins began their bombing raids on Paris. Gertrude Stein and Alice B. Toklas, tired of running for shelter, installed themselves in Palma de Mallorca, where they rented a large furnished house on a hillside with a garden full of tuberoses and carnations. They also acquired a dog - a large and shaggy deerhound – they called Polybe. *We had a dog, a mallorcan hound, the hounds slightly crazy, who dance in the moonlight, striped, not all one colour as the Spanish hound of the continent. We called this dog Polybe because we were pleased with the articles in the Figaro signed Polybe... He had an incurable passion for eating filth and nothing would stop him. We muzzled him to see if that would cure him, but this so outraged the russian servant of the english consul that we had to give it up. ..Cook was convinced that we did not know how to bring up Polybe. Polybe had one nice trait. He would sit in a chair and gently smell large bunches of tube-roses with which I always filled a vase in the centre of the room on the floor. He never tried to eat them, he just gently smelled them. When we left we left Polybe behind us in the care of one of the guardians of the old fortress of Belver. When we saw him a week after he did not know us or his name. Polybe comes into many of the plays Gertrude Stein wrote at that time.*

This hound was the first of Gertrude Stein's dogs. It too was a dog that could not be muzzled and a dog who mainly did what he wanted to do. Polybe not only creeps or leaps into the plays Gertrude Stein wrote at the time but into *Ida a Novel* too. It concerns a much-married woman and about fifteen dogs and their doings and their ways of dying.

After they left Polybe on Palma de Mallorca, Gertrude Stein and Alice B. Toklas did not have a dog again until much later, in 1929, when they had leased the country house at Bilignin in the Ain valley, where they would spend their summers to come: *We now had our country house, the one we had only seen across the valley and just before leaving we found the white poodle, Basket. He was a little puppy in a little neighbourhood dog-show and he had blue eyes, a pink nose and white hair and he jumped up into Gertrude Stein's arms. (...) Basket although now he is a large unwieldy poodle, still will get up on Gertrude Stein's lap and stay there. She says that listening to the rhythm of his water drinking made her recognise the difference between sentences and paragraphs, that paragraphs are emotional and that sentences are not.*

Basket was always well groomed and shaved around the head and paws and *the French men and women would all stop and look at him, they said each one as if it was a new idea one would think he was a lamb.* This would have pleased Alice B. Toklas, who had wanted a terrier that looked remarkably like a lamb. Gertrude Stein adds that *Basket liked it naturally it is always more pleasant to be flattered than anything and admiration is the most pleasing flattery* and of course, she also liked to be flattered and admired herself. She liked walking the streets of Paris *a good many hours in the evening* and she liked walking with a large and magnificent dog. She also liked the fact that poodles were circus dogs, [they] *have no sense of home and no sense of being a dog, they do not realize danger nor ordinary life because in a circus there is no such thing.*

When Basket died in 1938, friends had advised her to get another dog, one just like him, immediately: *"Le roi est mort, vive le roi,"* she said, went to a dog show at the *Porte de Versailles, acquired another white poodle, and named him Basket II.* Man Ray photographed Basket II, who looked exactly like Basket I, at least in photographs, posing on a low stool with a padded collar, his nose and feet cleanly shaven and the fur beautifully brushed.

Gertrude Stein walked through the blacked-out streets of war-time Paris with her beautiful poodle and the German soldiers would also stop and admire him and say that he was beautiful. Basket II barked. He barked at German soldiers. Towards the very end of the war, when the German army was in retreat he became too frightened to bark: *it was absolutely unbelievable that in July 1944 that the German army could look like that, it was unbelievable, one could not believe one's eyes, and then I came home having put my dog on the leash and when I got home there were about a hundred of these Germans in the garden in the house all over the place, poor Basket the dog*

was so horrified that he could not even bark, I took him up to my bedroom and he just sat and shivered he did not believe it could be true. But when the Americans arrived, and everyone cried 'Vive la France Vive les Americains' Gertrude Stein wanted her dog to participate: *so I took him down to the local barber and I said won't you shave him and make him elegant, it is not right when the Americans come along and when Paris is free that the only French poodle in Culoz and owned by Americans should not be elegant, so perspiring freely all of us including Basket, he had his paws shaved and his muzzle shaved and he was elegant and as such he took part in the evening's celebration and all the little children, said Basket Basket come here Basket, they do say it beautifully and then there was a blare of trumpets and naturally he was frightened and tried to run away, so I tied him with a handkerchief and the effort was not so elegant but we were all proud of ourselves just the same.*

Gertrude Stein did not only have beautiful and large dogs. She had much smaller dogs too. They had been presents. Francis Picabia gave them a little Mexican dog, after he had received two as a gift from a rich Mexican woman who had had them sent over by ship. *We called him Byron because he was to have as a wife his sister or his mother and so we called him Byron. Poor little Byron his name gave him a strange and feverish nature, he was fierce and tender and danced strange little war dances and frightened Basket. Basket was always frightened of Byron. And then Byron died suddenly one night of typhus.* Byron was followed straight away by another small dog; he looked just like Byron: *Basket was happy that Byron was dead and gone and then we had Pépé and as he had feared and dreaded Byron he loved Pépé. Pépé was named after Francis Picabia and perhaps that made a difference anyway Pépé was and is a nice little dog but not at all like Byron although in a picture of him you can never tell which is which one.*

From then on, until she died, Gertrude Stein lived with dogs or just a dog. She went for walks with them, they sat on her lap when she lounged in an easy chair, she listened to their barks and growls and tongues lapping, their playing and love-making and all this found its way into her writing, *I always write about dogs why not they are always with me.* During her period of depression in 1930s, she also often wrote the sentence *I am I because my little dog knows me.* This should probably not be taken as a snub to her big dogs, as if they wouldn't know, only the little dogs. She was pondering the question of what identity means, especially to her, now that people were interested in her as a person and not as a writer.

Mabel Haynes, just like Gertrude Stein and her old friend May Bookstaver, always preferred dogs to cats. She had a small dog called Tschin, who had a long ruff around his neck and I cannot identify what breed this was. There is just one photograph of Tschin, sitting next to my father when he was a boy of about eight years old, posing in a photographer's studio. Her husband, Major Leick, had him shot in front of the children, when he suspected him of having rabies. This must have been around 1923.

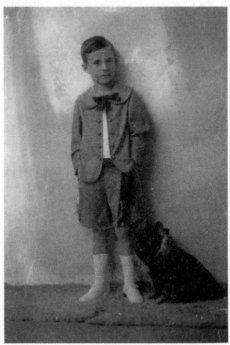

Wolfie, a German shepherd, came later. The family album preserves several snapshots of Mabel Leick, as she was then called, strolling in Graz with her youngest son and the large dog sagely wearing a muzzle.

Dreams

A novel is what you dream in your night sleep. A novel is not waking thoughts although it is written and thought with waking thoughts. But really a novel goes as dreams go in sleeping at night and some dreams are like anything and some dreams are like something and some dreams change and some dreams are quiet and some dreams are not. And some dreams are just what any one would do only a little different always just a little different and that is what a novel is.

You will say to me it has not happened and I will answer yes of course it has not happened and you will dream and I will dream and cream.

A while ago I dreamed that I was in the company of Gertrude Stein at some social gathering, outdoors in sunshine, and she smiled at me with a warm and sunny smile, saying something that I could not remember when I woke, but her smile had been enough to warm the day that followed that night and it lingered in my mind. It was a 'dream and cream' dream in the sense of something being added to the dream that like cream rises to the top in a more concentrated richness of feeling. *Some dreams are like anything and some dreams are like something* and some are quiet and some are not. My parents used to tell each other what sort of dreams they had had each morning and this habit made us children pay attention to the dreams we dreamed, so that we too could tell of our dreams and what they made us feel – excited or frightened or elated. The dreams we told each other resonated into the day, as the days and their emotions resonated into our dreams, in a kaleidoscopic scattering of what was being felt and seen and heard.

The waking thoughts that Gertrude Stein preferred to the dream work of novels, the ones that she thought belonged to the nineteenth century, the waking thoughts that resulted in her writing, her novels and plays and portraits and poems, do *go as dreams go in sleeping at night* in their evenness and circularity, their felicities and juxtapositions, their non-sequiturs and their stirring up of the banalities and profundities of lived existence. This may have something to do with the way she opened herself to what was happening in her mind while she was writing, following the trails of thought as they unravelled. Reading Gertrude Stein is also, for me, an activity not unlike that of dreaming, where one is carried along without being able to anticipate what will happen, and where critical or oppositional positions are of no avail. She was interested in writing in such a way so that it suggested *an existence suspended in time*. Her Novel *Ida* has a film or dream-like quality – *using a mode of narration so concrete and spare that the reader comes to feel that she is dreaming through Ida's mind the dream that is Ida.*

I like to read Gertrude Stein's writing in a state between wakefulness and sleep rather than wide awake; on long distance flights for instance, or in the middle of the night when sleep won't come. I recommend reading Gertrude Stein when struck by insomnia.

I dreamed this morning that I went to a picture show with you for the purpose of seeing several pictures that you had painted, and I was much excited you had done a most remarkable effect of Norwegian mountains, and above them in the sky, mixed up with clouds effects, you had outlined the word norvège. So, I thought I ought to write you today. Emma Lootz Erving wrote this to Gertrude Stein on June 6th, 1907, a time when paintings were much on Gertrude Stein's mind, and when the harassed Emma Lootz Erving, burdened by motherhood and her medical clinic, could only dream of her ancestral Norway. She was excited in her dream that Gertrude Stein had painted the landscape and had named it, and the dream made her write the letter.

Mabel Haynes suffered from insomnia and drugged herself to sleep so that she could not remember the dreams of the night. She turned to daydreams instead, even though daydreams are not proper dreams given that they are the product of willed fantasy. The lonesome Mabel Haynes, alone on Boston in 1947 writes to her daughter in Austria: *You may imagine what all my day-dreams consist of. When I shall see you again. Nothing else matters at all. I must keep my courage going for the great event.*

There is no mystery in daydreams as the desire that drives them is clear enough and they are more likely to remain unfulfilled. The dreams of one who labours or one who does the same thing all day long can be but prolonging that doing of the same thing over and over again, but as sleep deepens something else may rear up from the recesses of the mind and so add to the weariness sleep should remedy. This was something Gertrude Stein knew well as one who did much weeding and much writing.

When she shuts her eyes she sees green things among which she has been working and then as she falls asleep she sees them be a little different. The green things then have black roots and the black roots have red stems and then she is exhausted.

Eating

Eating is a subject and a habit and the country in which one lives needs the kind of eating everybody eats in it.

Eating was a subject that interested Gertrude Stein a great deal. She had a strong appetite and a sensual nature and eating the kind of food that she liked eating was very pleasant to her. She could be said to have been the same type of women as 'Miss Charles', whom she described in "The Making of Americans" as having *vigorous egotistic sensual natures, loving being, living, writing, reading, eating, drinking, loving, bullying, teasing, finding out everything.*

Given that with her strong appetite Gertrude Stein also had a delicate stomach, the subject of eating was also a matter of anxiety. There was a lot of anxiety about digestion in Gertrude Stein's family. Her father was also *a very hearty eater and was subject to bilious attacks.* Since these bilious attacks darkened his mood, his eating was a subject worth watching. Gertrude Stein and her brother Simon, like their father Daniel, were hearty eaters; Simon in fact liked eating so much that he died from obesity. The other brother, Leo Stein, had the most delicate digestion and the most nervous stomach, and he did not like eating as much as they did. Instead he ate either only nuts or raw vegetables, and at times he practised not eating at all and at other times chewed each mouthful for such a long time to make eating anything but a few mouthfuls intolerable.

Eating in the Stein household, where the mother slowly died of stomach cancer, one brother gorging himself and the other preferring to starve himself, was certainly a subject to think about.

There are many ways of eating, for some eating is living, for some eating is dying, for some thinking about ways of eating gives to them the feeling that they have it in them to be alive and to be going on living, to some to think about eating makes them know that death is always waiting that dying is in them, some of such of them have then a fear in them and these then never want to be thinking about ways of eating, they want their eating without any thinking, they never want to have the fear in them that comes to them with thinking about ways of eating, of ways of keeping health in them.

One of the qualities that made Alice B. Toklas indispensable to Gertrude Stein was her thinking about ways of eating that kept Gertrude Stein healthy. She naturally thought about her own eating - Alice B. Toklas was picky in her eating and her appetite could not be described as hearty; and she loved dainty and complicated dishes of which she ate little mouthfuls. But even more she thought of Gertrude Stein's eating and of Gertrude Stein's appetites and digestion. It was not just a matter of what was being eaten but whether it should be eaten hot or not hot. In "The Autobiography of Alice B. Toklas", Gertrude Stein has her say that *Gertrude Stein never likes her food hot and I do like mine hot, we never agree about this. She admits that one can wait to cool it but one cannot heat it once it is on a plate so it is agreed that I have it served as hot as I like.*

Alice B. Toklas also thought of what their guests should and could be eating; there were always guests to be expected for afternoon tea, when she served cakes and pastries on fine old China, for lunches in the country, formidable picnics, informal suppers and grand dinners. For most of the time, Alice B. Toklas did the thinking about their eating but did not cook herself as they usually had one or more people employed to see to that; as she remembers it was only during the war that she learned to cook properly: *The only way to learn to cook is to cook, and for me, as for so many others, it suddenly and unexpectedly became a disagreeable necessity to have to do it when war came and Occupation followed. It was in those conditions of rationing and shortage that I learned not only to cook seriously but to buy food in a restricted market and not to take too much time in doing it, since there were so many more important and more amusing things to do.*

One of the amusing things she could do with Gertrude Stein was talking about eating and about food. They could talk about the difference between peoples preferring moist food to dry food, speculate about why this might be the case, and they liked to talk with the people in the countryside about their eating, especially during the war, when talking about eating well was a consolation for not eating so well. The countryside they spent their summers in was after all *le pays de Brillat-Savarin* and people there took some pride in their table and their eating and they did not let the war and the Germans put a stop to that.

Gertrude Stein not only liked eating and talking about eating she also liked writing about eating. A whole section in *Tender Buttons* has to do with it, and almost all her plays and operas are set around a table where people are eating and talking or about to do so. As Dana Watson noticed only one of the sixteen plays published in *Geography and Plays* does not *contain any of the ingredients for a social gathering founded on food and talks.* Instead it reverberates like the sound-track to some continual *grande bouffe*, recording what happens when mouths open and shut, to bite, to chew, to swallow, to mutter, to shout, to shut up, to sputter, to mumble - two of them or four of them or a great many more: *It was a shame it was a shame to stare to stare and double and relieve relieve be cut up show as by the elevation of it and out out more in the steady where the come and on and the all the shed and that.*

It was a garden and belows belows straight. It was a pea, a pea pour it in its not a succession, not it a simple, not it a so election, election with.

Manners of eating reveal more than manners of speech and those who have been brought up to mind their manners of eating as much as their manner of speaking from a very early age, people like Mabel Haynes, would find the ways of people who had not had the same habits of eating repulsive: *And 35 years I have been horrified over the Austrian table manners – There isn't a mouthful that they manage properly – Blow the soup, push with their fingers, cut potatoes etc with a knife, the fork in the wrong hand – fill up their plates when finished – The one real lady I met here happened to be from Berlin.* The conflict between her Bostonian ways of eating correctly and the Austrian ways of eating correctly made eating in her Austrian home an often-unpleasant experience for the children; once my grandfather, Major Leick, was in such a rage about some infringement to his rules of eating properly that he threw the carving fork straight into his youngest son's forehead where it stuck and quivered.

Mabel Haynes described herself as a fussy eater, just as Gertrude Stein described herself as a fussy eater. She was always lean and, in her youth, when she knew Gertrude Stein at Baltimore, quite anorexic, as she remembered in a letter many years later: *Emma Erving (who was with me in Johns Hopkins) spoke this time of my eating next to nothing even then, just pecking like a sparrow. As my lungs were affected Professor Osler made me take 12 raw eggs a day and 2 quarts of milk. "After 6 months I hadn't gained an ounce, Emma said." "But think how you would have looked of you hadn't been stuffed like a goose".* When not being fed like a goose to ward off tuberculosis, Mabel Haynes liked eating very light food, briefly cooked vegetables with brown butter, a bit of fish or lean meat, and she took some effort to persuade her Polish and Austrian cooks to leave off their flour-based sauces. Back in America after the Second World War, she looked in abhorrence at her sister Cora's addiction to the American ways of eating, *eating like a teamster. Fried food, pork chops, lobster, mushrooms, the heaviest deserts.* Her sister was as self-indulgent, indolent and overweight as she was ascetic, self-controlled and under-weight, not unlike the contrasting natures of Leo and Gertrude Stein. What she found most difficult to bear was eating alone - *And always eating alone. My appetite has entirely* vanished she wrote from Boston, and *As to food it is mostly eating alone & economy – as well as continuing to be most fussy.*

Eating alone is quite different from eating in company. I tend to read when I am eating alone, so as to do something I can't do when eating with others and also to disguise the fact that I am eating on my own. Eating alone in the company of people who are not companions, as when eating alone in a restaurant, is even worse. It is something most men have no difficulty doing but a lone female diner invites pity. It is useful in such a situation to look purposeful and to suggest having a rich inner life.

Next to me next to a folder, next to a foldersome waiter, next to a folder some waiter and re letter and read her. Read her with her for less.

Emma Lootz Erving
(1875-1955)

Emma was not that one who said that she had been looking for some one. She was the one that had the same warm cloak that was hers when she bought her clothing and she had enough money that did not mean that if William were waiting he would not stand on the end of his ulster. He did not have that diagram. All the cabs were open. This did not make the night colder. This did not show the Lutetia.

Emma Lootz knew Gertrude Stein and Mabel Haynes from the time they both studied medicine in Baltimore. Her letters to Gertrude Stein, from the time between 1903 and 1927, form part of the Stein archive kept at Yale, and are an important source of information on the affair between May Bookstaver and Gertrude Stein and on the private life of Mabel Haynes, with whom she remained in contact until the latter's death. Emma Lootz' letters chart her friendship with Gertrude Stein, but as she keeps her also informed about the lives of other former classmates and friends from Baltimore days, she becomes a witness who adds her own comments and views about the emotional entanglements of her friends, at times exasperated, at times caustic.

Emma Lootz was born at Duxbury in 1875, the daughter of Norwegian parents, Gjert and Selma (née Wesenberg), who originated from Bergen and grew up in Boston. She attended Smith College, graduating in Physics 1897, and a year later went on to Baltimore to enrol at Johns Hopkins Medical School, at the same time as Mabel Haynes and Gertrude Stein, with whom she shared a house at East Eager Street. She was tall and blond, a handsome young woman with a high forehead and regular Norwegian features. She fell in love with William Erving, another medical student at Johns Hopkins, whom she married in 1903. They set practice together, first in Boston, then in Washington D.C. and had two children. They lived in financially straightened circumstances and

her letters describe her weariness of having to balance the demands of family life and the medical practice.

She was not a direct witness of the Stein-Bookstaver affair as she was living in Boston after her graduation but she was, along with Mabel Foote Weeks, one of Gertrude Stein's confidantes through correspondence.

Thanks for a letter from the cradle of Christianity. I did look disapproving when you said you had been marauding with your friends – but I may as well as well believe you when you say you were good – tho 'I'm afraid our conceptions of virtue differ, she wrote on August 10th, 1903, in response to Gertrude Stein's account about the complicated games of cat and mouse played between her and May Bookstaver, who was holidaying with Mabel Haynes in Rome. In February 1904, another rebuke: *Mabel Haynes is at present in N.Y. with May. Are you a trifle fierce with her, Gertie?*

By that time the affair between Gertrude Stein and May Bookstaver was over and Gertrude Stein was living in Paris with her brother Leo. Even two years (March 20th, 1906) Gertrude Stein's feelings were still troubled and she kept asking Emma Lootz about May Bookstaver and Mabel Haynes, prompting an impatient rejoinder: *Mabel Haynes and Mary Buckminster spent a couple of days in Washington a while ago – and I'd like to see you and talk a few things over with you. It's useless to write, cause you would just get me being up on some hook where I didn't intend to arrive and not let me get off again. Only I would remark that May Bookstaver would do as well not to show all the letters she receives from everybody to all her chance acquaintances.*

Gertrude Stein seems to have defended May Bookstaver, and Emma Lootz, who found herself in the position of a neutral arbiter, kept speaking up for Mabel Haynes. Her letters' answers are worth quoting at length, as they are the only account of Mabel Haynes' feelings. She wrote a further angry riposte on May 4th 1906: *I wouldn't be mysterious for twenty-five cents because that isn't my line.*

In plain English I think that May Bookstaver has been and still is running amok with her instinct for melodrama. Whatever else Mabel Haynes may have been, she has been honest in her feeling for May, and May has treated her like dirt. When Mabel was over here I freely told her that I considered that she had been the victim of a plot all the time, and that if she had any sagacity she would climb out. When she discovered that May had been showing her letters to most of her casual acquaintances and finally to her family, it helped her considerably. I say nothing about the nature of Mabel's affection for May, and I see the provocation in it, but all the same May hasn't been very decent. In the same vein, she might refrain from dissecting you at New York dinner parties and from showing your letters to her acquaintances. Her passion for conversation is boundless, apparently – and her remarks become less and less sane. As for her elaborate explanation of my mother for cheating in examination as she lays them before promiscuous assemblies, they are pictorial to a degree. She is welcome to dress me out in any fantastic dress that she pleases for the benefit of any one that she chooses, for she does me nothing. She is not justified in treating you the same way, whatever her motives, and she has been rotten to Mabel. She is becoming more and more of an adventuress and any trouble that Mabel has caused her, she brought on herself by making that fool bet with Grace Lounsbury. Meanwhile, her campaign between you and Mabel was fair to neither of you. – Now tell me anything you like of my ugly disposition, my perverted intelligence and general worthlessness. It may be all true what you think. There are six times as many sides as there are people.

Gertrude Stein obviously did not let the matter lie and seems to have lashed out at Emma Lootz for seeing both sides of the complicated love tangle, exasperating her friend enough to spell it out once more, in her letter from June 26th: *I reserve the privilege to resent it for you. I don't in the least extent feel sore at anything on my own account, and if were in N.Y. I should go and see May with the same interest that I have always felt. For what she has done to Mabel my feelings and opinions rather – are commentary not critical, for the nature of Mabel brings such things in itself. Mabel is now making a first class fight for her own sanity, and I respect decent fights. She's doing this for herself and as far as I can see, isn't sticking her claws in any one else. When you say that I sacrificed hospitality and loyalty to vanity, I frankly don't see it and I'm sorry that you do. My surface relations with Mabel have never varied by a shade of politeness, whether she was buying me with my knowledge and realization, of whether she was fighting you, without, if you please (and dense I probably was) my realization of what was actually the state of things – or of your feelings. Had you asked me then to suspend diplomatic relations with her for your sake, I might have done so on that account, but I shouldn't have considered you strictly rational. Nor, when she was knifing me, would it have occurred to me that your diplomatic relations with her would change. The thing that I do resent in the whole business is that it has by some occult means raised any question between you and me. I spit at both Mabel and May and myself on that account – and I think I'll forget it – if you will.*

Emma Lootz was wary of May Bookstaver - *I had a letter from May Bookstaver. Why?* – but maintained amicable relations with Mabel Haynes, keeping Gertrude Stein informed about her marriages, births, visits, and changing addresses, while news of May Bookstaver, especially after she had become May Knoblauch, becomes rare and ceases after 1927.

Her letters to Gertrude Stein reveal much about the ambivalence of a highly educated woman who chose to marry, have children and earn a living by practising medicine alongside her husband William Erving. She observed her own reactions with a self-deprecating objectivity one might adopt when writing to an old friend. She realises with despair how her world shrank to the confines of domesticity.

From the beginning she worried about William Erving's health; and her own lack of an independent income, such as that enjoyed by Mabel Haynes, whom she befriended while still in Boston, meant that she had to cook and wash dishes herself, as well as work in the laboratory. *I'm too poor to go to concerts or theatre, so I have no purple thought to impart.*

She writes with at times comical distaste about her pregnancies: *The trouble is just this. Since the first of January I have been dead to the world – flat on couch in an exaggeration of prostration and an ecstasy of nausea. I haven't been able to write or read or sew or play the piano or do a darn thing except wonder when my innards would come out. (…) I have thought of you sometimes but have been literally unable to hold a pen. Thanks for letter this morning. It aroused me to this spurt of energy. I'm not a sale vache. I'm a suffering woman and I appear to be a perfect lady. It's too much higher education – other people aren't so totally knocked out.* Did Gertrude Stein bring up the *sale vache*? The connection between a dirty cow, suffering, and appearing to be a perfect lady, summarises Emma Lootz' experience of becoming a mother. Once the child is born, she writes to Gertrude Stein: *I wanted a boy, Madam, and I got a girl, so don't tell me I got what I wanted. Now I have to make one more try for a boy. (…) My spirit being completely gone, lying in bed is my ideal of happiness, and I resent every stroke of work that life is going to get out of me – but the last few days I have begun to feel as if perhaps I could go on living for a while.*

She does not write often about her husband and, when she does, only in her customary ironical manner: *His parents certainly made a mess of him! More of a mess than even matrimony with me will ever straighten out.*

Three years after the first child, she gave birth to a boy, named Henry William: *I don't think much of this baby, poor little devil, but I hope he will flourish.* In the same letter she expressed the sense that her children are decidedly not an intrinsic part her own being: *It seems curious that I have two strangers in the family that I have to take care of. Selma is the spitting' image of her father, and I never knew him till he was partly grown; so she is quite strange to me. And the unfortunate apple-worm upstairs is still a surprise.* Further on, she tells Gertrude Stein that Mabel Haynes is expecting her second child and she contrasts her own attitude to motherhood with hers: *She seems to be the normal maternal female, anyhow – which is handy to be, in her situation, I wish I could show a spontaneous supply of the quality. But all my virtues are so fearfully forced – all born in travail from my intelligence, so to speak.*

Gertrude Stein, congratulating her on the birth of Henry William seems to have urged even more babies: *Don't tell to me about four children. I tell William that he can be casting an eye about for the mother to his next two. I'll take of them if he wants me to, but I'm too old and stiff and too bored to spend any more years of my life in the incubating business. Lord! I'm trying to exist with fortitude with a persistent cat-in-my-lap feeling and without a stomach but if William ever tries to do this to me again I'll leave him instantly. Weininger says there are only two types of women – the mother and the prostitute – and I know I'm not the mother-type. From which conversation you will discern that I am much better than I was, for I have strength enough now to sit up and blaspheme. But I'm not worth a darn – and I cheerfully give over both Selma and my patients to my cousin and ask only to be allowed to lie here on the couch and rot.*

Emma Lootz, while protesting her fate that bound her to house and hearth and nursery, in addition to seeing patients, learnt to cope with the pressures and tedium – *By keeping my eye firmly fixed on house patients and babies, I preserve my reason and my avoirdupois – but get as limited in my ideas as a clam.*

Hearing of the misfortunes and sufferings of her friends, such as those of Mabel Haynes (reporting to Gertrude Stein the death of her husband and her son), Marion Walker, and Mabel Foote Weeks, she wrote full of empathy. Emma Lootz did not manage to go to Italy or Paris more than just a couple of times, finding it much more convenient to take her children to stay with relatives in Norway. During the 1920s her correspondence with Gertrude Stein became reduced to one missive a year. At the age of forty she was widowed, in 1925 and wound up the practice a year later. She lived for a while with her son Henry in Washington and was finally able to visit Gertrude Stein in 1928, when she came to Bilignin.

Gertrude Stein's play *At Present,* from 1930, makes reference to various friends and people she had known who were dead, including William Erving.

When Gertrude Stein came to the States for her Lecture Tour in 1934 to 35, accompanied by Alice B Toklas, she did not seek out any her old friends from Medical School.

Mabel Haynes, living in Boston after the end of World War Two, wrote to her daughter in October 1946: *Emma Erving has dropped in. She has the same effect as May in New York in oiling my brain. Also a true friend.* By that time Gertrude Stein had been dead for three months. In 1950 Mabel Haynes writes about the death of May Knoblauch from an asthma attack and reflects that only Emma was still alive of the 'old set'. Emma Lootz Erving died a year after Mabel Haynes, in 1955.

Fathers and daughters

There is too much fathering going on just now and there is no doubt about it fathers are depressing.

The fathers of Gertrude Stein, Mabel Haynes and May Bookstaver were Victorian fathers, born in the first half of the nineteenth century, recognized as progressive men. Such men were prominent in society, successful in business, charitable, and above all respectable. They were to be respected and obeyed by their wives and their children. Such fathers who did their fathering as a way of asserting their authority were depressing to their children whose desires they curtailed. Gertrude Stein wrote about such fathers and especially her own father in *The Making of Americans*. She describes David Hershland, based on Daniel Stein, as one who *was very proud of his children but it was not easy for them to be free of him.* Such a father would pound on the table with his fists… *ending with the angry word that he was the father, they were his children, they must obey him, he was the master.* It has been suggested that Gertrude Stein's writing about the conflict between herself and her father was a cathartic process that *freed herself from the crippling emotional habits of the good daughter.*

Her father, Daniel Stein (1833-1891), was one of the nine surviving children of Michael and Hannah Stein who had left their Bavarian village in 1841 order to begin a new life in Baltimore. The three sons all worked in the family business that sold clothes and uniforms. Daniel Stein moved to Allegheny near Pittsburgh with his well-to-do wife Amelia Keyser and set up a shop with his brother. He never had much schooling and wished his five children - Gertrude was the youngest-, to have a better education. He took them all to Europe for some years to learn German and French and be tutored by native speakers. Then he struck out on his own to California to see what could be made of the opportunities in railroads and settled with the family in East Oakland, choosing a poor neighborhood to live in some style though in social isolation. When his wife died in 1888 the household all but disintegrated. Gertrude Stein's notebooks make references to her father's pursuing of governesses and to his becoming physically aggressive (*father angry hit her*); he would shut himself away and it was on one of these episodes of withdrawing to his own room that he suffered the apoplexy that killed him.

Then one morning we could not wake up our father. Leo climbed in by the window and called out to us that he was dead in his bed and he was.

When Daniel Stein died in these circumstances, on January 28th 1891, he was fifty years old and he left mainly debts behind. The eldest son Michael managed to put into practice some of his father's business ideas about street railways, which allowed Gertrude and Leo Stein to have an income. Gertrude Stein wrote that she was relieved when Daniel Stein died: *Life without a father began a very pleasant one.* They all went to live in San Francisco at first, under Michael's Stein's supervision: *we had our time with only a brother not a father and a father as Mike later so well explained to me is different after all he is a father.*

Gertrude Stein not only wrote about her own depressing father but about May Bookstaver's father, the Judge Henry Weller Bookstaver, another man of high standing and respectability. In *Q.E.D.* she quotes Mabel Neathe as giving an account where she *drew a very unpleasant picture of that parentage. Her description of the father as a successful lawyer and judge as an excessively brutal and at the same-time small-minded man who exercised great ingenuity in making himself unpleasant was not alluring.* He was a descendant of Swiss reformer and the family had settled in Orange County in the 18th century. He attended school in Montgomery, obtained a doctorate in law from Rutgers College, moved to New York City, joined a law firm and was made a partner at a young age, with a reputation as an eloquent pleader. He was elected justice of the Common Court of Pleas, and in 1896 of the Supreme Court. He had two children with his wife Mary Bailey Young, but only the younger daughter, Mary (May) survived to adulthood. He died a wealthy man in 1907, but he settled his will in such a way that it benefitted Rutgers College rather than his only descendant. Her attempt to challenge the will in court was not successful. May Bookstaver was given an expensive education but little financial freedom or affection. In her second literary variation of the theme of the Gertrude, Mabel and May affair, in "Melanctha" in *Three Lives*, the subject of the brutal father and unloving mother occurs again. The incident of Helen having broken her arm after falling from the haystack that she must have climbed in defiance of her father's word, and her father's subsequent refusal of having it treated by a doctor, occurs in both books. Gertrude Stein has Helen/May depend financially on Mabel, who had a more benevolent and generous father. May Bookstaver went on to defend the rights of women to know about birth control and to exercise their vote. When she married a stockbroker she called herself henceforth Mrs C.E. Knoblauch. There are several ways relinquish to the Name of the Father.

Mabel Haynes's father, John C. Haynes (1829-1907), father of six daughters, was by all accounts a man who liked to be loved and he seems to have loved his children and been loved by them. His ancestors came from England in 1635 and they stayed close to where they had landed on the Massachusetts coast, and prospered as farmers. Having lost his father to an infected rat bite, John C. Haynes entered the employment of a music publisher in Boston and, like Henry Weller Bookstaver, quickly advanced to be made a partner in the business. He had a talent for being very much liked, as much by those who employed him and by those he employed, and he was adroit in his investments. Under his directorship the company he had entered as a teenager became the largest music publisher in the United States and he added a form under his own name that made musical instruments of high quality. He also lost his only son at a very young age, but, unlike Henry Boookstaver, did not withhold affection from his surviving daughters. He encouraged the intellectual ambitions of his most gifted daughter, Mabel, by sending her to excellent schools and provided her with enough funds to travel, to live well and to support a friend. Mabel Haynes, who thought that her mother had not been the right sort of wife for her father, spoke of her father with affection and admiration for his ability to assert authority with kindness and by example. She wished to emulate him, as these lines from a letter suggest: *I went to see an old family friend this week – Fannie Plympton. A most intelligent person who saw us all grow up. She told me not to get excited over Cora's obstinacy, that she had always been incapable of seeing another person's point of view and also of meeting any problem; in other words an "evader". The friends spoke of her as the 'light-weight" of the family. But then this opinion is tinged by her admiration and affection for me – "just like your father" she kept saying. Anyway the greatest compliment I could be paid.*

Did Mabel Haynes' father depress with his kind authority as much as Mr Hershland by being angry? May Bookstaver stayed in New York but changed her name and became a public figure, standing up for the sort of things her father did not stand up for. Mabel Haynes always kept the name Haynes, merely adding the name of her husbands after 'Haynes'. Yet she went as far from this good father as any of his daughters ever did. She crossed the ocean and lived on the margins of the Austrian Empire. Judge Bookstaver and John C. Haynes, the brutal and the kind father, both died in 1907 when their daughters were thirty-three and both were married. Gertrude Stein's father had died much earlier, when she was seventeen in 1891. Her father had died unexpectedly, and she was to turn this sudden death into the slow death, the depressing father slowly dying inside her until through the long exorcism of writing he grew into just one of *all the men and women who ever lived.* My own father was the youngest son of Mabel Haynes, the only son to survive to adulthood. We loved each other dearly and he died before I was of an age when his fathering could have become depressing.

Films

My life has been troublous enough for a movie that no one would take to be true.

Gertrude Stein did not care for the cinema and never refers to any particular film in her writing. It is clear from what she did write about cinema that she had seen some, but she preferred not to profess an interest in it.

Gertrude Stein's lack of interest in film was not based on snobbish disdain as Edith Wharton's, who in 1928 declined the invitation to appear in a short documentary feature about notable American women because this list also included film actors, notably Mary Pickford. Edith Wharton may have disliked being ranked alongside mere movie stars but she was not averse to making deals with Hollywood about her novels being made into motion pictures. Gertrude Stein's novels did not become motion pictures, but she was not averse to meeting movie stars in person. She wrote about encounter meeting with Mary Pickford in a way that reads like a movie script in "Everybody's Autobiography": *Well however we went to tea and there were a good many writers and others there I drifted around and then I saw a short little woman with a large head and there were curls but I did not notice them. We were asked to meet each other, Mary Pickford and I. She said she wished she knew more French and I said I talked it all right but I never read it I did not care about it as a written language she said she did wish she knew more French, and then, I do not quote know how it happened, she said and suppose we should be photographed together. Wonderful idea I said. We were by this time standing near a couch where Belle Greene was seated (...) Mary Pickford said it would be easy to get the Journal photographer to come over, yes I will telephone says some one rushing off, yes I said it would be wonderful we might be shaking hands. You are not going to do it, said Belle Greene excitedly behind me, of course I am going to I said, nothing would please me better of course we are I said turning to Mary Pickford, Mary Pickford said perhaps I will not be able to stay and she began to back away, Oh yes you must I said it will not be long now, no no she said I think I had better not and she melted away. I knew you would not do it, said Belle Green behind me. And then I asked every one because I was interested just what it was that went on in Mary Pickford. It was her idea and when I was enthusiastic she melted away. They all said that what she thought was if I were enthusiastic it meant that I thought that it would do me more good than it would do her and so she melted away.*

Mary Pickford's melting away preoccupied Gertrude Stein for a long time as she thought about identity and celebrity. In the account above she not only avers not to have been aware of who Mary Pickford was or to know what she looked like, she also describes her as a *'short little woman with a large head'*, exposing the reality behind the screen fantasy that made short little women and short little men into idols of perfection. She then exposes the superficiality of the movie star who fails to recognize Gertrude Stein as someone who would need no endorsement from an actress, and she keeps repeating that she melted away, that she fades out, just as they do on screen. She wrote rather differently about meeting Charlie Chaplin at a dinner in Hollywood; she likened him to a Spanish gypsy bullfighter. *Charlie Chaplin was like that, gipsies (sic) are intelligent I do not think Charlie Chaplin is one perhaps not but he might have been, anyway we naturally talked about the cinema. And he explained something. He said naturally it was disappointing, he had known the silent films and in that they could do something that the theatre had not done they could change the rhythm but if you had a voice accompanying naturally after that you could never change a rhythm you were always held by the rhythm that the voice gave them.*

In her telling of that conversation, Gertrude Stein did not take the subject of silent film versus talkies up but instead explained to Chaplin, at some length, what she was trying to do in her opera *Four Saints in Three Acts, where nothing was happening and that that was exciting,* and that she wanted to write a drama where no one did anything. *He said yes he could understand that, I said film would become like the newspapers just a daily habit and not at all exciting or interesting, after all the business of an artist is to be really exciting and he is only really exciting when nothing is happening.* And then at the end when people ask her what she thinks of the cinema *I told them what I had been telling Charlie Chaplin, it seemed to worry them but almost anything would worry them and at last I found out what was bothering them they wanted to know how I had succeeded in getting so much publicity...*She answered with some subterfuge that the *biggest publicity comes from the realest poetry,* which has a small audience but is really exciting. She did not really believe that herself and nor did the guests at the Beverly Hills party. She was well aware that publicity needed quite a different effort. In a radio interview that has been archived, Bennett Cerf, the American publisher, had a good deal to say about Gertrude Stein's interest in publicity and the lengths she was prepared to go to get exposure, and how she enlisted the services of another movie star, Miriam Hopkins. Asked if her books sold well he replied *Not really. We made money on Gertrude, but she had a very limited audience. Nobody knew what the hell she was talking about. I wangled for her an NBC interview--coast-to-coast radio. There was no television then. I acted as M.C. We went to the studio, and Miriam Hopkins came with us. Miriam adored Gertrude, and Gertrude adored Miriam. She had Miriam running errands for her, day after day. This amused her - having a movie star calling for shoes for her and having her clothes dry-cleaned. She ordered* everybody *around and got away with it.*

Before Gertrude Stein had arrived in the Unites States, where she was greeted as a celebrity, she had passed through a period of depression and writer's block. Eventually the lectures she was writing for her American tour helped her concentrate. In these four lectures that she read to various audiences across the continent, she tried to explain her methods of writing. In the one entitled 'Portraits and Repetition' she made several references to the cinema: *Of course I did not think of it in terms of the cinema, in fact I doubt whether at that time I had ever seen a cinema but, and I cannot repeat this too often any one is one's period and this our period was undoubtedly the period of the cinema and series production. And each of us in our own way are bound to express the world in which we are living.*

Gertrude Stein was telling her American audience, who had certainly been to a cinema, what she had come to feel of being in *one's period* from quite a different side; that she too, by simply writing in a radically new way, could get at the secret of existence and movement.

Meanwhile the movies had caught up with Gertrude Stein now that she had become a household name in America. Two films from 1935 use Gertrude Stein's literary style to comic effect. In *The Man on a Flying Trapeze* the hapless W.C. Fields, noisily munching on a piece of toast at breakfast, is made to listen to his wife reading the latest piece by someone called Gertrude Smarts – but closer to the mark is the scene in *Top Hat,* when Ginger Rogers listens to her friend reading a telegram: *"Come ahead stop stop being a sap stop you can even bring Alberto stop my husband is stopping at your hotel stop when do you start stop,"* and reads and then comments with bewilderment: *"I cannot understand who wrote this."* Dale declares brightly *"Sounds like Gertrude Stein!"*

Gertrude Stein found that amusing, but she did not bother to see either of these films. She did go to see the Pathé newsreel of her reading one of her texts. It was an experience she may not have enjoyed - *it gave me a funny feeling and I did not like that funny feeling.*

Gertrude Stein did not allude then to the fact that she had written a film script years ago, in the 1920's, simply entitled 'A Movie'. It is a wartime spy story about an American painter who takes up driving a taxi to make a living and is enlisted by the Americans once they enter the war to find some stolen money. There is plenty of slap-stick humour, a car chase with two American crooks with motor-cycles trying to escape over top of the Pont du Gard (great stunt), and a final scene in which the American painter with his Breton housekeeper in their taxi bring up the rear of the victory march through the Arc the Triomphe, waving the American flag and the tricolour.

Clearly Gertrude Stein was not as ignorant of the silent movies of the time, with their inter-titles and frequent changes of location. The scenario was also a way to pay homage to a friend, as she explains in "The Autobiography of Alice B. Toklas", *it was William Cook who* inspired the *'only movie she ever wrote in English*. William Cook was a painter. He had been nursing, and he drove a taxi. He gave driving lessons to Gertrude Stein so that she could drive her Ford truck about for the War Wounded Fund with Alice B. Toklas, and dispense not just medicines but gifts and good cheer, being *two such nice ladies*.

If that first movie script was the result of a friendship with an American, the second script (*Deux soeurs qui ne sont pas soeurs*), that she wrote in French, owes much to her friendship with the French poet George Hugnet, whom she met in 1927, whose languorous and rather louche poem *Enfances* she re-worked in English – one could not call it a translation – as *Before the Flowers of Friendship Faded Friendship Faded*. As in *A Movie* Gertrude Stein and Alice B. Toklas appear, simply *'deux dames'* in car. The location is a boulevard outside Paris, where a washerwoman with her basket of laundry stops to examine rapturously a photograph of two white poodles. A car comes to a stop beside her, two ladies get out to look at the photo too. A pretty young woman (beauty queen) sees the empty car, gets in and starts to cry, but the two ladies throw her out and she falls on the washerwoman, who realizes that the photo of the dogs is gone, a fact she relates to a young man passing by. *After some hours* another washerwoman stands before an employment agency. The car with the ladies pulls up and they show her the photo of the white poodles. The beauty queen appears and with a cry of joy moves towards the car with the two ladies who speed off. *The day after next* the washerwoman, still standing with her laundry, sees the beauty queen carrying a small packet and the young man. All three are together, and suddenly, the car arrives, and in it is a real white poodle and in the poodle's mouth is a small packet. The three on the pavement watch it pass and understand nothing.

Mabel Haynes, the American who was becoming increasingly less American the longer she lived in Austria, was decidedly a fan of movies and of some movie stars. In the letters she sent to her daughter Gabrielle she often wrote of the latest film she had been to see. In the late 1940s, when she had gone back to Boston after the war, the cinema was her main diversion: *"Gone with the Wind" has been put on again with the original cast, all much changed. Clark Gable, Vivien Leigh, Olivia de Haviland and another good one. There had been big scroll put out in the theatre for those to sign who wanted this film re-released. Feel all excited about it. …Don't ever miss "The Ghost and Mrs Muir" if it comes your way. I saw it four times and fell completely for that irresistible ghost (Rex Harrison). Also saw "The Seventh Veil" 5 times with Jack Mason and Anna Todd. The English would seem to be beating the Americans in the cinema line. Did "Brief Encounters" come to you? A perfect production. The English leave individuality in their women's faces. This last picture is about most everyday people, but breathtaking…Clark Gable will be here soon in "Command and Decision" – some war part and only men in it. There one will again see that gorgeous figure. Marlene Dietrich set the country agog with "A Foreign Affair".*

Mabel Haynes could get quite lost in the cinema, engrossed in the action on the big screen, weeping into her handkerchief, forgetting her loneliness as she looked at the gorgeous figure of Clark Gable, a short little man in real life, and at the sad eyes of Greta Garbo, at the mischievous lips of Vivien Leigh. She was ready to give herself up to the emotions stirred by close-ups and music. In the darkness of the cinema, Mabel Haynes could forget about being Mabel Haynes as she became submerged in the human stories conjured up on screen. She was not trying to do anything with cinema in the way Gertrude Stein had done, who did not allow herself to be so seduced by a movie as to forget that she was Gertrude Stein. Gertrude Stein may have been gratified to learn that some filmmakers would try to do with their movies what she had done with her writings. Her insistence on composition and repetition, on completely expressing the actual presence, the elimination of narrative, of plot, made much of her writing unreadable. Montage works better on the screen; simultaneity is only possible on screen. It has been argued that *her theories are ideally, and only realisable in film* although only unusually bookish directors were interested to make such films, like, for instance, *L'année dernière à Marienbad,* and that they're rarely a smash hit, even with someone as beguiling as Delphine Seyrig

Friendship

Gertrude Stein made and unmade a great many friendships in her lifetime. This is one of the main themes in *The Autobiography of Alice B. Toklas*, which presents the perfect and enduring friendship between 'Gertrude Stein' and 'Alice B. Toklas' as the foil to the various other friendships they engaged in - friendships that could only be secondary in importance and virtue, while at the same time showing the excellence of 'Gertrude Stein' measured by her ability to inspire friendship in good men and good women. The only person however, who appears as a truly worthy friend to 'Gertrude Stein' is Pablo Picasso, whom Gertrude Stein acknowledged to be a genius. Since she recognized this quality in herself, they *were resembling each other in virtue* and could therefore be said to be perfect friends. This perfect friendship is contrasted in the *Autobiography* with the one to Ernest Hemingway, described as an *extraordinary good-looking man,* as well as one promising to become great as a writer, who was later found to be lacking in genius and hence too unequal to remain a worthy friend.

In their daily living Gertrude Stein and Alice B. Toklas made and unmade many friendships. These were often the more heartfelt and friendly the greater the social distance - as with soldiers or country people or those much younger or older. The combination of some distance, say in age or status, with personal charm and an eagerness to be of service to her genius, proved useful for the preservation of such a friendship. It was essential that their friends showed an appreciation of Gertrude Stein's work and would do what they could to get it better known; those who failed in this appreciation, such as Mabel Weeks, for instance, could not continue to be called friends. It is telling that two of the titles of two published volumes of correspondence between Gertrude Stein and her friends reflected the fragility of the bond: *A history of a great many times not continued to be friends* and *The Flowers of Friendship*, which refers to Gertrude Stein's book *Before the Flowers of Friendship Faded Friendship Faded*. She needed to be reassured that her friends delighted in her company, and that she should always rank highest among their friends, as in this letter to Carl van Vechten, a beloved friend, though not much younger nor from a different class, but who retained her affection until the end of her life, not least because of his unceasing loyalty and successful promotion of her oeuvre: *There is no doubt about it Carl that you have awfully good taste in friends and it's a great pleasure to me that I am one of the oldest and best of them because I feel it to be proof of how charming and gentle I am it's true alright.* It was true that Gertrude Stein could be charming and gentle and that she enjoyed bestowing affection on those she counted as her friends; she wrote thousands of letters and cards in her life - only a fraction of them survive – and they show her vivid interest in the minutiae of the lives of those she befriended. She was also a generous friend who liked sending presents and invitations. Alice B. Toklas has been held responsible for keeping the benevolence and professions of friendship that Gertrude Stein inclined to by nature under some restraint; that she acted in defence of their perfect union can be surmised. Alice B. Toklas was to remain the most congenial of friends not least because she was the most devoted to the genius of Gertrude Stein.

Friends who were no longer to be called friends became just 'people': *Sometimes in Paris people used to turn up that I had not seen for many years. I remember one year two or three that I had not seen for eighteen years turned up. Certainly there is no use in seeing anybody you have not seen for eighteen years, and I hoped it would not happen again. Alice B. Toklas always liked a poem that used to go, Give me new faces new faces I have seen the old ones – and just then well there did not seem any reason why one should see the old ones any more.*

Gertrude Stein's early friendships, begun before she set out to serve her genius by writing, were friendships of youth, where the motive of friendship is pleasure. As she delighted in conversation with interesting people and was interesting and stimulating herself, she met people who would become close friends, with whom she maintained contact for long afterwards; Emma Lootz Erving, Mabel Weeks, Marion Walker, Dr Claribel Cone and Etta Cone, Mabel Haynes. Gertrude Stein wrote about friendships and especially friendships between women in *Three Lives,* and her difficult relationship with May Bookstaver and Mabel Haynes found echoes in all her early writing. She was most concerned with the power dynamic in friendships and importance of winning. In this passage from 'The Good Anna' she even anticipates a situation of balance, one she was to experience much later with Alice B. Toklas:

In friendship, power always has its downward curve. One's strength to manage rises always higher until there comes a time one does not win, and though one may not really lose, still from the time that victory is not sure, one's power slowly ceases to be strong. It is only in a close tie such as marriage, that influence can mount and never meet with a decline. It can only happen when there is no way to escape.

Gertrude Stein's desire for May Bookstaver was not equal to the power that she thought Mabel Haynes exerted over her. When neither of them was in a position to wield power over anyone involved, their friendship changed to distant benevolence. The married May Bookstaver came to be of service to Gertrude Stein's genius by helping her to get her work published, something Mabel Haynes living in Austria could hardly offer.

Eventually after decades of at least sporadic correspondence, Gertrude Stein's fame in the mid-fifties and Alice B. Toklas' sifting of friends for their worthiness, made but old faces of them.

The old faces remaining - Mabel Weeks, Emma Lootz Erving, May Bookstaver and Mabel Haynes - held on to their mutual friendship that had begun in their youth across the distance of time and place. When she was in her seventies, Mabel Haynes, having returned to Boston after having lived through the war in Austria, met Emma Lootz and May Bookstaver again. She found that talking to them had the effect of *oiling her brain* and she referred to them in her letters as *true friends* and *simply brilliant.* They were true friends for they had remained true to what they had seen in each other when they first formed their friendship, and they took pleasure in each other's company more than fifty years later. Mabel Haynes was to discover that her old chum Mary Buckminster was not to be trusted, but her other two friends were still treasured and that their special bond was still working: *I am really finally glad myself that I have discovered Mary Buckminster's inside workings. I want nothing of her. Think of May in New York and Emma Erving in contrast. As Emma hasn't heard from me for 3 weeks she autoed way up to Boston. It was when I had that cold, and she had just a "feeling" that something was wrong. Too bad both are so far away.*

Grace Constant Lounsbery

(1876 – 1964)

...a valiant little thing whose intellect had been trained at Bryn Mawr who detested feminine weakness, and dresses herself in severe tailor-made frocks in the fond belief that they made her look like a boy

Grace Lounsbery is an important if tantalizingly elusive presence in the annals of Mabel Haynes, May Bookstaver and Gertrude Stein. According to her obituary *she was born in New York to a distinguished New England family* and *spent her early years leading a country life and riding often with her father on the extensive family estates.* A couple of years younger than Mabel Haynes, she also attended Bryn Mawr College and she graduated at the same time as Mabel Haynes on June 2nd, 1898, also in Chemistry and Biology. However, she was less narrowly focused on science than Mabel Haynes. Shortly after their graduation, Grace Lounsbery accompanied Mabel Haynes to Europe. Thereafter they both enrolled as students at Johns Hopkins Medical School in the autumn of 1898 and shared an apartment on St Paul Street. During this period, May Bookstaver's address was listed as her parent's house in New York City. Mabel Haynes and Grace Lounsbery entertained at their rooms where Gertrude Stein, as one of the fellow students at medical school, was one of their guests.

Grace Lounsbery does not appear on any of the Johns Hopkins student records and certainly never graduated. She seems to have been abandoned medicine for literature and was frequently absent from Baltimore. The Californian novelist Gertrude Atherton remembered her inhabiting the same apartment building she lived in, the new and fashionable 'Iroquois' near Times Square in New York City. Gertrude Atherton was much taken with Grace Lounsbery and wrote to John Lane, her own publisher: *I find her so solidly clever and so natural and unassuming that I feel a personal interest in seeing her started.* Gertrude Atherton had invited Grace

Lounsbury to accompany her on a trip to the West Indies, where she was hoped to find material for a biography she was writing. This was not a luxurious voyage, and the two women had to share not just a cabin but a single bed. Grace Lounsbery was known to be an agreeable travelling companion and later that year, in 1901, she joined Mabel Haynes once more to go to Europe. I wonder whether it was in her company that Mabel Haynes toured the *very lovely English Riviera with a coach and four.*

1901 was an important year for Gertrude Stein, *the fateful twenty-ninth year the straight and narrow gateway of maturity and life which was all uproar and confusion narrows down to form and purpose and we exchange a dim possibility for a big or small reality.* Gertrude Stein had met May Bookstaver the year before, in Baltimore, most likely in the company of Mabel Haynes and Grace Lounsbery. By February of 1901 she had begun to neglect her medical studies, which alarmed her brother enough to encourage her to persist. Her desire for the impetuous, handsome, Gentile, May Bookstaver brought on enough uproar and confusion to jeopardise her ideas about herself and her professional direction. Which role Grace Lounsbery played remained enigmatic and hinges on a comment Emma Lootz Erving made in a letter to Gertrude Stein, where she talks about May Bookstaver: *She is becoming more and more of an adventuress and any trouble that Mabel has caused her, she brought on herself by making that fool bet with Grace Lounsbury. Meanwhile, her campaign between you and Mabel was fair to neither of you.*

It is not at all clear whether Mabel Haynes' relationship with Grace Lounsbery was one of friendly comradeship or an erotic attachment at that time or indeed at any time. May Bookstaver, who had known Mabel Haynes for longer, since the time they spent at Miss Peebles Preparatory School at Bryn Mawr, while living in New York between 1898 and 1901, would have to rely on mutual visits to maintain whatever bond she had with Mabel Haynes that so enraged Gertrude Stein who clearly identified her as her main rival.

Did Grace Lounsbery make a bid to encourage May Bookstaver to seduce the bright but sexually naïve Gertrude Stein so as to divert May Bookstaver's attention away from Mabel Haynes? Was Mabel Haynes in another complicated love triangle with May Bookstaver and Grace Lounsbery?

During the summer of their tumultuous twenty-ninth year, in 1901, Gertrude Stein went to Spain with her brother Leo, while Mabel Haynes was in England with Grace Lounsbery. John Lane published her first book of poetry *An Iseult Idyll and Other Poems* that year, thus vindicating her decision to devote herself to literature. After Europe, Gertrude Stein went to New York, staying with Mabel Foote Weeks, where she continued her bid for May Bookstaver's undivided devotion. Just when she began to see *the narrowing down to form and purpose* that year remains unclear – she started writing seriously and obsessively about the affair in 1902, still in New York. In 1903 she had made up her mind to leave America and to join her brother in Paris but she kept on being preoccupied with May Bookstaver for years afterwards, as Emma Lootz Erving's letters make clear.

Grace Lounsbery, also in New York, continued to write. John Lane published *Delila, a drama in Three Acts* in 1904 another book of her poetry, entitled *Love's Testament: A Sonnet Sequence,* two years later. *Poems of Revolt, and Satan Unbound,* appeared in 1911, with Moffat, Yard and Company of New York.

During a stay in Venice in 1908, - again it is unclear whether Grace Lounsbery went there alone; she met Jean Cocteau and she seems to have been interested in producing his play, *Le portrait surnaturel de Dorian Gray* (based on Oscar Wilde's novel); it never came to fruition. However, the abandoned project spurred Grace Lounsbery's interest in writing her own, English version of this play. It is unclear when she began to work on it.

In May 1913 she left the United States for Paris where she became part of the Parisian literary scene. Her version of Wilde's tale was a novel published by Simpkin Marshall in London that year. Lou Tellegen, the French matinée idol, was intent of producing and directing her play on the theme, in which he was to perform the leading role. It opened at the Vaudeville Theatre in London on August 28th, 1913 and ran to 96 performances, to mixed reviews.

In 1922 she came back to *The Portrait of Dorian Gray*, by collaborating with Fernand Nozière on a French adaptation that introduce *a heterosexual subplot involving a romance between Dorian and Lady Gwendoline*, performed at the *Comédie des Champs Elysées* on December 20th. She had written her own plays, *L'Escarpolette, Delila* (1904), as well as poetry (*Poems of Revolt and Satan Unbound*, 1911). Grace Lounsbery could be theatrical herself and presented staged readings of her poems and some of her plays in her flat at 12, rue Guynemer. The American composer Henry Cowell, who watched a performance of her *Poèmes Vecus*, described her as *a striking figure in rich Indian robe and a turban*.

Gertrude Stein did not give performances of her work and she is likely to have scoffed at the efforts of Grace Lounsbery, whose literary work she never mentioned, although she seems to have maintained a friendly enough social contact. Alice B. Toklas in her own memoir has this to say about her: *Grace Lounsbery, an early acquaintance of Gertrude from the Johns Hopkins' days, was frequently about at this time. She was an intimate friend of two of Gertrude's intimate friends. Gertrude thought she was a false alarm. She was small and not unimpressive in her funny little way. She considered herself a Greek scholar and wrote Greek plays. When she was young, she came to Paris and fell in with Jean Cocteau. They were two infant prodigies of the social world. Her plays were produced in a semi-professional manner and she took great satisfaction from this. Grace Lounsbery amused me, but Gertrude found her very tiresome. In those days she lived in a flat in the rue Boissonade, which was painted in the fashionable manner of the day in black. She considered herself an aesthete and a gourmet. Later she moved, with the beautiful Esther Swainson, down the rue d'Assas into a charming little pavilion.*

Alice B. Toklas pokes fun at the artistic and aesthetic pretensions of their fellow American but does not mention the hospitality she and Gertrude Stein enjoyed at the country house of Grace Lounsbery and Esther Swainson in the Loire valley.

What Gertrude Stein would have found tiresome was Grace Lounsbery's Eastern mysticism and what she called *free spiritual research*, and especially Buddhist meditation.

In 1928 Grace Lounsbery had heard a lecture given by the Chinese Buddhist Master Taixu (Tai-Hsu) and this meeting was to give her life a new direction. She founded the Paris branch of the World Buddhist Institute, under the name *Les Amis du Bouddhisme* in 1929, largely financed by her own means. She seems to have given up writing poetry or plays in the post-war period, immersing herself instead in studying the Dharma, publishing translations of Southern (Theravada) Buddhism, which were written in a straightforward manner and reprinted many times.

Her obituary writer mentions the impact of a woman, Mme La Fuente, whom Grace Lounsbery was to have met at the hospital she founded during the Great War, and who later became the General Secretary of *Les Amis du Bouddhisme*. Grace Lounsbery and Marguerite La Fuente had been, so her friends remembered *like two fruits of the same tree.*

Grace Lounsbery's own health declined after her friend's death in 1958, and she entered a clinic where she remained until her death five years later, on September 24th, 1964, at the age of eighty-eight.

Hair

A package and a filter and even a funnel, all this together makes a scene and supposing the question arises is hair curly, is it dark and dusty, supposing that question arises, is brushing necessary, is it, the whole special suddenness commences then, there is no delusion.

Gertrude Stein had dark and wavy, even frizzy, hair. As a child this was gathered into a ponytail and allowed to hang loose, as was the custom at the time. By the time Gertrude Stein, Mabel Haynes and Mary Bookstaver put their hair up, they no longer, like their mothers had done, parted the hair in the middle and arranged the bulk of the hair low at the nape or massed behind the ears. The 1890s style favoured an apparently natural, though precarious piling up of tresses and curls, often on the front part of the head, and on this artful construction perched an equally artfully arranged hat, secured by hair pins stuck into the core of the heaped-up hair.

Gertrude Stein adopted a more natural manner by wearing her plaits further back on apex of her head, in a style sometimes called 'cottage-bun'. Pablo Picasso painted Gertrude Stein with her hair like that.

Ernest Hemingway, who was very taken with Gertrude Stein when he met her in 1922, wrote of *her lovely, thick, alive immigrant hair which she put up in the same way she had probably worn it at college.* Gertrude Stein did not invest much effort in doing her hair, but Mabel Haynes always looks, at least when posing for photographs, as though she had relied on crimping irons.

The time-consuming ways of dealing with hair were abandoned once women began to do things that had been done only by men before. Alice B. Toklas had bobbed her hair before the war, adopting the long fringe she was to keep all her life, but Gertrude Stein still had a long plait until 1926.

In her memoir, Alice B. Toklas describes how Gertrude Stein was moved to cut her hair after a visit by the dashing and also newly short-haired Duchesse de Clermont-Tonnere: *That night Gertrude said to me, Cut off my braids. Which I agreed to do. The following day I spent gradually cutting it off, because I did not know how you did it, and it got shorter and shorter. The more I cut off, the better Gertrude liked it. I was still cutting the next evening, I had been cutting a little more all day and by this time it was only a cap of hair when Sherwood Anderson came in. Well, how do you like it, said I rather fearfully. I like it, he said, it makes her look like a monk.*

(…) Later Gertrude forgot that she ever had two long braids.

It is of course significant that it was Alice B. Toklas who performed this shearing and not a coiffeur, and since Alice B. Toklas did not know anything about cutting hair, she ended up cutting it all off, to Gertrude's delight we are told. When Picasso first saw her like this, he was only thinking that his portrait of her might no longer work but on close inspection of her cropped head, he pronounced that *it was all there*, that he had allowed for that aspect of her face and appearance. Soon after she had cut her hair, Man Ray took some new publicity photographs and one image shows Gertrude Stein with her hair not quite a short as on later pictures. It is slicked back and shows the 'short back and sides'.

She wears lipstick and mascara and is dressed in a patterned gown with a white soft scarf held together by a brooch. It is interesting to compare this picture with the one taken by the Arnold Genthe of Mrs Charles E. Knoblauch, the erstwhile May Bookstaver, taken in New York on January 22nd, 1927. Mrs Knoblauch too has her hair brushed back and wears make-up; her look is as defiant as Gertrude's imperial profile, only with the self-assurance befitting a *femme du monde.*

Mabel Haynes not only had fairly thin hair, it also turned grey before time: *My hair got grey early. But not so bad, with 38. Then I began to dye it, chiefly when I married Rudolf who was so much younger.* She dyed it with henna until the Second World War, when survival was difficult enough for her, as an enemy alien in Austria, without having to worry about hair. In her last photographs that she had professionally made in Boston 1946, she had visited a hairdresser beforehand and her white hair had been permed into fluffy curls.

When I look at the various babies' hair, which Mabel Haynes had placed in little envelopes and pasted into the chronicles of her children, they appear now as little sacrifices made to memory. Her daughter Gabrielle cut off a little strand of her mother's hair after she had died; it still had some dye in it, and I still have that little envelope, marked with the date, August 22nd, 1955. In the nineteenth century it had been a custom to wear one's lover's lock in a locket, or a dead child's curl; one could look at it and remember the touch, the scent of it, and the irrevocable loss, as one realizes that *the whole special suddenness commences then, there is no delusion.*

Handbags

In none of all the many photographs of Gertrude Stein does she hold anything other in her hand than a hat, or a book, or a dog on a leash. It was Alice B. Toklas who carried a handbag, sometimes several bags; various but generally commodious handbags. Gertrude Stein may have had deep pockets in her voluminous outfits to hold at least some of the smaller items, a bit of cash, a cheque-book, scraps of paper and a pencil, hardly a lipstick. She did write a poem entitled *A Purse,* in the collection *Tender Buttons: A purse was not green, it was not straw color, it was hardly seen and it had a use a long use and the chain was never missing, it was not misplaced, it showed that it was open, that is all it showed.*

Was this her own purse, the one she never displayed, the one *hardly seen* but showing that *it was open?* Or one of Alice B. Toklas', one that had *a long use,* and if so who's use? The poem has been subject of some exegesis, its analysts making reference to Freud's interpretation of Dora's fiddling with her reticule as indicating masturbation; another reader preferred to see the poem, as the product of a writer, who is *androgynous in her self-understanding, both male and female, who is virile and masculine in defiance of her society, who is a mannish seductive lesbian, who is unashamed of masturbation, who is less interested in protrusion than flowing and wetness and the orgasmic body beyond genitalia, who is creating a continuous present from the plenitude of lesbian pleasure.* Another reader saw it as a signal of Stein's distancing herself from '*the promiscuity and venality of Left Bank Parisian lesbian in favour of a monogamous and exclusive relationship*'.

The etymology of the word 'purse' points to an article made of leather. In English usage, a woman carries her money in a purse, a man in a wallet. A purse that is open shows its content or lack of content, the fluctuations of value, the flows of money or desire. Gertrude Stein eschewed the handbag but gave due credit to the purse, the strings of which she and Alice B. Toklas, and before that she and her brother Leo Stein, pulled, together and separately.

I have in my possession a beaded bag lined in light blue silk that had belonged to Mabel Haynes. The pattern shows roses and pansies in profusion and a brown twisted silk cord is threaded through the finely crocheted mouth of the reticule. At the bottom a beaded knot gathers the folds together. It is quite a commodious bag, large enough to hold opera glasses, a handkerchief, a powder compact. It is a splendidly feminine object - the tiny beads must have taken some female hands long hours to sew - its soft contours would bulge with its contents or hang limply from the wrist. The tassel on the cord is frayed and shows signs of wear or having been fiddled with. When I turn the bag inside out and sniff the lining there is a slight scent of perfume. Yet it has been sturdily made, and is not a dainty object but a reticule that conveys a sense of substance, not a trifle. I have a hunch that this bag had been a present, and I like to imagine that May Bookstaver had given to her and that it had been used when they were together, at the opera or concert hall; possibly on the night when they heard *Carmen* at the Met in New York, an awkward night described by Gertrude Stein in *Q.E.D.* A gift carries not just the obligation to reciprocate, but some responsibility to do the gift justice, to put it to use, and to keep it.

May Bookstaver, once she was Mrs C. E. Knoblauch and had money, would have had dainty clutches and fashionable handbags to see her through all of her numerous social engagements in Manhattan, but in her role as an activist for the women's suffrage movement she would have needed the sort of practical canvas bags, strapped across the body, that could be filled with pamphlets, or a bag big enough to hold the manuscripts of Gertrude Stein's writings. When she succeeded in getting *Three Lives* published, it was the first Gertrude Stein book to be published. *The chain was never missing it was not displayed.*

Handwriting

writing automatically in a long weak handwriting—four or five lines to the page—letting it ooze up from deep down inside her, down onto the paper with the least possible physical effort; she would cover a few pages so and leave them there and go to bed, and in the morning Alice would gather them up.

Gertrude Stein had the same trouble as I had at school in producing neat and legible handwritten work, as related in "The Autobiography of Alice B. Toklas": *They asked the children in the public schools to write a description. Her recollection is that she described a sunset with the sun going into a cave of clouds. Anyway it was one of the half dozen in the school chosen to be copied out on beautiful parchment paper. After she had tried to copy it twice and the writing became worse and worse she was reduced to letting some one else copy it for her. This, her teacher considered a disgrace. She does not remember that she herself did. As a matter of fact, her handwriting has always been illegible and I am very often able to read it when she is not.*

Gertrude Stein does not remember to have felt that getting somebody else, whose handwriting was better, to do the job for her, was a disgrace. As far as she was concerned, she had written the description of the sunset with the sun going into a cave of clouds and that was what mattered to her. She was then as she was to become later, somebody who wrote things that were to be read for the words written rather than for words beautifully written on a piece of paper. When she was a child, millions of people toiled as clerks, their detachable cuffs splattered with ink, standing at their desks, scribbling from dawn to dusk, making copies, and copies of copies; they had to be able to write very fast as well as neatly and above all legibly in a 'good hand'. Gertrude Stein's handwriting was not considered a good hand, though she could write fast enough, and had *large, loose and looping* characters.

Alice B. Toklas had very neat and legible handwriting herself but her special talent, with which she served Gertrude Stein almost from the beginning of the time together, was the ability to decipher Gertrude Stein's large, loose and looping letters. She transcribed them onto a typewriting machine and Gertrude Stein corrected the typed sheets with more handwriting.

Gertrude Stein never used a typewriter herself.

Gertrude Stein wrote in lined or squared exercise books that were comparatively small for her large letters, but this was a restraint she liked to work with; keeping to short words, five would fit a page, writing words one underneath the other, using indentions. She allowed her pen the range of the page. It mattered how it worked on the page and Alice B. Toklas worked out a manner to type so as to convey that, but the format of the typewriting paper is quite different. It was even more difficult to set it in type for the books.

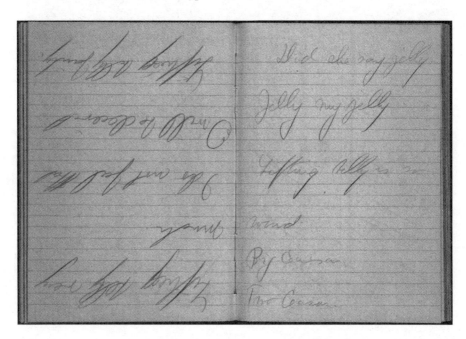

I have been transcribing hundreds of letters Mabel Haynes had written to her children, as well as the much fewer she had written to Gertrude Stein. It is quite remarkable that her elegant and rather forceful handwriting hardly changed over the years. She loops her letters together and she crosses her t's with long horizontal strokes that sometimes extend the whole width of the word. Her handwriting is easily legible and has the fluidity of long practice. She never wrote anything but letters, but she wrote a great many of these, given that she spent her life far away from her relatives and friends back in America. She never used a typewriter.

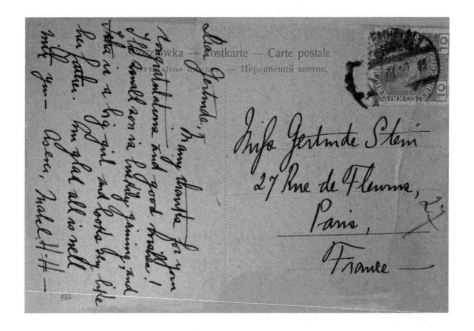

Alice B. Toklas destroyed all the letters that May Bookstaver had sent to Gertrude Stein. I found a short note addressed to Mabel Haynes inside a letter she had sent to her daughter. She seems to have been fond of wide nib fountain pens and the bold strokes convey something of her temperament, not florid but forceful.

Dear Mabel:

How glad I shall be to see you on Tuesday about five thirty. Shall I be prepared with tea, cocktails or a nightball. Mabel Weekes is coming to see you on Wednesday. I am sure you are all agog. All best. Yours

Mary Knoblauch.

Hats

In 1905 Henri Matisse painted his wife Amélie, sitting in a chair and looking crossly from under a huge hat, a composition of feathers, ribbons, artificial buds and fruit. It was shown at the Salon d'Automne and received with much derision: *Having gone to the opening day of the salon and heard what was said of his picture and seen what they were trying to do to it he never went again.*

Gertrude and Leo Stein liked the picture of *La Femme au Chapeau* and they bought it for $400.00 to hang on the wall of their studio at 27, rue de Fleurus, where they had set up house together. Matisse' career owes something to his wife's taste in hats – she was working as a milliner at the time to help make ends

151

meet; it precipitated the new phase in his painting and, for the first time, had made him some money.

Alice B. Toklas, trying to improve her conversation in French, turned to Picasso's mistress Fernande Olivier. They talked about fashion and hats: *She liked hats, she had the true french feeling about a hat, if a hat did not provoke some witticism from a man on the street the hat was not a success. Later on once in Montmartre she and I were walking together. She had on a large yellow hat and I had on a much smaller blue one. As we were walking along a workman stopped and called out, there go the sun and the moon shining together. Ah, said Fernande to me with a radiant smile, you see our hats are a success.* Alice B. Toklas, so the artist Pavel Tchelitchew remembered, loved hats and bought lots of hats. He said that *Gertrude Stein used to comment on her hats that Alice had three or four kinds of hats. There's the hat of a great success. This hat can go for long years and sometimes be worn — that's a great love. The second hat was the kind good, very good, it would go for three months. Then, the hat which was a failure. It saw half a day's time,*

it arrived, it was put on, and – it died that day. And so Gertrude would say, 'And so with art.'

Gertrude Stein, impatient with dresses and hats in her youth, was in her later life as interested in them as in all details of domestic life, her happy domestic life with Alice B. Toklas. *Colored hats are necessary to show that curls are worn by an addition of blank spaces, this makes the difference between single lines and broad stomachs, the least thing is lightening, the least thing means little flower and a big delay a big delay that makes more nurses than little women really little women. So clean is a light that nearly all of it shows pearls and little ways. A large hat is tall and me and all custard whole.*

When women bobbed their hair after the war and did many things that women had not been doing before, the hats changed too. The cloche hats of the 1920s echo the hard helmets worn by soldiers during the First World War. They were tight fitting and made of felt and were worn pulled well down the forehead like visors. May Bookstaver, by then Mrs Charles E. Knoblauch, looks like a silent movie Valkyrie in a photo by Arnold Genthe, square jawed and tightly helmeted, she epitomizes the sort of woman who had helped to bring about female suffrage and kept the world going during the great carnage.

Mabel Haynes looks melancholy from under her summer hat that accentuates her large nose.

Gertrude Stein had a great many hats; there was the awkwardly balanced velvet hat worn in Venice on her first visit with Alice B Toklas, to the homburgs, panamas and fedoras she came to wear once she had cut her hair short.
She particularly liked her leopard skin cap, which was one of the hats she took to America.

When Gertrude Stein flew about America for her lecture tour in 1934 she liked to wear a close-fitting but peaked hat and it was this hat, which Alice B Toklas never mentions, that was to become a favourite trope for some enthusiastic journalists approach her whole puzzling persona: *The hat was a Stein hat, a hat as persistent as the repetitions which are a feature of her abstruse writings. Peaked in front above her candid brown eyes, it roamed backward tightly about the close-cropped head to a fold at the rear; a gay hat which gave her the appearance of having just sprung from Robin Hood's forest to enunciate another word pattern of her own literature - literature which she said must await the reverence of our grandchildren's children.*

Gertrude Stein said: *'It's just a hat.'*

Itha Heissig Thomas Karminski-Pielsticker

(1908-1982)

Mabel Haynes thanked Gertrude Stein for congratulating her on the birth of her first child:

March 7ᵗʰ, 1908

My dear Gertrude,

Your letter reached me while still in the sanatorium in Vienna and I was glad of your good wishes and your thoughts of me. The baby daughter is all kinds of healthy and weighed nearly nine pounds at the start. She is all father as yet and when I get a chance you shall have a snap-shot of both of them. I was well cared for in the sanatorium and escaped without any complications and am nearly myself again. We want to go to America but it would scarcely be advisable for a year to come.

Mabel Haynes was thirty-four when she gave birth to Itha Heissig. Unlike Emma Lootz Erving, who loathed being pregnant, she did not find this state irksome and she had enough of an income to afford nursery maids and later governesses to take on the tedious aspects of child rearing. Mabel Haynes thought that her daughter took after her father, Konrad Heissig, the Austrian captain, she as fair as he was, and had the same deep-set eyes.

This is the last official picture of the family, taken in 1912, when Mabel Haynes' second child was two years old. When Konrad Heissig died in November that year, Itha was four.

Mabel Haynes got married again, in October 1913, to another Austrian officer, Rudolf Leick. As Emma Lootz Erving wrote to Gertrude Stein, Mabel Haynes had married again with the same unseemly haste as Queen Gertrude in *Hamlet*.

The head trauma that Rudolf Leick sustained during the war - some shrapnel or stone splinters were lodged in his brain - triggered violent and erratic behaviour, especially towards the children. Mabel Haynes seems to have tried to shield Itha from her husband's erratic behaviour by sending her to be schooled abroad. In 1925, when Itha was seventeen, she came to the United States, as reported in the Bryn Mawr Alumnae Bulletin from 1927: *Mabel Haynes Leick's daughter, Itha Heissig, came over to this country a year ago with Clara Vail Brooks, after Peggy Brooks had spent some weeks at the Leick's home in Graz, Austria. Last winter Itha lived in Boston with Mary Miller Buckminster and studied at Boston University. She has now returned to Austria.*

Itha was thus away during the difficult time when Mabel Haynes fought to secure her divorce. It is not known what Itha studied while she was in Boston, or indeed if she pursued the opportunities to develop her intellect with any zeal. When Itha returned to Europe in October 1927, she was to spend some time with her mother in Paris to meet interesting people. Mabel Haynes also contacted Gertrude Stein: *I am here for a time with my 18-year-old daughter Itha who has just returned from America. Could we come and see you some afternoon? Just drop me a line at above address. Am so looking forward to seeing you. Wish you might have some men on deck – as my offspring will have nothing to do with the good Americans –*

Gertrude Stein had just come back from spending the summer in the Bugey and agreed to meet them. An undated brief note in the Yale Stein archive states how much Mabel Haynes and Itha had enjoyed the evening, with or without young men to attract Itha's attention. Itha did not accompany her mother to Graz, as the next letter Mabel Haynes sent to Gertrude Stein explains:

March 2 1927

In the short three months since Paris many changes have come over my life – I have secured a divorce from my husband and custody of the children, so all is peaceful here after many years of torment. Itha went straight from Paris to Palermo to visit an old friend of mine, Mrs Gallotti, and within 8 days I got a telegram that she was engaged to Eduardo, the only child, whom I had always a great affection for – His father was Italian and Eduardo is intelligent, all gold inside and an Adonis out. As far as I can see, they are well suited and are to marry in September – She just 19, he 22! Now I am wondering if the U.S. government can refuse, at my death, at least to give her her share of the inheritance. The little ones are well and I shall stay on in Graz. How is everything with you and charming Miss Thecla? I can't tell you what it meant to sit around and talk as of old in that heavenly peace, all the more where everything was so tangled up for me. – It seemed a pity to break the spell and talk of the miseries of my existence. I am getting back my equilibrium and hope I find wisdom for all these children. Do write. Warmest greetings to your friend and to you both from Itha. Much love as of old and ever, Mabel

Mabel Haynes may not have opened her heart to Gertrude Stein to reveal the full extent of her troubles when they met by preferring not to *break the spell* that conversation with Gertrude Stein could weave. Gertrude Stein did react to their meeting and the letter from March by writing a text that she incorporated in the work she was engaged in at the time:

Mabel Haynes American four Austrian children. Four Austrian children are children of Mabel Haynes America Mabel Haynes American's four Austrian children. The eldest of Mabel Haynes American's four Austrian children would if she were obliging marry an American and so reduce Mabel Haynes American's four Austrian children to three Austrian children. Mabel Haynes American's three Austrian children if Mabel Haynes American's three Austrian children two Austrian children were born Italian children Mabel Haynes American's three Austrian children being born two Italian children Mabel Haynes American's one Austrian child four Austrian three Austrian children one Austrian child Mabel Haynes American's eldest Austrian child two Austrian children of Mabel Haynes American's eldest Austrian child four Austrian children did not marry and American two

Austrian children being born Italian three Austrian one Austrian child four Austrian children.

Gertrude Stein knew that Mabel Haynes' third and fourth child (Enid and Gabrielle) had been born in what in 1927 was Italy; only her last son, my father Reginald, was born in what was still Austria. Itha, whose inheritance Mabel Haynes worries about if she were to marry an Italian, could have married an American and thus rebalanced some of Mabel Haynes' Austrian offspring. As she wrote to Gertrude Stein, with evident relief that she was to find her equilibrium again after *years of torment,* Itha was to wed the handsome young Eduardo, the only son of her American friend. Mabel Haynes planned a grand wedding in Graz to which numerous people were invited. Itha duly went to the altar, sat down at the wedding banquet and boarded the train with her husband to set off on the honeymoon. Eduardo waited in vain for her to return to their sleeping compartment. Itha had disappeared. A few days later she announced that she had no intention to live with Eduardo and that she wished to marry Leopold von Thomas, a habitué of Mabel Haynes' salon in Graz, a man considerably older than Itha, whom she married when the union to Eduardo Gallotti was annulled. She later told her family that her mother had forced her to marry Eduardo but they she could not bring herself to do so as she did not love him.

Itha went on to have two daughter, Solveig and Dagmar, who both became stage actresses in Germany. Her marriage with Leopold von Thomas ended in divorce and in 1937 and she married Artur Karminski-Pielsticker, a lawyer, also a Viennese, and the best friend of von Thomas. According to Dagmar von Thomas, Mabel Haynes was very much against Itha's marriage to Artur von Pielsticker *because he was Jewish* and she threatened to disinherit Itha should she do so against her will. Since Itha defied her wishes she refused any further contact with her daughter.

Gabrielle Leick, Mabel Haynes' fourth child, always talked about her sister Itha as one who liked to torment her mother. She also spoke about the time Itha spent in America and that she had nearly succeeded in destroying Mabel Haynes' long friendship with May Bookstaver by *spreading lies* about her mother when she came to visit 'Aunt Mary' in New York'. What sort of lies they were I could never find out. It could have been the issue of Mabel Haynes being thought a Nazi.

Itha survived the war in Vienna and the difficult years of the occupation, protecting her beautiful daughters from the Russians.

According to Mabel Haynes' letters to Gabrielle from Boston, where she moved to in 1946, she was *being hounded by Itha* with requests for money and assistance, which she refused. She had cut off all relations and altered her will so as to leave her firstborn daughter only the obligatory one US dollar.

Itha Heissig died in 1982 and buried in the same vault as her father in Hietzing Cemetery in Vienna.

Jealousy

In loving some one is jealous, really jealous and it would seem an impossible thing to the one not understanding that the other one could have about such a thing a jealous feeling and they have it and they suffer and they weep and sorrow in it and the other one cannot believe it, they cannot believe the other one can really mean it and sometime the other one perhaps comes to realise it that the other one can really suffer in it and then later that one tries to reassure the other one the one that is then suffering about that thing and the other one the one that is receiving such reassuring says then, did you think I ever could believe this thing, no I have no fear of such a thing, and it is all puzzling, to have one kind of feeling, a jealous feeling, and not have a fear in them that the other one does not want them, it is a very mixing thing and over and over again when you are certain it is a whole one some one, one must begin again and again and the only thing that is a help to one is that there is really so little fundamental changing in any one and always every one is repeating big pieces of them and so sometimes perhaps some one will know something and I certainly would like very much to be that one and so now to begin.

I was a sad resisting depressed jealous one and now I am telling this thing.

The telling this thing took up the first few years of Gertrude Stein's life as a writer and by the time she was writing the last few hundred pages of *The Making of Americans* she was no longer sad resisting depressed and jealous. She had found the woman who unequivocally wished to be her love object, Alice B. Toklas, who was to make sure that Gertrude Stein would never doubt for a minute that she would only allow herself to be the beloved of Gertrude Stein:

> *Baby preciousest, sweetest adorest, allest*
> *Mine and I am allest thine precious baby*
> *Mine…*

Gertrude Stein would apparently no longer experience jealousy but Alice B. Toklas, certainly in the early years of their time together, was at times wary of any one she thought might attract Gertrude Stein in such a way as was to be felt like a loss to her. She did not approve long of Gertrude Stein's attachment to the young Hemingway, who seems to have been oblivious to the sexual nature of their relationship, which repelled him. Ernest Hemingway later wrote that Gertrude Stein's affection cooled because *she was just jealous* of his success as a writer. That would have made her envious, but it seems to reveal something about Ernest Hemingway that he ascribed jealousy to her.

Alice B. Toklas remained vigilant, quietly discouraging the cultivation of some contacts on some occasions, or putting her foot down firmly on others, but she was ill prepared for the revelation that Gertrude Stein had loved, and loved deeply if unhappily, another woman before her. When Bernard Faÿ and Louis Bromfield found the manuscript of *Q.E.D.* in a cupboard, where Gertrude Stein said she had forgotten it, as well as the note-books and letters written by May Bookstaver, Alice B. Toklas was beside herself. *She destroyed - or made Gertrude destroy - May's letters, which had served as the basis for the early novel. She became, as she put it, "paranoid about the name May."*

She also seems to have forced Gertrude Stein to make alterations to a composition she was working on at the time (1932) 'Stanzas in Meditation', as Ulla E. Dydo, working on the original manuscript discovered: *Throughout the stanzas, Stein, who was not in the habit of revising, had laboriously and consistently changed her original phrasing, replacing not only the <u>auxiliary</u> <u>verb</u> "may" with "can" but the word 'may" or "May" in all its forms.* Considering the devoted care Alice B. Toklas took of all of Gertrude Stein's writing, this was an extraordinary thing for her to do. Thereafter Alice B. Toklas vetoed any contacts with the people who had any knowledge of the May Bookstaver affair, such as Emma Lootz or Mabel Weeks, and of course with Mary Knoblauch, once she realized that this was none other than May Bookstaver's married name. Visits from Mabel Haynes and any correspondence also cease after this time.

Mabel Haynes eventually realised that Gertrude Stein had not diminished the affection May Bookstaver held for her and she for May Bookstaver, and she continued to write friendly letters to Gertrude Stein. She would later counsel her grown-up children against losing their composure over the infidelities committed by their lovers or spouses. As her daughter would say, *what's the use of being unhappy over it? It won't stop them doing it or wanting to do it.* A Stoical response I have myself tried to adopt, successfully, more often than not.

My mother, who was given to resent those who drew my father's amorous attention, learned not to show her jealousy of his numerous paramours. Only in her jealous resentment of her mother-in-law, Mabel Haynes, did she have her way, as Mabel Haynes withdrew from the field, wise to the fact that her son's love for his mother could not be diminished by his love for his wife, but also knowing that his wife could forgive his fleeting affairs but begrudged the admiration and affection her husband showed for his mother.

Jewellery

Please be please be get, please get wet, wet naturally, naturally in weather. Could it be fire more firier. Could it be so in ate struck. Could it be gold up, gold up stringing, in it while while which is hanging, hanging in dingling, dingling in pinning, not so. Not so dots large dressed dots, big sizes, less laced, less laced diamonds, diamonds white, diamonds bright, diamonds in the in the light, diamonds light diamonds door diamonds hanging to be four, two four, all before, this bean, lessly, all most, a best, willow, vest, a green guest, guest, go go go go go go, go. Go go. Not guessed. Go go.

A diamond can be a girl's best friend, and to lay down a stock of such easily disposed of investment might seem a suitable strategy to pursue if you have little to go on but looks and charm. Mabel Haynes was not such a girl. She bought her own diamonds and sapphires and pearls. They were, so she told her daughters, good for showing off when times were good and good for selling when times were bad. On the photographs taken of her in professional studios, she wears pearls and gold and bracelets and rings on fingers and in earlobes as befitting a woman of substance. None of these jewels have come down to my generation as they were either sold or stolen; her daughters later made do with imitations since they knew how to carry them off as if they were real. I never acquired a taste for valuable jewellery, unlike my sister, who happily wears the golden necklaces our father gave my mother to make up for his infidelities.

Gertrude Stein and Alice B. Toklas liked to rummage in flea markets and *bric-à-brac* shops and were just as delighted with rhinestone, as with coral, pearls or old silver. Gertrude Stein did not wear earrings or bracelets, but she was very fond of brooches and long heavy necklaces, like the heavy Chinese mandarin chain of lapis lazuli that Alice B. Toklas mentions in her memoir, which seems to have been a present from Mabel Weeks since Leo Stein writes to Mabel Weeks that Gertrude Stein *says that I am to say that it's very beautiful.* Gertrude Stein's most emblematic piece of jewellery was the bright red coral brooch set in silver that she wore when Picasso painted her portrait.

This brooch is quite large (3 x 3.8 cm) and holding together a low white collar, it marks the only bright spot, set right in the geometrical centre of the painting and thus *forming the only ostensibly "feminine" element of the picture.* She also wore it when Alice B. Toklas first set eyes on her and Alice B Toklas *thought that her voice came from the brooch.* According to Nancy H. Rummage's research, this brooch had been a present from Leo Stein. Gertrude Stein stopped wearing it after she fell out with Leo Stein, and she wore instead a lapis lazuli brooch, possibly one made in the Parisian jewellery making establishment that her older brother Michael Stein had opened. Alice B. Toklas wrote in her own autobiography that Michael Stein had asked her to sell his jewellery, made from designs by his wife Sarah, to the people she had been meeting and that she was relived to find that French law prevented the sale of objects in a private house and that Michael Stein found it easier to export them to the United States.

The most extraordinary image of Gertrude Stein wearing jewellery is the 1907 painting of her by Félix Valloton. Seated against a bare wall, her large body swathed in a brown velvet robe, resting a fat fingered hand on each thigh and looking sternly imperious, she wears a long necklace that may have been a string of prayer beads made of lapis lazuli with a coral red, lips-shaped appendage that looks like a displaced vulva in a vast expanse of cloth. Furthermore, this gown is held together at the neck by a viciously sharp pin. Gertrude Stein never liked that painting and she disparaged Valloton as the *Manet for the impecunious.*

Gertrude Stein took pleasure in strongly coloured semi-precious stones and their smooth polished surfaces. Her brooches and chains were a source of sensual delight, as much as adornment, and not an investment to be sold in times of want. Alice B. Toklas, who had a theatrical bent - she liked to impersonate the popular singer Lillian Russell at times – wore plenty of jewellery and she favoured large, pendulous earrings. Mabel Dodge describes her appearance at the Villa Curonia: *Alice wore straight dresses made of Javanese prints – they are called batik nowadays. She looked like Leah, out of the Old Testament, in her half-Oriental get-up – her blues and browns and oyster whites – her black hair – her barbaric chains and jewels – and her melancholy nose. Artistic.* Alice B. Toklas liked to create an effect, one that brought out her daintiness and delicacy in contrast to Gertrude Stein's earthy massiveness, and she favoured finely wrought and precious adornments, befitting her as *baby precious always shines.*

Mabel Haynes bought her own jewellery, to serves as an adornment for occasions that demanded the full effect as an investment. Her diamonds, sapphires and strings of pearl could be sold when the need arose. My only memory of her is that of eagerly fingering her pearls as a three-year-old perched on her lap.

Jews

Can a Jew be wild.

Nobody in Krumpendorf and only Jews in Pörtschach.

Gertrude Stein was Jewish, Mabel Haynes and May Bookstaver were not. Gertrude Stein and Mabel Haynes lived most of their adult lives in Europe and always thought of themselves as Americans. Gertrude Stein also thought of herself as a Californian and as a genius. Her Jewishness was not something she made much of in her writing, as she did not make much of being homosexual. Even when she was living in German occupied France during the Second World War, living as a Jew with another Jewish woman, she never mentioned it. For the Gentile Mabel Haynes, living in German-annexed Austria meant living with anti-Semitism in its most virulent manifestation. May Bookstaver, Colonial Dame, living in New York, could look at what was going on in Europe from a safe distance.

When Gertrude Stein studied at Radcliffe in the 1890s, she came fresh from the warm, extended Jewish relatives in Baltimore who had taken her in after her father's death. Her older sister Bertha would end up marrying and setting up a kosher household. An early essay of Gertrude Stein's is entitled *The Modern Jew who has given up the faith of his Fathers can reasonably and consistently believe in Isolation,* where she stresses the superior intellect and nobility of the Jewish race and argues that in order to maintain Jewish identity Jews should remain strictly endogamous: *The Jew shall marry only the Jew. He may have business friends among the Gentiles, he may mix with them in their work and in their pleasures, he will go to their schools and receive their instructions, but in the sacred precincts of the home, in the close union of family and of kinsfolk he must be a Jew with Jews; the Gentile has no place there.*

Gertrude Stein may have repeated some of the talk she heard among her Baltimore relatives, or her perhaps her close friendship with her Jewish fellow-student Leon Solomons contributed to her idea that for a Jew real intimacy is only possible with another Jew.

When Gertrude Stein went on to study medicine at Johns Hopkins in Baltimore, she became friendly and ultimately intimate, with a number of non-Jewish women, some of whom were, like Mabel Haynes and Emma Lootz, fellow students. And she fell in love with the Gentile May Bookstaver. When that relationship ended in an impasse, and she had given up medicine and had moved to Paris, she used her diary notes, as well as letters she had written and received from May Bookstaver, to compose her first literary works. The emotional dynamics between a wayward and immoral beloved, who is never free enough from other attachments, and the earnest and self-disgusted *dependent independent* lover, are played out in several variations in *Three Lives*, as well as in 'Fernhurst' and in the middle section of *The Making of Americans*. Concetta Principe has suggested that Gertrude Stein's obsessive preoccupation with what could be seen simply as unhappy love-story, had to do with Gertrude Stein's ideas about Jewish identity and its potential to bring forth people of genius. Intimacy with Gentiles in *the close union of family and kinsfolk* would mean not only a betrayal of racial solidarity but thwart the possibility of becoming a genius herself. In *Q.E.D.* Adele (the Jewish woman based on Gertrude Stein) exchanges a passionate kiss with Helen Thomas: *Adele was aroused from it by a kiss that seemed to scale the very walls of chastity. She flung away on the instant filled with battle and revulsion…. she lost herself in the full tide of her fierce disgust.* According to Principe's analysis, Adele's reaction is not revulsion at discovering her response to lesbian sex, but that *while the reaction is about the physical touch, the issue is not the homosexual encounter but is more unconscious than that. The sexual bond between them began to reveal to Adele the dangers of their intimacy in terms of her Jewish identity.*

Tracing the various narrative strands in *The Making of Americans*, which constitute the variation on the theme of the Bookstaver affair, Principe detected the same theme: *This representation of barren sexual relations between a Jew and an American Anglo-Saxon reflects Stein's conscious or unconscious race-centered objection to mixed marriages. Both marriages stand as counterpoint to Stein, the narrator of* The Making of Americans, *as someone who, in a crisis of spiritual identity, rejected the Gentile from her private life to keep her Jewish identity. Stein's love for and marriage with Alice B. Toklas is proof of this decision and the narrator's claims of happiness in the heart of Alfred's portrait may be seen to confirm it.* Gertrude Stein's long inner struggle could thus be seen to have ended once she had established a close union with Alice B. Toklas. This not only allowed her sexuality to be lived according to her desire, but to do so with a partner whose Jewishness would provide the nurturing environment for Gertrude Stein's destiny to become a genius to be realised. Although in the long making of the 'The Making of the Americans' (between 1903 to 1911) she *filled dozens of manuscript books with notes and diagrams codifying the characteristic behaviors of Jewish and Anglo-Saxon types of people. The published volume, however, contains no explicit references to Jews, for Stein dropped all mention of Jews and Anglo-Saxons in lieu of purely descriptive behavioral terms.* This suggests that Gertrude Stein had managed to solve the conundrum of the Bookstaver affair and of Jewish identity by the time she had finished her *magnum opus*. She had, so Amy Feinstein suggests, aligned herself along the continuum of outstanding personalities of genius (from Goethe to Picasso) whose very genius and consistent behaviour she marked as typical for a 'Jewish type', in so far as *"they persistently and consciously educated themselves, consciously ran themselves by the minds, their minds". While none of these men were Jewish, all of them, according to Stein, were behaving like Jews or performing one variety of the platonic Jewish type of her schema, with their exhibitions of intellectual keenness. By casting non-Jews in the Jewish role of genius, Stein confirmed a practical and racial conflation of Jew and genius while nonetheless beginning to distance herself from racial understandings of human nature more broadly.*

When she later, in *The Autobiography of Alice B. Toklas,* describes a rather vulgar American as *looking like a Jew,* knowing that he wasn't Jewish, she again reveals for own categorization of what being Jewish means for her.

In the year of Gertrude Stein's greatest success and public recognition, at the end of her American tour, in 1935, the Nazi government in Germany announced new laws that defined a Jew as someone with three or four Jewish grandparents and that forbade Germans or people *of related blood* from marrying or having a sexual relationship with Jews. Regardless of how assimilated, how German they felt, whether they had abandoned the faith of their ancestors, whether they had converted to Christianity, even become a genius, having three to four Jewish grandparents alone determined who was to be classified as Jewish in the Nazi world. Mabel Haynes, American and resident in Graz, was obliged, as everyone living in Austria after 1938, to furnish an ancestral passport (*Ahnenpass*). Her New England Puritan ancestry did not endanger her.

Gertrude Stein and Alice B. Toklas, living in Vichy and then in occupied France, had only Jewish ancestors and they were in danger of having their possessions confiscated, and, in the final years of the war, being deported and sent to concentration camps. Gertrude Stein had made some flippant comments in the American press about Hitler in the 1930s, which were interpreted as evidence that she owed her survival to collaboration. She had translated some of the speeches by Marshal Pétain, the Vichy Head of State, and she was a close friend of Bernard Faÿ, an intimate of Pétain's. Faÿ's personal devotion to Gertrude Stein and Alice B. Toklas was genuine, based on his admiration for Gertrude Stein's work – he had translated parts of *The Making of Americans.* He was able to protect Gertrude Stein's collection of art during the war and may have had some influence in keeping the existence of the two elderly Jewish women below the radar. In *Wars I Have Seen* she never mentions the fate of Jews, and she does not credit Bernard Faÿ as someone who used his connections to keep her and

Alice B. Toklas safe. Instead, her account suggests that they saved themselves by being sensible, by keeping up friendly relations with their French neighbour, and she gives free expression to her admiration to the local mayor: ... *it was the mayor, the sub-prefect, and the townspeople who chose to look the other way when official anti-Jewish legislation trickled down to the villages of Bilignin and Culoz.*

At any rate, Gertrude Stein and Alice B. Toklas survived and returned to Paris, where they discovered their flat to be almost entirely intact. Gertrude Stein only survived the war by less than a year before she became *a dead one.* The fact that in Jewish tradition of a *dead one is a dead one* had been troubling to Gertrude Stein, whose mother's untimely death had caused a repressed and traumatic response in her. *Dead is dead yes that is certain and they go on having their religion and they are not believing and their religion is believing that dead is not dead, to be dead is not really dead, dead is dead of that they are really certain some of these then and they go on then having their religion doing everything of that their religion is almost certain and they are almost certain in them that in them, they know it in them.*

For Alice B. Toklas, who had survived her beloved Gertrude Stein, the Jewish concept of death that does not allow for the hope of being re-united with a beloved dead one, was troubling. It happened that through the mediation of Bernard Faÿ, who had done what he could to save their skins, she found a way to escape having Gertrude Stein being so decidedly and everlastingly a dead one by converting to Catholicism.

Mabel Haynes also survived the war in Austria, as did her children. Most of her Jewish acquaintances there did not. Some of her remarks in letters show that she had absorbed the anti-Semitism of her adopted country even when she lived in the United States again: *I have discovered that a doctor lives here on the ground floor, an Austrian. Seeing his name is Hiegels, he's of course a Jew, but in an emergency I shan't hesitate to phone him up.*

Konrad Heissig
(1864-1912)

Konrad Heissig was the first husband of Mabel Haynes. They were married for only five years until he died November 1912.

No letters of his survive, and what is known about him personally comes from letters written by his wife and her friends. However, his personal records as an officer of the Austro-Hungarian army, the so-called *Qualifikationslisten*, though conforming strictly to the bureaucratic norms of such documents, contain basic biographical information and reveal something of his character and his abilities.

Konrad Heissig was born on February 10th, 1864 as the son of the leather-goods manufacturer Josef Heissig and his wife Anna, née Smetana. He attended the infantry cadet school at Karlstadt (now Karlovac in Croatia) from 1879-1883and joined the imperial-royal army on April 10th, 1881. He belonged to the generation of officers who served in period of peace (from 1867-1914) and who went through the ranks without seeing any combat, with no opportunity for rapid promotion by valiant conduct in battle.

These reports show that Konrad Heissig was a successful peace-time officer, steadily rising through the ranks, faintly praised as not exceptional, but never admonished either, fulfilling his duty to keep his battalion in good order and to make his men fit for a fight that was to come after his death. He had good manners and apparently no vices, preferring to move in 'good society' and not incurring debts and getting embroiled in duels. He was, until the sudden collapse of his health, of sound physique and, as an officer of the Austrian army, considered and comported himself as a gentleman, though he was not of noble birth.

He made the acquaintance of Mabel Haynes in the winter of 1904/05 in Vienna. It is not unlikely that they met at one of *marvellous balls* she later fondly recalled. He was forty, his blond hair had started to thin. A photograph portrait from around this time shows him in uniform wearing the three stars of a Captain.

It was a time when Mabel Haynes had been working on her career as a physician by studying in Europe and working various dispensaries in Boston. Meeting Konrad Heissig opened new perspectives for Mabel Haynes. She had turned thirty in 1904. Although marriage to an Austrian officer meant sharing a garrison life in the wide-flung and hopelessly provincial provinces of the empire, giving up her medical career, and separation from family and friends, it seemed the only way out of the emotional torment.

As her friend Emma Lootz Erving wrote to Gertrude Stein, the whole thing very nearly came to naught: *She met the man when she was in Vienna, and saw something of him, and they kept up quite a correspondence. Then a year or more ago he came over to this country and May Bookstaver intercepted him in N.Y. (Mabel had sent him a letter to her) and he returned to Vienna without seeing Mabel. Then he was on deck when she went back to Vienna in the summer and then Mabel decided that he was the whole thing. When they became engaged he told her some perfectly astounding unpleasantnesses about May. I am shaking myself like a duck to avoid having the spray of any of these tales soak in. I should be inclined to believe a direct statement of Heissig's (his pictures are rather nice and he has evidently been pretty straight) but I refuse to believe Mary Buckminster or May Bookstaver or even Mabel who was making a fine stab at being sane.* Just what May Bookstaver had been up to remains unclear. However, even without the interference of a jealous former lover, it was by no means easy to marry an Austrian officer and twice as difficult for an unbaptized American. Konrad Heissig had to explain the complicated process, and the fact that wives had to pay a deposit and provide substantial additional income for the army to grant permission to marry. Perhaps these difficulties provided a spur to their resolution. Konrad Heissig obtained leave to cross the ocean in order to meet Mr John C. Haynes. The meeting must have been a success, for soon Mabel Haynes was officially engaged and her father agreed to provide the necessary funds. The captain went back to his regiment to obtain the required permits from his superiors, and Mabel Haynes made preparations to become a baptised and confirmed Lutheran, to disengage herself from her dispensary, and prepare to move her belongings to Austria.

It is not known how much Konrad Heissig had wanted to marry and to have children before he met Mabel Haynes. The reality was such that few officers were able to marry at all: *The army severely limited the proportion of those in each unit who could have a family and it ruled that marriages ought to be contracted only with women who would neither be a drain on the treasury nor demean the lofty social status and dignity of the corps. Overcoming the triple obstacle of numerus clausus, financial requirements, and acceptable social standing made a nightmare of an officer's existence.* The income of Austrian officers was lower than those in France and Germany and the state did not wish to support widows and orphans. Dr Mabel Haynes, daughter of the wealthy Boston music publisher, had sufficient status and money and once she had become baptised and confirmed, her side of the exigencies was fulfilled. Konrad Heissig managed to obtain the permission of his superiors and the requisite leave and so they were married on January 6th, 1907 in the Neo-Gothic Votive Church in Vienna. Their data were duly entered in the army's *Trauungsbuch* Vol XXXI Folio 22, carefully listing the fourteen documents and permissions that had been required. They had succeeded to overcome all the obstacles thrown into their path. She wrote, with some elation, to Gertrude Stein: *Your letter has just come, it was good to hear from you, and I am grateful, my dear, for your good wishes and your so sincere congratulations. I don't know what Emma may have written you – but the whole point is that I am immensely happy, and at peace. What more can I say? The Captain is an Austrian, a Viennese, forty-two years old, and we met here two years ago. I hope you will soon see for yourself how really right it all is. I don't wonder that ask where Przemysl is! It is in Austrian Poland, very near the Russian frontier, a garrison town with 50,000 soldiers and 1,000 officers. More details I can't give you yet, as I shall see it for myself for the first time in a week from now. We are at present in Vienna, after a delightful stay in the mountains at the top of the Semmering Pass, two hours from here.* Konrad Heissig and his wife, who now called herself Mabel Haynes Heissig went to Przemysl, where he continued to carry out his duties as an officer. Their first child, a girl named Itha, was born a year later. A son, named Oswald, followed after three years. It was, so Mabel Haynes would write to her friends, a successful marriage.

On April 1st, 1910 Konrad Heissig transferred to the Infantry Regiment Ernst Ludwig Grossherzog Hessen und bei Rhein No.14 that was stationed in Linz. In the autumn of 1912 Konrad Heissig fell ill with what was described as severe neurasthenia and was on sick leave for three months. The whole family went to Boston for the summer, where the beautiful children were much admired. As Emma Lootz Erving wrote to Gertrude Stein, it was clear now that he was suffering from General Paresis, an irreversible degeneration of the nervous system caused by a much earlier and possible unnoticed case of syphilis. On their return to Vienna he was too ill to be looked after at home and was admitted to the newly built sanatorium at the edge of the Vienna Woods, Steinhof. Konrad Heissig died there of a paralysed heart on November 21th at the age of forty-eight.

Laughter

Go red go red, laugh white.

When Gertrude and Leo Stein went to the Petit Palais to look again at the painting of Matisse called *La femme au chapeau,* which they had liked the day before and wished to buy, they found *people roaring with laughter at the picture and scratching at it. Gertrude Stein could not understand why, the picture seemed to her perfectly natural.* They bought the painting and they hung it on the wall of their studio in rue de Fleurus. Gertrude Stein had been *upset by them all mocking at it. It bothered her and angered her because she could not understand why because to her it was so alright, just as later she did not understand why since the writing was all so clear and natural they mocked at and were enraged by her work.*

The mocking laughter, especially the mocking laughter of a crowd of people, is the type of laughter that means to show superiority of taste or morals over somebody or something that offends generally held views. It is a laughter that rejects understanding or sympathy, and Gertrude Stein, who was, as she said, to experience mockery and misunderstanding of her work for many years, was upset and bothered, especially when to her it all seemed natural and alright and so clear.

Being bothered by mockery and ignorant laughter did not make Gertrude Stein despair of her work and of trying to show people how to look at modern art. Henry McBride, an art critic for the New York State *Sun,* who did much to promote the work of Gertrude Stein, would say to people who were likely to mock her work: *Laugh if you like…but laugh with and not at her, in that way you will enjoy it much better.*

Hostile criticism did not stop Gertrude Stein laughing her own laugh. By all accounts Gertrude Stein was a great laugher. People who were introduced to Gertrude Stein were, so her biographer James R. Mellows contends, *charmed by the lightness and suavity of her voice, by the irresistible fullness of her laughter. It was laugh, as one of her friends remarked, "like a beefsteak" – juicy and solid. Another thought it was like the fire kept banked up in the studio's cast iron stove. A sudden burst of inspiration could fan it into a roaring blaze, spreading a general warmth.*

In a televised interview recorded in 1952, Alice B. Toklas wistfully remembered Gertrude Stein's *deep, rich, contralto voice* and said that she especially liked her laugh: *she had an exceptional, a rare laugh. It was hearty and very loud and oh, it was music to my ears.*

Gertrude Stein liked to laugh. She could burst into roars of pleased laughter and she liked to laugh with Alice B Toklas: *Gertrude rocking happily in her wicker chair and Alice quieter but just as thoroughly amused.*

Alice B. Toklas wrote of Gertrude Stein's *fine large laugh* and that she really did laugh *a good deal.* She laughed when something delighted her, and a great many things could delight her in her life with Alice B Toklas. She could make herself laugh by her own writing; Eric Sevareid described a scene of Gertrude Stein reading aloud from her recently finished *Faust: She walked heavily up and down her study in front of her dark Picassos and read the script aloud to me, carried away by her own words and breaking off into ringing laughter which so overcome her at times that she would stop to wipe her eyes.* She could laugh with herself and she could laugh with Alice B. Toklas and with her friends. She may have laughed at herself and at her friends but that would have been a different laughter.

Laughter was a part in her early writing, when she was still writing about her experiences with May Bookstaver. The characters in the story *Melanctha* in *Three Lives* are distinguished from each other by their laughter. Melanctha herself *had a hard-forced laughter,* one that *just rattles.* Only Jeff Campbell has the right laugh: *He sang when he was happy and laughed and his way the never abandoned laughter that gives the warm broad glow to negro sunshine.* Jeff Campbell as the bewildered and ultimately frustrated lover in the story could be seen as Gertrude Stein's *alter ego* and while he fails to hold Melanctha, only he could bring forth the type of laughter that induced the *warm broad glow.* Only Gertrude Stein had the gift of such laughter, a laughter that is abandoned to itself, not constrained by conventions of politeness, neither forced nor hard, but bursting forth like sunshine. She describes negro workers who could fall into paroxysms of laughter, falling *full on the earth and roll in an agony of wide-mouthed shouting laughter.* Negros could laugh like that, with full abandon despite their oppression and miseries. Gertrude Stein saw that she had the same ability and that this type of laughter was a rare quality, certainly among the sophisticated college women of Baltimore who were not used to such displays of unrestrained hilarity. Gertrude Stein put her own laughter into the laughter of Jeff Campbell, the earnest doctor who woos the ever-wandering Melanctha with her hard laugh. However, while at the beginning of the story we hear a lot about sunshine and laughter, soon all this laughter is never heard again. It is drowned by the agonized discussions and the complete inability to understand one another. In the other, the Northern version of the same story in *Q.E.D.,* Gertrude Stein's persona is called Adele, and there is not much room for laughter in this version. There may be a short angry laughter, but no wide and warm glow-spreading one. It is a sad story and although Gertrude Stein liked sad stories and liked to tell sad stories she really was very sad and confused and angry and that is a mood that leaves little room for laughter.

Then a lighter, brighter, Parisian rather than Southern laughter appears in her writing. This laughter and the happiness that caused it to appear occurred after she had set up house with Alice B. Toklas. By then the past had become the past and the unhappiness had passed, and she was quite ready to be happy and to write about things that would provoke the delighted laughter. Alice B. Toklas' famous Haschisch Fudge, which she wrote was liable to produce *euphoria and brilliant storms of laughter*, may have helped as well. Gertrude Stein's wrote *The Long Gay Book* and this book has a tender minstrel-like tone, it is a happy Troubaritz who writes here: *Place the laughter where the smile is lending what there is of expecting that attention.*

From then on, the ghost of the author's laughter at her own inventiveness and at the sheer wonderful absurdity of existence is never far away. Whenever bafflement sets in among the *non sequiturs,* a hard and hearty (beefsteak) laughter arises. Sara Crangle has very carefully traced the nuances of the socio-dynamics of Gertrude Stein's laughter, from the solitary to the shared. She sees quite clearly that the lack of laughter or the right sort of laughter is characteristic for the inability to communicate and hence typical for the relationship of Adele and Helen in *Q.E.D.* She also sees that *Stein knew that a laughing life is not a stagnant one, and that she sought to underscore the continuity in her writing by eliciting laughs.*

A *rire gaie* in all its exuberance and charm fills *The Long Gay Book* and much of *Tender Buttons,* but once that first nuptial first tenderness was gone, there was need to play to a particular gallery, the smart people who thought they were smart people who sought Gertrude Stein's company, especially once she had become a notoriety, even, eventually, at the time of the American lecture tour, a celebrity. The laughter now feels more like a self-satisfied laughter at the expense of those who don't get the joke.

I know nothing about the sound of Mabel Haynes' or May Bookstaver laughter, as it had not been noticed much. One can be pretty sure that their laughter did not sound at all like Gertrude Stein's laughter in any of its variations. Mabel Haynes was a Bostonian from a New England Puritan lineage. She may not have been quite as reserved as Henry James' singular example of a Bostonian spinster, Olive Chancellor in *The Bostonians,* described as *a woman without laughter; exhilaration, if it ever visited her, was dumb.*

As for May Bookstaver, she was a New Yorker, and by all accounts excitable and as she was a New Woman, an emancipated woman, she could have indulged in less restrained manifestation of mirth and certainly her husband, Mr Charles 'Chas' E. Knoblauch was known for his propensity for practical jokes and merry making. However, at the time when May Bookstaver was entangled with Gertrude Stein, they did not seem to have much to laugh about as their relations lacked gaiety and the sort of delightful sharing of the pleasant moment conductive to Gertrude Stein's deep and hearty laugh.

Gertrude Stein ended up having the last laugh and her laughter, her Dionysian laughter, continues to ring from her pages.

Letters

Next to me next to a folder, next to a folder some waiter, next to a folder some waiter and re letter and read her. Read her with her for less.

The Yale Collection of American Literature's holdings of the Gertrude Stein and Alice B. Toklas Papers consists of 173 boxes, taking up 93 feet of linear space. The boxes contain manuscripts, artworks, photographs, items of personal use, newspaper clippings, and correspondence – postcards, telegrams and, above all, letters. Handwritten letters and typed letters, letters from people who became famous and letters from people no one remembers. Her letters, so Norman Pearson wrote, *are like roundelays of sprightliness* and he quotes Gertrude Stein: *"I write a good many of them,"* she has said. *"I like to write them."*

There are quantities of letters from and to Gertrude Stein in other archives too - in the Baltimore Museum of Art, the Bancroft Library, the Harry Ransom Humanities Research Center in Texas. Letters written by Gertrude Stein and Alice B. Toklas, bequeathed by their recipients, can also be read in these archives. I read the letters, the postcards and announcements that Mabel Haynes had sent to Gertrude Stein in the Yale archive.

The letters and postcards that Gertrude Stein had sent to Mabel Haynes have not survived. Mabel Haynes did not keep letters; she always said letters should be read carefully, several times, indeed many times if they were love letters. After that, she said, they should be torn up and thrown away. I have tended to follow her example. A bundle of letters Mabel Haynes wrote to her daughter Gabrielle survived as they had been stashed away in a store cupboard and forgotten. The letters that May Bookstaver sent to Gertrude Stein were destroyed by Alice B. Toklas in 1931. Just one postcard May Bookstaver sent to Mabel Haynes' daughter survived in my aunt's postcard album and one short note to Mabel Haynes. It's a pity because May Bookstaver was an enthusiastic correspondent and often wrote to Mabel Haynes: *May is so good to me, sends me such interesting letters almost every week. It is hard to have her so far away. She belongs to the "brilliant" women.*

May Bookstaver and Gertrude Stein, by contrast, considered a letter that has been sent and received as a document over which neither the writer nor the recipient had exclusive rights. They thought that they were testimonies to personalities, to character and attitude. A letter could be read not just for its contents, but for clues as to the state of mind of its sender. In a passage from "The Making of Americans" Gertrude Stein describes this interest: *Some men and women are inquisitive about everything, they are always asking, if they see any one with anything they ask what is that thing, what is it you are carrying, what are you going to be doing with that thing, why have you that thing, where did you get that thing, how long will you have that thing, there are very many men and women who want to know about anything about everything. I am such a one, I certainly am such a one. A very great many like to know a good many things, a great many are always asking questions of every one, a great many are to very many doing this with intention, a great many have intention in their asking, a great many just have their attention caught by anything and then they ask the question. Some when they are hearing any one talking are immediately listening, many would like to know what is in letters others are writing and receiving, a great many quite honest ones are always wanting to know everything, a great many men and women have a good deal suspicion in them about others and this has in them not any very precise meaning.*

The letters May Bookstaver wrote to Gertrude Stein during the period of their love affair may have been ripped up or burnt by Alice B. Toklas, but many passages from these letters were quoted verbatim in Gertrude Stein's texts, certainly in *Q.E.D.* and "'Melanctha'" in *Three Lives,* in *The Making of Americans.* May Bookstaver, so Emma Lootz Erving told Gertrude Stein, read passages of Gertrude Stein's letters aloud during dinner parties. Gertrude Stein had made Annette Rosenshine show her the letters Alice B. Toklas had written to her San Franciscan friend and Gertrude Stein read them all and used them as *a first close-up to Alice's psychological makeup.* While Annette Rosenshine described Gertrude Stein to Alice B. Toklas in her letters, Alice B. Toklas did not have access to anything Gertrude Stein had written. It took her a while to overcome the impression that Gertrude Stein had formed of her on the basis of the letters to Annette Rosenshine.

The content, the form of expression, the handwriting, even the choice of paper convey the sender's state of mind, but the recipient responds to all this with emotions conditioned by the relation between them – with relief, indifference, joy or sadness. Reading an old letter again after some years, results in a different reading: *Sometimes one reads a letter that they have been keeping with other letters, and one is not very old then and so it is not that they are old then and forgetting, they are not very old then and they come in cleaning something to reading this letter and it is all full of hot feelings and the one, reading the letter then, has not in them any memory of the person who once wrote that letter to them. This is different, very different from the changing of the feeling and the thinking in many who have in them real realisation of the meaning of words when they are using them but there is in each case so complete a changing of experience, some one once alive to some one is then completely a stranger to that one, the meaning in a word to that one the meaning in a way of feeling and thinking that is a category to some one, some one whom some one was knowing these then come to be all lost to that one sometime later in the living of that one.*

Reading a love letter not addressed to oneself but to another lover not only causes pain but serves as evidence for what may have been suspected while at the same time it violates trust. In the story called 'Fernhurst' Gertrude Stein retold the triangular affair between a married young lecturer at Bryn Mawr and the companion of the college dean, which had caused quite a scandal in the 1890s: *Mrs. Redfern arose and went into his room. She walked up to his desk and opening his portfolio saw a letter in his writing. She scarcely hesitated so eager was she to read it. She it to the end, she had her evidence. She turned with the letter still in her hand and faced Redfern who had come back. Their eyes met, Redfern was sinful, she was dishonourable, her eyes fell and she was ashamed. "I found it by accident" she stammered in confusion. "I did not know it was private." Redfern received the paper in silence and she hurried from the room. "That was a brutally discourteous act" Redfern said to himself some hours later, "I should have accepted her apology, of course she lied but I ought not to have shown that I thought so..."*

In 1916, by then blissfully united with Alice B. Toklas, writing furiously, she also composed a text entirely of letters, short letters nobody replies to.

I am not satisfied with a letter. Not at all. Not what I intended. Not at all what I intended.

Mabel Foote Weeks

(1872-1964)

Mabel Weeks was born on December 14th, 1872 in Whitesboro, New York. She attended Radcliff College where she read English, graduating with a B.A, *magna cum laude* in the first class of 1894, and then started her long career in teaching. She met Gertrude Stein not at Radcliffe, but in Baltimore, in the late 1890s, when she came down from New York City to visit her friend Emma Lootz. Mabel Weeks hit it if off with Leo Stein and saw much of him when he came to stay with his relatives in New York. In the summer of 1900 she accompanied the Stein siblings on a holiday to Europe, which took them to Paris to see the Great Exhibition, and to Italy. While Gertrude Stein was to return to Baltimore at the end of their travels, Mabel Weeks went from Paris to England, where she spent the winter studying at Cambridge.

If Mabel Weeks was able to divert herself from her emotional woes, not more clearly defined perhaps even to herself - by looking at paintings, this did not work as successfully for Gertrude Stein, who by that time had fallen in love with May Bookstaver. In the autumn, Gertrude Stein, having spent some weeks with Leo Stein in Spain, delayed her return to Baltimore and stayed with Mabel Weeks at the so-called White House that she shared with two artist friends. In this house Gertrude Stein began working on the notebooks that were to become *Q.E.D.* Leo Stein had left Baltimore by then and gone to study art in Italy. Having tired of Italy, he went to London and Gertrude Stein joined him there. Like Mabel Weeks had done, she spent most of her time reading, mainly in the British Museum, but unlike Mabel Weeks, she did not take to London and was not able to overcome her emotional turmoil by looking at Rubens paintings. She once more sought the company of Mabel Weeks and went to live with her again in the White House, while making occasional visits to Baltimore to see May Bookstaver.

Eventually Gertrude Stein would take Mabel Week's prescription of the tonic that looking at painting could afford, when in spring 1903 she joined Leo Stein in Paris and went to live with him in his atelier in Rue de Fleurus. She felt lonesome in Paris, *and the allure of seeing May Bookstaver once more drew Gertrude to the United States* and again she descended on Mabel Weeks for a four months' stay. After she went back to Paris in June 1904, she was not to return for another thirty years, but Mabel Weeks continued her relationship with Leo Stein and with Gertrude Stein, though not quite as long.

In 1907 Mabel Weeks began her long association with Barnard College on New York's Upper West Side. Her position was at first Adjunct Professor and then as associate in English, teaching a course in her favourite subject, the eighteenth century. In addition to her teaching, she also held the post of Assistant to the Dean in Charge of Social Affairs, which entailed a formidable workload. Mabel Weeks seems to have had an appetite for work and an aptitude for administration. That same year Gertrude Stein, having had no luck in finding anyone willing to publish *Three Lives*, sent the manuscript to Mabel Weeks, who handed it over to May Bookstaver (by then married and known as Mrs Charles Knoblauch), who got Grafton Press to bring it out at the expense of the author. Mabel Weeks liked *Three Lives* well enough, but when Gertrude Stein sent her the *Portrait of Mabel Dodge* she was puzzled: *The Portrait I am very glad to own though I should be disingenuous if I said I either understand or enjoy it. It puzzles me because you seem to have gone back on the principles that have guided you in your other writing and that were bringing you to such a point of success. For the other things do seem very successful. The Matisse more than Picasso to the mind of one who really knows nothings about either, but in the Portrait you seem to be doing something entirely different, and I feel rather sad because it evidently marks your taking a path in which I can't follow you. I shall, I suppose, have to adopt Leo's course and simply not read you, and considering the pleasure I've had in reading you in the past I am naturally cast down. This isn't criticism, I admit; only a definition of limitation. I'm long past trying to make myself over and I'd have to, to enjoy the Portrait.*

Mabel Week's admission that she could not 'follow' Gertrude Stein on her new path eventually eroded the friendship between them. She had before insisted in being included in the 'real readers' of Gertrude Stein's texts that they were not only written *for myself and* strangers but *for yourself, strangers, and Mamie Weeks*. Secure in her shared life with Alice B. Toklas, Gertrude Stein was able to jettison old friends who, had as she saw it, lagged behind; Mabel Weeks and Emma Lootz were just some of those whom she broke with when they no longer interested her. When Mabel Weeks tried to get to see Gertrude Stein on the occasion of her lecture tour, when she and Alice B. Toklas were much fêted in New York, Gertrude Stein refused to see her and told her gruffly to come and see her in France, as a very upset Mabel Weeks wrote to Leo Stein. She continued being a confident of Leo Stein's for all his life. When his papers and letters were published in 1950 with her Foreword, she concludes this with her belief with that his work *will endure long after Gertrude's work is forgotten. Leo may appear as the more significant of the two when time has weakened the impress of Gertrude's remarkable personality.*

Mabel Weeks retired in from Barnard College in 1939 at the age of sixty-seven. An academic career that spanned more than thirty years was followed by another period of time, nearly as long, of active and happy retirement. She remained in touch with Mary Knoblauch, a widow since 1934, and with Mabel Haynes.

Reflecting on her life and weighing up what it had meant to have been part of the generation of women who had to fight to have access to education, to birth-control, to have the vote, she wrote a response to a polemical article entitled 'Are American Women making the most of the rights and privileges for which they fought' by Agnes Rogers: *It is in the variety and scope of the demands that women are making on life that I find their courage most in evidence. They demand in ever-increasing numbers a college education and feel no more committed by it to a special career than men do. They expect and want early marriage and children, although they know that they must get along without service. Often, to help out, they take a part-time job, and in addition most of them ask an active part in the cultural and community life of their time.*

Who shall say that the task of harmonizing all these aspects of living is not enough to challenge the adventurous spirit of women? And it is perhaps a more truly creative job than following in the beaten track of a professional career.

Mabel Weeks, the lifelong spinster and successful academic, could see a creative spirit in the often compromised and harassed lives of women who wanted to pursue careers as well as have families. She died at the age of ninety-two in 1964. Before she died, she had bequeathed the letters she had received from and written to both Stein siblings to the Yale archive.

Marian Walker Williams

(No dates available)

Marian Walker studied at Radcliffe with Gertrude Stein, and they graduated on the same day, July the second, 1898. She came from Cincinnati, Ohio, and was the daughter of Judge Bryant Walker and his wife Frances Tyng. Her father, who had never recovered from an injury sustained during the Civil war, died 1874. This means that Marian Walker, whose date of birth or death, I have been unable to verify, was probably born around 1873 or 1874.

Marian Walker had her mind set on becoming a medical doctor. She enrolled at Johns Hopkins Medical School at the same time as Gertrude Stein and was in the same class as Mabel Haynes and Emma Lootz. She graduated a year earlier, in 1901, and on February 9th that year she had married Allen Hamilton Williams, who completed his medical degree at Harvard Medical School also in 1901.

Years later, on June 28th, 1928, she wrote to Gertrude Stein reminiscing about their student days: *I have been in Baltimore for two weeks – a ghost among ghosts who were more real than the realities and the most real of all was your own vigorous self, tramping across town or into the country, swinging down corridors, full of life and sanity and humour. (…) I should like to see you and be sand-bagged on the head when I didn't agree with you and sand bag you back again. It was a good life we led, that student life, and it is still a good life that we lead in our individual ways. The world whether in Paris or California – is a great place and full of interest to actors and on-lookers. (…) Good bye Gertrude. Congratulations on all you have achieved.* The sand-bagging arguments that the two women had had concerned subjects dear to Marian Walker, a feminist and active supporter of women's suffrage. They were also dear to May Bookstaver but not to Gertrude Stein. In *The Autobiography of Alice B. Toklas* she writes about her decision to leave Johns Hopkins without finishing her degree: *There was great excitement in the medical school. Her very close friend Marion Walker pleaded with her, she said, but Gertrude Gertrude remember the cause of women, and Gertrude Stein said, you don't know what it is to be bored.* And a few paragraphs later she comes back to her arguments with Marian Walker, whose name she never spells right: *It was only a few years ago that Marion Walker, Gertrude Stein's old friend, came to see her at Bilignin where we spend the summer. She and Gertrude Stein had not met since those old days nor had they corresponded, but they were as fond of each other and disagreed as violently about the cause of women as they did then. Not, as Gertrude Stein explained to Marion Walker, that she at all minds the cause of women or any other cause but it does not happen to be her business.*

Looking back on that encounter a year later Marian Walker writes affectionately: *It was good to see you last summer, & find you still the same old Gertrude, battling all the heads that come your way. The reason we get on is that my head is tough and I too like the game of battling.*

It was not true that they had not corresponded in the meantime. Like her other friends from the Baltimore days, Marian Walker did keep in touch with

Gertrude Stein. She was the first of their set to get married and, like Emma Lootz, she combined working in practice with having children. In 1901, less than year after the wedding she wrote to Gertrude Stein: *Marriage is an admirable institution. I highly recommend it if accompanied by steady work outside the sphere of home. But don't talk to me about wife & whole end of woman! I wouldn't have believed you capable of it except that you are the victim of moods which at times resemble fixed ideas…*

After some years Marian and Allen Walker moved to Hartford, Connecticut, where they opened a practice. In June 1906 Emma Lootz Erving writes rather sardonically about the days she had spent there: *Marian was looking badly. She had had three very good months and had handled her practice all right, but then came a couple of weeks when she felt pretty mean and she was dreading the possibility of giving up for a few months. She expects the baby in about five months now. Meanwhile I perhaps feel better than either Mabel [Haynes] or Marian, I was a sorry specimen. (…)*

Marian had mastitis first in one breast and then in the other, with symptoms of general infection – and in the first place because she had to be dilated with a bag – and she is still out in the country. But bless me – she still believes that a woman can be a man and a woman too. The baby thrives apparently.

Marian Williams was determined to have her babies, her husband and her career. She may have had more domestic help that Emma Erving, who felt overwhelmed by the demands of mothering, housekeeping and working. She even found time to write some scholarly articles, such as one entitled 'The Feeding of Sick Children.'

At some point they left Hartford as Allen Williams was offered work in Taos, Arizona, looking after Pueblo Indians. Emma Erving wrote to Gertrude Stein on June 30, 1912: *Allen & Marion are living in elegance without glass in their windows or furniture of any sort. (…) I'm afraid they are in for some hard days – but if Marion will get well enough to enjoy life it will be worthwhile. She is impossible. When flat on her back in Saimac she was organizing a Suffrage club.*

Emma Erving wrote to Gertrude Stein a few months later, on September 10th, at a time when her husband and her son were suffering from tuberculosis and when Mabel Haynes had to deal with her husband's terminal illness: *Marian seems to be picking up out in New Mexico. She is up to camping trips of several days, which is a great gain – and she has some chance to enjoy life – if she has learned to accept it exclusive of the practice of medicine and every other damned philanthropy and altruism & socialism combined.*

Allen and Marian Williams did not stay in Taos but settled in Phoenix, where Marian Williams opened her own practice in 1916 and where they were jointly appointed as medical directors of tuberculosis sanatorium. She remained active in the suffrage movement and is listed as a member of the national advisory panel of the National Women's Party. The last records I could find all refer to California. There is a letter to Gertrude Stein suggesting a serious illness, dated April 22nd 1927: *I've been in California seven weeks this winter and saw Allen and Marion. Poor old Marion was in bed without a trace of voice, in a state of exhaustion. For one with her ardor it's a poor life – and I wondered as I looked at her, how long she was going to hold on.*

I have not discovered whether Marian Williams recovered and how long she held on to her exhausting, fulfilling life. Her husband Allen most likely outlived her; he died in 1960 at the age of ninety-one of cerebral arteriosclerosis.

Money

It is a very difficult thing to have your being in you so that you will be doing something, anything you are wanting, having something anything you are wanting when you have plenty of money for the buying, in clocks in handkerchiefs, so that you will be thinking, feeling anything that you are needing feeling, thinking, so that you will be having aspirations that are really of a thing filling you with meaning, so that you will be having really in you in liking a real feeling of satisfaction.

When Gertrude Stein writes about the desire for clocks and handkerchiefs, especially gaily coloured handkerchiefs, such as the ones servant girls like to buy, she might have meant to say that it is more difficult for those that have plenty money to get such a sense of satisfaction in buying. Gertrude Stein's family was used to *rich American living,* and so was May Bookstaver's, while Mabel Haynes grew up in a family that enjoyed *very rich American living.* Gertrude Stein was seventeen when her father died, and she depended on her eldest brother to put the finances of the family in order so that she and her brother Leo could count on having an income. Mabel Haynes' father was wealthy and generous, and the allowance he gave her allowed her to be generous with her friends, such as May Bookstaver, whose own father was not as wealthy and certainly not as generous as Mabel Haynes'. The notion that May Bookstaver relied on the generosity of Mabel Haynes and thus preferred not to relinquish this friendship for monetary reasons was one cause for Gertrude Stein's worries.

May Bookstaver, Mabel Haynes and Gertrude Stein never worked in order to earn a living. Mabel Haynes worked for some years as a doctor in Boston dispensaries where she would have been paid very little, if anything. May Bookstaver worked for a number of political organisations and as an editor of the *Birth Control Review,* without being paid a salary. Gertrude Stein was active for *Fund for the War Wounded* on a voluntary basis and spent a good deal of her own money on it too. May Bookstaver married a dynamic stockbroker on Wall Street, who had various streaks of good luck when money flowed into his pocket. He could buy a modern and spacious apartment on Seventh Avenue and they could live it up, travelling abroad, giving parties – they were on the

Social Register. Eventually, during the Depression, his firm went bankrupt, and he lost all his money. When he died, he left his wife with the apartment but little money to live on. In her later years, after the war in the 1940s and 50s, she was very hard up and had *no money for taxis*. Yet she sent Mabel Haynes packages of books she might find interesting all through the war years.

Mabel Haynes did not marry men who made any money. On the contrary, she had to ask her father for a substantial sum in order to pay for the marriage licence required for the Austro-Hungarian officer she wished to wed. Like Gertrude Stein, who had her family's money tied up in trust funds in the United States, she could not always access her money while living in Europe, as when Austria was at war with America. They both found their funds depleted and their money worth much less when the dollar fell during the Depression. In these times they both resorted to liquidising their assets. Gertrude Stein sold the paintings she had bought at a time when her allowance was sufficient to buy art from still unknown artists, and Mabel Haynes sold her houses and her jewels. When Mabel Haynes returned to the United States after the Second World War, she kept her family in Austria going by sending food, clothing, and money. Her letters from this period convey her anxieties about any of these reaching their destination, as they often didn't; her efforts to liquidate stocks, which were often thwarted by the Trustees; the high taxes she paid, etc. My father died before he could enter into his inheritance of what was left of Mabel Haynes' money, and hence my siblings and I received the share of the investments made by our great-grandfather that had passed through Mabel Haynes. This American money kept our family going once my mother was widowed, and when I came of age, I could buy a property, and since that time I always had a roof over my head.

Gertrude Stein and Mabel Haynes could be said to have been *rentiers*, who lived on the capital that had accrued through the capitalist ventures of their fathers.

It allowed them to live the sort of lives they wished - being an artist, raising a large family, supporting other artists, supporting family members and friends, taking vacations, entertaining, buying books and furniture, keeping dogs, keeping cars, keeping servants. None of these activities generated money, and whatever effort was spent on doing any of these things, they were not labour. Gertrude Stein could be said to have laboured over her writing, but there was no market for her products. Instead she spent money to have her first book published by Grafton Press, and she kept a careful record of all the manuscripts she had sent off, the postage that was paid, and the rejections she received. In the early 1930s she decided, with Alice B. Toklas, to publish her works themselves, and they sold Picasso's *Girl with a Fan* in order to start Plain Edition, bringing out *Lucy Church Amiably* as the first book in 1930, followed by *Before the Flowers of Friendship Faded Friendship Faded* and by a thousand copies of *How to Write*. They were nice looking books and they did not sell well. Gertrude Stein thought they were not in the right time for writers: *There is no doubt about it, in the twentieth century if you are to come to be writing really writing you cannot make a living at it not by writing (…) In the eighteenth century not enough read to make any one earn their living and in the twentieth century too many read for any one to make their living by writing, the nineteenth century was just right it was in between.*

There were of course some writers, such as Edith Wharton and Willa Cather, whose books sold very well and they made a good living from writing them. On a whim, so she made out, Gertrude Stein decided to try another form of writing, the *money-making* writing, and produced *The Autobiography of Alice B. Toklas*. Having been published in *Vanity Fair,* she had grown used to being packaged and to packaging herself, as a collector of modern art, the friend of Picasso and Matisse, somebody who has done sterling work during the Great War. Writing it from the point of view of Alice B. Toklas and referring to herself always as 'Gertrude Stein', contributed to her commodification.

As she reflected some twenty years after, in *Everybody's Autobiography*, the fact that this book came to be such a success was troubling: *Before one is successful that is before any one is ready to pay money for anything you do then you are certain that every word you have written is an important word to have written and that any word you have written is as important as any other word and you keep everything you have written with great care. And then it happens sometimes sooner and sometimes later that is has money value I had mine very much later and it is upsetting because when nothing had any commercial value everything was important and when something began having commercial value it was upsetting, I imagine this is true of any one.*

At first however, she was excited at having made money and being able to spend the money she had made: *I had never made any money before in my life and I was most excited…. I bought myself a new eight cylinder Ford car, and the most expensive coat made to order by Hermes and fitted by the man who makes coats for race horses for Basket and two collars studded for Basket.*

Gertrude Stein became troubled and she could not carry on writing. Even once she had begun again, writing the lectures she was to give on her American tour, she still puzzled over the question of money. She had made the experience of having become herself a commodity, a celebrity, somebody everybody knew and whose work hardly anybody read. She did not read works on economy, she certainly did not read Karl Marx, or any critique of the capitalist system; her ideas about money were shaped by her Republican conservatism: *Every now and then there is a movement to do away with money. Roosevelt tries to spend so much that perhaps money will not exist, communists try to live without money but it never lasts because if you live without money you have to do as the animals do live on what you find each day to eat that is just the difference the minute you do not do that you have to have money or if the money isn't money and sooner or later they always do decide that money is money.*

At the height of the Depression, in 1936, she published a series of five short articles on money for the mass circulation paper *The Saturday Evening Post* where she rather flippantly argues against any government 'handouts' and suggests that the unemployed are lazy.

In *The Geographical History of America,* where she mulls over human nature and human mind, money comes up too: *money who likes money money is what we all agree, to be happy and make money, is anything.* Making money and having money and not having money is a distinctively human concern: *I know a lot about money just because I never earned my first dollar and now I have…I have been writing a lot about money lately, it is a fascinating subject, it is really the difference between men and animals, most of the things men feel animals feel and vice versa, but animals do not know about money, money is purely a human conception and that is very important to know very very important.*

Meanwhile, there was the pleasure of spending: *It did not frighten me, I was enjoying myself I was spending my money as they had spent their money all the other painters and writers that I had blamed and condemned and here I was doing the same thing. And then the dollar fell and somehow I got frightened, really frightened awfully frightened just as all of them had gotten frightened really frightened these last years, but luckily for me being older the fright has made me write. I say luckily for me because I like to write. It is what I like best. I like it even better than spending money although there is no pleasure so sweet as the pleasure of spending money but the pleasure of writing is longer. There is no denying that.*

Having become a household name in America, Gertrude Stein was offered lucrative lectures, at rates of a thousand dollars for an appearance, but she turned that down in much quoted quip: *There is not enough money in the world to persuade me to stand up before a horde of curious people who are interested in my personality rather than my work.*

She did accept commissions to write articles for the American press, such as those for the *Saturday Evening Post*, but she had decided, as anticipated on one of her lectures 'What is English Literature', *to serve god and not mammon* in literature: *If you write the way it has already been written the way writing has already been written then you are serving mammon, because you are living by something some one has already been earning or has earned. If you write as you are to be writing then you are serving as a writer god because you are not earning anything. If anything is to be earned you will not know what earning is therefore you are serving god.*

This decision also solved her crisis of identity and her writer's block that the financial and popular success had triggered. She succeeded in having *The Geographical History of America* published and it did not sell more than a few copies and it was derided as incomprehensible.

During the last years of the war, Gertrude Stein and Alice B. Toklas had to rely on the kindness of friends to lend them money when they could not get at theirs invested in America and they had to get over to Switzerland to sell a Cézanne in order to survive. Gertrude Stein's book about her war experiences, *Everybody's Autobiography*, was written in a confidential and confiding tone rather than the god-serving *haut ton* of her other works of the period and did make some money. When Gertrude Stein died in 1946, she left all her paintings to Alice B. Toklas, and Alice B. Toklas lived quietly and in increasing penury, once the Stein descendants had taken from her the last and only means of production, the paintings Gertrude Stein had left her.

Music

A cup is readily shaded, it has in between no sense that is to say music, memory, musical memory.

The father of Mabel Haynes, John C. Haynes, became the president of the oldest and largest publishing company of printed music in the United States, with some 20 million musical publications per year. John C. Haynes and his firm, Oliver Ditson and Co., by printing and disseminating music, were said to have had a significant influence on the development of musical culture in the United States.

Mabel Haynes played the piano, and her daughter Gabrielle remembered her fondness for Chopin, though not being at all musical herself, she did not really know what it was that her mother played, or indeed how well she played. Mabel Haynes attended concerts and operas wherever she found herself, in Boston, Baltimore, New York, Vienna or Graz. She engaged music teachers for her children but none of them had the ability and patience to persevere.

The printed music in Gertrude Stein's family home most likely came from Oliver Ditson and Co. Although Gertrude Stein's mother recorded the expenses for musical tuition in her diary, none of the children were particularly musical. Gertrude and Leo Stein went to the opera in San Francisco. Gertrude Stein was to say that she had only been interested in music at that time: *I came not to care at all for music and so having concluded that music was made for adolescents and not for adults and having just left adolescence behind me and besides I knew all the operas anyway by that time I did not care any more for opera.*

Gertrude Stein liked to profess that she did not care much for music once she had come of age and that she was more attuned to the visual and intellectual properties as relevant for her work: *Music she only cared for during her adolescence. She finds it difficult to listen to it, it does not hold her attention. All of which of course may seem strange because it has been so often said that the appeal of her work is to the ear and to the subconscious. Actually it is her eyes and mind that are active and important and concerned in choosing.*

In Paris Gertrude Stein met Eric Satie, *a charming dinner guest,* though *Gertrude Stein really became a Satie enthusiast* some years later, after Virgil Thomson had played the whole of *Socrate* for her. She also attended one of the first performances of *Le Sacre du Printemps,* but generally she and Alice B. Toklas were more interested in painters and writers than musicians. They rarely ventured out to see what was new, preferring to be visited and they were quite particular whom they wished to see more than once. It was not easy for the young composer Virgil Thomson to get to meet Gertrude Stein again after their first meeting in 1926, despite the fact that she had liked his idea to set some of her works to music. He persevered and composed and when she heard him play and sing *Susie Asado, Preciosilla* and *Capital Capitals,* texts that she had written, *she delighted in listening to her words framed by his music.* She defended him from criticism that his music was superficial by remarking: *He frosts his music with a thin layer of banal sounds to put people off, but what's underneath is very pure and special.*

Virgil Thomson was persistent enough to have the opera *Four Saints in Three Acts* performed, to great critical and popular acclaim, in 1934 and Gertrude Stein was very pleased with that success and with the production she saw in Chicago that year. She wore a bright red dress and white stockings for the occasion. Virgil Thomson also composed *The Mother of Us All,* the opera about Susan B. Anthony that Gertrude Stein had written for him to be set to music, but it was not performed during her lifetime.

At Bilignin, so she wrote in *Everybody's Autobiography,* she was at ease and began to play again: *to improvise on a piano I like to play sonatinas followed by another always the white keys I do not like black keys and never two notes struck by the same hand at the same time because I do not like chords, but most of the time I have no piano and I do very nicely without it.* She was very fond of the American popular ballad *The Trail of the Lonesome Pine.* Such songs reminded her of America and what she liked about America. When the Second World War was coming to an end and the first US soldiers arrived in France, she loved to hear the names of the places they were from: *Just as we were sitting down to lunch, in came four more Americans this time war correspondents, our emotions were not yet exhausted nor our capacity to talk, how we talked and talked and where they were born was music to the ears Baltimore and Washington D. C. and Detroit and Chicago, it is all music to the ears so long long long away from the names of the places where they were born.*

Alice B. Toklas had had real musical training and her sophisticated taste complemented Gertrude Stein's assumed musical barbarism in the same way as her general fastidiousness complemented Gertrude Stein's roughshod ways. In her own memoir she does not dwell long on her musical background: *I had received a parchment certifying me as a bachelor of music. Now I commenced to study piano with Otto Bendix, a pupil of Liszt, and harmony with Oscar Weil.* When she was twenty-six, she gave two recitals, one in Seattle where she played with Elizabeth Hanson, Schumann's variations for two pianos, and Schubert's *Wanderer* in San Francisco. Laconically she adds: *Soon after that, Otto Bendix died and my musical career came to an end.* She had discovered that she was actually 'commonplace.' Her finely tuned ear would be able detect the musical qualities in Gertrude Stein's voice – in her speech and her laughter. When the French critic wrote an article *le Contrepoint poétique de Gertrude Stein,* in which he compared Gertrude Stein's work to a Bach fugue in its crystalline integrity, Alice B. Toklas was happy to concur: *For what he said about Bach is true. She introduces her theme contrapuntally and turns to the minor key and has the same exactitude.*

Negroes

"Negro" is a fine word. Etymologically and phonetically it is much better and more logical than "African" or "colored" or any of the various hyphenated circumlocutions.

I am afraid that I can never write the great American novel. I don't know how to sell on a margin or do anything with shorts or longs, so I have to content myself with niggers and servant girls, and servant girls and the foreign population generally.

I was brought up to believe in the North.

Gertrude Stein, Mabel Haynes and May Bookstaver were all brought up to believe in the North, in the Unionist, abolitionist North of the United States that were divided by the issue of slavery. They were born after the Civil War, and growing up in their prosperous Northern homes in Boston, East Oakland, and Upper East Side New York City, they knew nothing about the real lives of Negroes until they came to Baltimore and were sent to assist in the medical treatment of impoverished black families.

Mabel Haynes came from a line of Puritan activists; her maternal grandfather was the Reverend Charles Spears who campaigned for the abolition of the death penalty and the abolition of slavery: *Spears contended that the numbers of Negro executions made them a legal instrument of evil whose real purpose was to intimidate and terrorize slaves and thus maintain and enforce slavery.* His son-in-law, John C. Haynes, was known for his liberality to towards black Americans: *Originally associated with Theodore Parker in the anti-slavery movement, he was particularly generous toward the colored race. Many of their schools of the South knew his kindness, and many a colored man and woman in the North was helped over a difficult place by his generosity.*

There is no record of Mabel Haynes' views on the matter; it was not a subject that arose in the letters she wrote to her Austrian daughter or to Gertrude Stein.

It is likely that she talked about the plight of American blacks with May Bookstaver, who was not only an activist for female suffrage but a committed socialist. As the editor for Margaret Sanger's *Birth Control Review,* she brought out an issue entirely dedicated to Negro women. She also commissioned the Harlem Renaissance writer, Angelina Weld Grimké, to contribute to the journal to lend support to the treatment of poet and novelist Jean Toomer. In her letter to Grimké she writes: *Of all the crimes with which our history is blackened, it is the most. I don't see how, as a nation, we can ever live it down.* These snippets of information suggest that May Bookstaver, known for her leftish and progressive views, could see some of the shame of American race relations.

Gertrude Stein's attitude towards Negroes is far better documented and much has been said about it. She was always proud of the fact that she had written what she always called *my Negro story - Melanctha,* published as the second of *Three Lives* in 1909. She had, she said, made use of her experience of working as a medical student among poor blacks in Baltimore. Yet this is not simply a story about poor blacks in Baltimore, nor did she intend to address the relationship between whites and blacks or the issue of segregation. When she wrote *Melanctha,* in 1905, she was still working through her failed romance with May Bookstaver. Her earlier attempts (later published as *Q.E.D.*) had cast her experience of loving May Bookstaver in a Jamesian paradigm; this time, perhaps as a way to gain more distance, or as an experiment in writing in a different style, she transposed the situation into a Negro milieu. She transformed May Bookstaver, a Colonial Dame, into the sexually explorative (always wandering), half-caste, *pale yellow* Melanctha: *She had youth and had learned wisdom, and she was graceful and pale yellow and very pleasant, and always ready to do things for people, and she was mysterious in her ways and that only made belief in her more fervent.* Much of the dialogue between Melanctha and the doctor, Jefferson Campbell, who falls in love with her, concerns the nature of feeling and right and wrong behaviour in love, the right and wrong ways of gaining wisdom in the matter of sex.

Melanctha reiterates the conversations and letters between Gertrude Stein, May Bookstaver, Mabel Haynes and Mabel Weeks, that had formed the basis of Gertrude Stein's first work *'Things as they Are'* (later published as *Q.E.D.)* to such an extent that Leo Stein wrote to Mabel Weeks that he thought 'Melanctha' *to have nothing to do with Negroes.* He also depreciated praise for Gertrude Stein's grasp of Negro psychology: *This brings to mind to fact that a very intelligent writer – Eric Walrond – said to me once that Gertrude was the only white person who had given him Negro psychology. I laughed and said, of course, the book was really not about Negroes and had only Negro local color. And as the psychology of whites and Negroes of the same cultural grade is essentially the same. The extra psychology will give Negro psychology, provided the understands the cultural group.*

The *local color* in Gertrude Stein's text is first of all a matter of skin colour – each character is defined by the degree of blackness, from Jane Harden, *a negress but so white hardly one would guess it,* and Melanctha Herbert's *pale yellow* to Rose Johnson's *real black.* It is also conveyed by the way some of the characters talk about themselves: *"No, I ain't no common nigger", said Rose Johnson, "for I was arised by white folks, and Melanctha she is so bright and learned so much in school. She ain't no common nigger either.*

Local colour is also laid on with the thick brushstrokes of racial stereotyping, from *the warm broad glow of negro sunshine* to negligent mothers, drunken and violent fathers, promiscuous daughters, and Bible reading good black people. Much has been said about the racist undertone that is thus built up and to what extent Gertrude Stein was intentionally or naively doing so. Some scholars have *disparagingly or approvingly suggested that these representations are closely connected to Stein's own position as "other" and to her feelings of "otherness" as a Jewish American lesbian.*

Gertrude Stein's rueful comment that she had to content herself with *niggers, servant girls and the foreign population* could also be seen as her refusing to write about the white upper-class milieu that is the setting of most of Henry James' and Edith Wharton's novels. She would soon abandon any attempts at specific social and cultural settings altogether. Living in Paris, she met some of the black celebrities who had also made a life for themselves in Europe, notably Josephine Baker and Paul Robeson. She met them, like so many other interesting or exotic people she invited to her place, just once. Having entertained Josephine Baker and the other female stars of the Révue Nègre, as well as the actor Paul Robeson and his wife, to tea at rue de Fleurus, there was some mix-up about who was to come on the Wednesday and who would come on Friday. This inspired Gertrude Stein to write 'Among Negroes', that begins with the lines: *The story of the Three of you Josephine Baker Maud de Forrest and Ida Lewelyn and Mr. and Mrs. Paul Robeson as they never met and as they never met. Naturally. They were made to be alike they were not made to be alike. Naturally.*

The text collages snippets of conversation, the desire of the black artists to see her, and her own relish at having kept the two groups apart, while celebrating the *encounter between the high literary and artistic modernism represented by Gertrude Stein and the vernacular modernism embodied by jazz, Josephine Baker and Paul Robeson.*

Some years later she wrote about the occasion again in *The Autobiography of Alice B. Toklas,* and her disappointment with Paul Robeson gives rise to one of her categorical pronouncements on Negroes: *Carl Van Vechten sent us quantities of negroes beside there were the negroes of our neighbour Mrs. Regan who had brought Josephine Baker to Paris. Carl sent us Paul Robeson. Paul Robeson interested Gertrude Stein. He knew american values and american life as only one in it but not of it could know them. And yet as soon as any other person came into the room he became definitely a negro. Gertrude Stein did not like hearing him sing spirituals. They do not belong to you any more than anything else, so why claim them, she said. He did not answer. Once a southern woman, a very charming southern woman, was there, and she said to him, where were you born, and he answered, in New Jersey and she said, not in the south, what a pity and he said, not for me.*

Gertrude Stein concluded that negroes were not suffering from persecution, they were suffering from nothingness. She always contends that the african is not primitive, he has a very ancient but a very narrow culture and there it remains. Consequently nothing does or can happen. Of course, a great deal could and did happen, especially to those who were not lucky enough to have been born in New Jersey. Paul Robeson told the writer Claude McCay who thought of Gertrude Stein that *she had nothing to offer'*, that he, Paul Robson, *thought she was alright.*

One of Gertrude Stein's close friends, the American writer Carl van Vechten, was an enthusiastic habitué of the clubs and cabaret scene in Harlem during the 1920s. He wrote a novel, a love story without a happy ending, called *Nigger Heaven.* His female heroine, Mary Love, is a librarian, who enjoys reading. reads *Melanctha* and deplores the poor taste in literature of her readers. Gertrude Stein wrote him a letter, saying she was *delighted delighted, Nigger Heaven came and I just read it, it is awfully good and made up of light and delicate work and I am pleased and proud to be in it. You have never done anything better it is rather perfectly done and that is one of things I like about it most, a thing like the best niggers the Sumners that is actually perfection neither too delicate nor too anything and yourself in it. It is really in a big and delicate way and the Sill man comes forward and back from being nigger to being white really Carl the way you have kept it delicate and real.*

When Gertrude Stein returned to the United States for her lecture tour of 1934-35, she and Alice B. Toklas also visited the South and she wrote about that in her own autobiography. They went to Charleston and she saw that *there were school houses with white children and school houses with Negro children… the houses where Negroes were living had a fire burning which showed as if the house was burning as it was on the floor.* In New Orleans she found that *New Orleans Negroes were more French than American* and in Houston she talked to a Negro chauffeur *about the Negroes as they were in Texas* and who told her *he does not get the same justice as a white man* and that when it comes to professionals, he thought white professionals were more conscientious than negro professionals.

The black Americans she encountered most were performers. Having watched a performance of 'Porgy & Bess' in Fort Worth she wrote that *the man who played Porgy did it so well any Negro actors act it so naturally that it is natural that it should be done very well and why not since they might be any one as they are never any other one that is with Negroes a natural thing, with many of them with most of them, publicity does not hurt them because they can be what anything makes them and it does not make anything else of them because they are the thing they are then. So it is not acting it is being for them, and they have no time sense to be a trouble to them.*

Her view that Negro actors *might be anyone as there are never any,* refers to her notion that Negros were suffering from nothingness. When Virgil Thomson decided to cast only black singers for his opera he had composed to her libretto *Four Saints in Three Acts,* she was very gratified to hear that they had no trouble saying her words. As he said: *The whites always kind of resisted Gertrude, whereas the blacks understood her perfectly well and took to it like ducks to water.*

In the autumn of 1945, when Gertrude Stein and Alice B. Toklas had moved back into their flat in rue Christine, a young American reporter who had been sent to cover the initial meetings of the World Federation of Trade Unions in Paris, asked to interview Gertrude Stein on the subject of the black soldiers. She had become very interested in G.I.s at the time and was working on a book about them that was later published as *Brewsie and Willy.* Many of these common soldiers, including black soldiers, came to her flat to talk to her about their aspirations and their lives. She agreed to see the journalist, Ben Burns, who often passed himself off as a light skinned black man. They spent the whole afternoon talking and he recorded their conversation, as they talked about the Negro and "the problem".

It was, he said, *as if she had herded her thoughts for years and must suddenly release them.* She was more concerned about the whites: *I'm worried about the white man. Don't worry about the Negroes. They holler a little but they take care of themselves. Being pushed around makes them strong. It's the whites who suffer spiritually.* She told Burns that she considered *the nonsense* of race abominable, the black sense of inferiority as well as white sense of racial superiority, and explained that she considered race an attribute, as a particular ethnic characteristic and a form of cultural heritage that can be learned and passed on. Reflecting on the fact that whites move out from neighbourhoods once blacks had moved into it, she thought that showed that blacks had greater resilience: *The Negro has the advantage over the whites. They are the only people in America still pioneering. In the last 50 years they have pioneered up from the South. In a kind of way the Negro is much more lively minded than the white. If you pioneer, you're alive. The mass of white Americans have forgotten how to pioneer. Jews because they are also prosecutors keep on pioneering. Persecuted races have to pioneer. That's poverty. It's a very urgent matter. Americans have to get to do something about it. I'm ashamed of the.. ashamed that the only people who pioneer are Negroes and not whites. The more whites persecute Negroes, the more Negroes have to pioneer to live. They have lost their own liberty in holding down the Negro.* They also talked about some of the black actors and writers she had known and expressed dismay over Paul Robeson's *leftish inclinations,* but she had nothing but highest praise for Richard Wright, whom she considered *the best American writer today:*

He is a Negro who writes about Negroes but he writes like a man rather than a Negro. The material is within him but he is outside the material. The ordinary Negro isn't outside of this material. Wright's material doesn't dominate him. With most Negro writers, the Negro is on top of him. (…) he is without question the best master of English prose since myself (…) in the tradition of creative writers like Twain, Henry James, Howells, Walt Whitman and Gertrude Stein.

Gertrude Stein helped secure an official invitation to Richard Wright to come to Paris and met him off the train. Their wills clashed, as Wright later told Burns: *We were wonderful friends until we met. But then our relations were just one long argument. And then she up and died on me in the middle of the argument.*

In this way Gertrude Stein's last argument was one about Negroes and race conducted with a black writer she had thought a worthy successor of a literary line she traced from the writer of *Huckleberry Finn.*

Nerves

Some have all their living nervous being, nervous feeling. Julia Dehning had a quite a great deal of nervous being the bigger part of her living. Some have nervousness from sensitive being in them, some do not have nervousness from sensitive being in them. Some have nervousness from ambition in them. Some have nervousness in them pretty nearly all of their living.

A great many Americans of the generation of Gertrude Stein and Mabel Haynes had nervousness in them. In fact, the state of nerves, exhausted, frayed, frazzled or restored, soothed, and replenished, was a constant concern, especially to the social classes who could afford to have nerves in the first place. Once the American physician George M. Beard, who suffered from poor nerves himself, had identified the exhaustion of nerve energy as Neurasthenia, in 1869, it became not only an affliction suffered by the most distinguished men and women of the country, but a sign of American superiority and progress that no other civilization had as yet experienced it; as George Beard wrote: *not Great Britain, nor all Europe, nor all the world could assemble so large an army of sufferers from this distinguished malady.*

Nervous energy was a capital that circulated freely but could be possessed initially in fixed amounts, determined largely by heredity; once demand exceeded supply, *even a tiny excess could cause the entire system to break down,* like an *overloaded electrical circuit board* and an overdrawn bank account.

Neurasthenia was at once a disease of capitalism and a capitalist disease, subject to the same cycles of boom and bust. The medical response reacted to current notions about male and female responses – women became neurasthenic through the constant demands of their bodies (weakened by menstruation, parturition, menopause), while men squandered their naturally greater nervous energy in the pursuit of profit or glory. A prestigious doctor, such as Silas Weir Mitchell, would accordingly proscribe 'rest cures' for the former and 'West cures' for the latter, who were sent to ranches where they had to *engage in vigorous physical activity … and to write about the experience.* Women were promised not just a cure of their nervous conditions but to learn to accept the proper conditions of being female and submissive (no pen, no brush, no book allowed), while men would become truly manly; so Theodore Roosevelt was helped to overcame the stigma of his effeminate looks by being sent to rope steers and endure the hardships of the Western frontier; and he returned a new and virile man, a persona he went on to embody for the rest of his life; the sharp-shooting, hard-drinking Rough-Rider. Those American men and women of a nervous disposition, whose sensitivities made them reject these forms of therapy and who had sufficient incomes, could instead go to Europe. Here their nerves were soothed by ancient landscapes and fine art; while their moral and vital superiority could be confirmed by their encounters with the decadent and enfeebled aristocracy.

Gertrude Stein had developed an interest in nervous disorders in women from a medical point of view. She had worked on hysteria at Radcliffe, and her move to Johns Hopkins Medical School was partly inspired by this. Her experiences of working in a hospital for insane women were traumatic, and she preferred to do laboratory work on the brain with Dr Franklin Mall's assistant, Lewellyn Barker, who wrote the book *the Nervous System and its Constituent Neurons*. Barker, some forty years later, wondered *whether my attempts to teach her the intricacies of the medulla oblongata had anything to do with the development of the strange literary forms with which she was later to perplex the world.*

Gertrude Stein eventually abandoned her laboratory work, her medical degree, her scientific career, in order to find out what she really wanted to do, to get the glory she had wished to obtain from an early age. She suffered from confusion, listlessness, boredom, the symptoms of a neurasthenic. Following her *extremely neurotic* brother Leo Stein to Europe, she began life as a writer and henceforth experimented with words and language. *The Making of Americans* shows a dogged determination to account for the great variety of human experience as a total system; as patient and systematic an undertaking as any scientist would have been able to muster. As she develops her scheme of *bottom nature,* the trope of *nervous being* and *nervous feeling* appears time and again: *Some of them have in them nervous feeling, this is different from an impatient feeling, this is different from anxious being, many have all of these mixed up in them.* She punctuates the 925 pages of her book with admissions of despondency and tries to cheer herself up too: *I am all unhappy in this writing. I know very much of the meaning of the being in men and women. I know it and I feel it and I am always learning more of it and now I am telling it and I am nervous and driving and unhappy in it. Sometimes I will be all happy in it.*

Living with Alice B. Toklas instead of with her brother made for an atmosphere that was congenial to Gertrude Stein's writing and happiness. She had then little reason to be nervous. Unlike her brother, she never admitted to being neurotic, and if she attempted to cure her nervous being, she did not resort to psychoanalysis and self-analysis like Leo Stein. She simply avoided any occasion that would make her feel nervous, like the theatre. The theatre made her feel out of step, as she explained in a lecture on plays: *Then also beside the curtain there is the audience and the fact that they are or will be or will not be in the way when the curtain goes up that too makes for nervousness and nervousness is the certain proof that the emotion of one seeing and the emotion of the things seen do not progress together.*

Nervousness consists in needing to go faster or to go slower so as to get together. It is that that makes anybody feel nervous.

Gertrude Stein kept her *sang-froid* during the First World War, and while she noticed the dog getting nervous at times during the Second World War, she resorted to reading medieval prophecies, and the long walks in search of food kept her in good health and good spirits. Her sudden success as an author after years of obscurity did trouble her, and so did a prolonged spell of writer's block. Then she went to America, with Alice B. Toklas, to do her lecture tour: *New York was coming nearer and we were nervous but not really nervous enough. You never are nervous when a thing is really happening. If things happen all the time you are never nervous it is when they are not happening that you are nervous.*

Gertrude Stein found that things were happening at last and that everybody knew her, and that people wanted to listen to her. She was not nervous before her lectures and she was not nervous going up in airplanes even in bad weather. When she was interviewed for an article in *The New Yorker* and the journalists were interested in her daily routine, she could be amusing about being nervous, having quite got over her nervousness about being nervous: *Miss Stein gets up every morning about ten and drinks some coffee, against her will. She's always been nervous about becoming nervous and she thought coffee would make her nervous, but her doctor prescribed it.*

Mabel Haynes' doctor prescribed cocktails as a tonic for her heart and her nerves when she lived alone in Boston after the Second World War had ended. She had by then given up cigarettes and she bore her loneliness and anxiety over the grown children she had left behind in Austria with her customary forbearance, alternating with bouts of irritability. She did not talk about the state of her nerves much; she thought that it was her heart that had suffered from the hardships and grief she had experienced. Her daughter Gabrielle and her son Reginald were highly-strung and excitable, easily roused to a passion, impatient and impetuous. Mabel Haynes worried about Reginald's frayed nerves from overwork and told Gabrielle: *Don't ever try to slim off. It would be bad for your already poor nerves.*

My mother, whose slovenly domestic habits got on Mabel Haynes' nerves, did not have an excitable nature, was not easily provoked, and preferred sullen resentment to confrontation. She never had a nervous breakdown and coped with her grief and confusions without resorting to tranquilisers. I was a restless child and given to fidgeting at school, which made the teacher so nervous that she could not bear it. My father made me take a pill each morning to calm the fidgets, though I now think he might have done better to give them to the teacher instead.

Pens and pencils

My dear Carl,

Voici a new fountain pen I have not had one since you were last in Europe and I am very pleased with the same it was almost time wasn't it.

Peeled pencil, choke.

Rub her coke.

She refused to accept any fountain pens as gifts, explaining that she could get one, from any company merely by writing an endorsement:" When I write with this pen anyone can understand me."

When Gertrude Stein made that remark about everybody understanding what she writes with a certain kind of pen, she showed that she knew how advertising worked and that she could, on occasion, send herself up.

I also associate advertising with fountain pens because of the ink blotters printed with pharmaceutical adverts that my father was sent to induce him to prescribe the drugs they promoted. He let me use these colourful blotters and my exercise books were slightly less full of blots. My father's fountain pen, a sleek red Parker pen, had a golden triangular nib I liked to lick furtively.

Mabel Haynes, May Bookstaver and Gertrude Stein, like most of their contemporaries who had time on their hands, spent hours writing letters and sending cards. Letters were always written in ink with some elegant fountain pen. I still use Mabel Haynes' red Parker Slimline to write my much less frequent letters.

It could be said that Gertrude Stein's writing emerged from her habit of writing letters, her habit of copying out letters. She became a woman of letters who wrote not just letters but literature. She wrote in French school exercise books with a soft rather than a sharp pencil, in flowing loops that are hard to read and sometimes she transcribed what she had written into another exercise book with a fountain pen that did not need to be an expensive one: *I am writing all this with an American dollar pen.* Alice B. Toklas typed it all out. Gertrude Stein continued to write postcards and letters and some of the thousands of letters that Gertrude Stein wrote were published in book form, but it is quite a different experience to read them as retrieved from an archive, just as she had written them - hastily or carefully, on various types of letter writing paper, sometimes hardly legible when the ink bled through the page to overlay what had been written on the other side.

She used fountain pens to write her letters and to make a neat copy and to sign books, but the tool that she thought most conducive to respond to inspiration was the pencil. A pencil with a rubber end has its own suggestive connotations, a double instrument for making marks and erasing them, its soft tip can stroke a lip, the sharpened end pricks the skin; it can be peeled like an apple. Lisa Ruddick subjected Gertrude Stein's poem *PEELED PENCIL, CHOKE. Rub her coke* to extensive psychoanalytical exegesis. Within the 'paternal script' under attack in Gertrude Stein's writing *one may hear a defiant voice condemning the death-dealing pencil itself to death: peeled pencil, (go) choke* and that *"rub her" suggests erasure in the sense of rubbing "her" out.* But she concedes that this may also be light-heartedly subversive, that Gertrude Stein *is able to have fun at the expense of the glorious phallus that is causing all the damage* and that it becomes *just a "rubber cock", a sort of dildo.* Other possibilities of reading might refer to Lesbian sexuality: *In "Peeled Pencil", it is by a sort of lead game, a scribal sleight of hand, that Stein barely veils the words "her cock" with "her coke: the art of punning enables her to mix genders with impunity. A similar lead game, the deletion of a single character, get her from "Choke" to "coke" – from (perhaps) the vaginal image of an artichoke to a male "cock".* And she concludes that *Stein's experimental pencil plays past the father's categories.*

Who would indeed dare to offer Gertrude Stein the gift of a fountain pen after she had shown that there was lead in her pencil?

The one postcard and the single written note I have of May Bookstaver were written with a large-nib fountain pen in black ink. She was almost but erased from the Gertrude Stein's collection of missives, but the imprint she made resisted being blotted out.

Perfume

Of course to have a lesson in french one has to converse and Fernande had three subjects, hats, we had not much more to say about hats, perfumes, we had something to say about perfumes. Perfumes were Fernande's really great extravagance, she was the scandal of Montmartre because she had once bought a bottle of perfume named Smoke and had paid eighty francs for it at that time sixteen dollars and it had no scent but such wonderful colour, like real bottled liquid smoke.

What is a sentence a sentence should have no perfume like hyazinths

What is a cook a cook is a cross between odor and perfume. What is an odor and what is perfume. An odor is a singular glance and milk and lightening, a perfume is an article and expected space and even an authority.

Alice B. Toklas, who talked about perfume with Picasso's mistress Fernande Olivier, had acquired a taste for perfume and furs herself while still living in San Francisco. It was thus a fine subject to talk about in French. Alice B. Toklas set great store by her appearance, from her elegant fingernails to her small feet, and although she let Gertrude Stein have the limelight, she could make her presence felt. She could make her presence felt by her sharp comments and darting glances but also by olfactory means. She smoked her American cigarettes incessantly and scented her body with French perfume. She liked heavy flowery perfumes, especially those evoking tuberoses and her friends tried to indulge her preferences: *Fania has discovered that Guerlin had no tuberose, and so she sent Alice Champs-Elysées.. Floris has a tuberose. I wonder if she would like that?*

The beautifully bottled luxury fragrances by Parisian perfumeries promised exclusivity, they were customized to suit complexions and temperament, and they were purchased not just by courtesans, but also by respectable women wealthy enough to afford them, such as Mabel Haynes. Her perfume was sent by her request in plain bottles to be decanted into atomisers, and she never changed it. Her daughter Gabrielle remembers that her mother's perfume permeated her rooms and the objects of her daily use. As a child she would hold one of her mother's handkerchiefs to her nose in a vain futile attempt to overcome the pain of separation. All the silk scarves she left me are impregnated with her own perfume and evoke her presence, in turn, to me.

Gertrude Stein did not talk much to the wives and mistresses of her friends and she would have found a conversation about perfumes and hats tiresome. She liked to have a hot bath and it was her sort of luxury to have hot running water installed in the Bilignin country house. She preferred odours to perfume and thrilled to the erotic appeal of pheromones - *singular glance and milk and lightening* - and she was critical of the commercially produced article with its *authority*. Would she be amused to hear that she is now credited as having had a 'signature smell' called *Jolie Madame* by Balmain? In fact, *Jolie Madame* was only released in 1953, quite a while after her death, and while Pierre Balmain may have been inspired by Gertrude Stein to ask his 'nose', Germaine Cellier, to a create a 'Leather fragrance for Women' it is more likely that *Jolie Madame* was a present to the then seventy-six-year-old Alice B. Toklas. It is hardly likely to have helped to bring back a sense of Gertrude Stein's presence to the lonely Alice B. Toklas.

Photographs

A regret a single regret makes a door way. What is a door way, a door way is a photograph. What is a photograph a photograph is a sight and a sight is always a sight of something.

Gertrude Stein never had a camera and is not known to have taken any pictures. She was photographed first as a child, with her family, then as a young woman, a Radcliffe student, on holiday in Europe, and in later life as a celebrity. One of the first professional photographers she posed for was Man Ray:

It was one of the little, tiny hotels in the rue Delambre and Man Ray had one of the small rooms, but I have never seen any space, not even a ship's cabin, with so many things in it and the things so admirably disposed. He had a bed, he had three large cameras, he had several kinds of lighting, he had a window screen, and in a little closet he did all his developing. He showed us pictures of Marcel Duchamp and a lot of other people and he asked if he might come and take photographs of the studio and of Gertrude Stein. He did and he also took some of me and we were very pleased with the result. He has at intervals taken pictures of Gertrude Stein and she is always fascinated with his way of using lights. She always comes home very pleased. One day she told him that she liked his photographs of her better than any that had ever been taken except one snap shot I had taken of her recently. This seemed to bother Man Ray. In a little while he asked her to come and pose and she did. He said, move all you like, your eyes, your head, it is to be a pose but it is to have in it all the qualities of a snap shot. The poses were very long, she, as he requested moved, and the result, the last photographs he made of her, are *extraordinarily interesting.*

Gertrude Stein liked the photographs Man Ray took of her at that time so much that she put one of them on the cover of the *Autobiography of Alice B. Toklas* when that book was first published.

Gertrude Stein is seated at her wooden table that resembles an altar with its candlesticks and stacked books. Light falls from the high windows of the studio onto the sheet of paper that Gertrude Stein is writing on. In the doorway, Alice B. Toklas appears. She wears a large white collar that lends her the air of a Flemish housewife. Her entrance does not interrupt the stillness of the room, where the writer is held by the arms of the wooden chair, like a carthorse by the shafts. Alice B. Toklas' apparition, ghostlike in the washed-out light, marks a passage from one space to another – the vestibule to the studio – but also of time, the contingencies of daily life and the moment erupting on the suspended time of reading. Gertrude Stein's resistance to this interruption is the *punctum* of this photograph.

In 1914 Gertrude Stein met Alvin L. Coburn, who had taken photographs of George Meredith and Henry James, published in a volume called *Men of Mark* (1913). He wished to include her image in a volume of pictures of prominent women: *At any rate he was the first photographer to come and photograph her as a celebrity and she was nicely gratified. He did make some very good photographs of her and gave them to her and then he disappeared and though Gertrude Stein has often asked about him nobody seems ever to have heard of him since.* He photographed Gertrude Stein in 1913, wrapped in a velvet robe, looking intent, but he never published the book.

Gertrude Stein liked the photographs Man Ray had taken of her well into the 1920s; some appeared in magazines like *Vanity Fair,* but she did not like to pay him for taking photographs of her and he stopped doing so. Instead Cecil Beaton became the favourite *operateur*, shooting Gertrude Stein and Alice B. Toklas in their Balmain suits and with their photogenic poodle.

In 1920 Gertrude Stein wrote a short play called *Photograph. A Play in Five Acts*, which takes up the subject of doubling, the way a photograph could be said to double a subject and be itself subject to enlargement, editing, printing, copying and distribution. She makes a link between the reproduction people engage in to produce babies, who could be said to be versions, at least partial genetic copies of their parents, and some of the babies could be twins, who may present if identical, copies of each other:

Act III

A photograph. A photograph of a number of people if each one of them is reproduced if two have a baby if both babies are boys what is the name of the street.

Madame.

Gertrude Stein was more interested in playing with the way language can create echoes and rhymes, associations and repetitions, which cannot simply be reproduced. She may have looked at the pictures of the babies that some of her friends had sent her, babies that had been reproduced mechanically: *Photographs are small. They reproduce well.*

I enlarge better.

Mabel Haynes had some photographs that she always kept near her: *For all your small photographs I have bought frames and there you all are on my bureau*, she wrote to her *third daughter*. Others she put away, some glued into the albums; there might have been some that she destroyed to avoid the sight of them for good. I don't know when she took the photograph of May from its frame, nor if she ever had one of Gertrude Stein.

Not just portraits of people evoke emotional responses.

Mabel Haynes had her favourite house in Graz photographed, all the rooms she had furnished, the outside, the garden; she made postcards of some them and sent them to her friends. Looking at them now, more than eighty years after they had been taken, I recognize objects - candlesticks, pictures, vases, and other ornaments, that form part of my surroundings now. The sight of each empty room is *a sight of something.*

Reading

She read anything that was printed that came her way and a great deal came her way.

I do like reading writing.

All our family needs endless fruit – and (as you say) reading matter.

It was funny that about reading, I had never read anything aloud much, all the letters of Queen Victoria to Alice Toklas when we were in Majorca at the beginning of the war and I had never thought of myself as reading and I had never read anything I had written and then when they asked me it seemed very strange to me and then somehow I came to like it, it sounds very interesting as I read it, quite so to me.

Children like being read to before they become readers themselves and some children like being read to more than others and these are likely to become adults who cannot do without reading for pleasure. May Bookstaver, Mabel Haynes, most of their friends, and Gertrude Stein of course, did read voraciously, avidly, greedily, obsessively from an early age, and they never lost the habit: *From her eighth year when she absorbed Shakespeare to her fifteenth year when she read Clarissa Harlowe, Fielding, Smollett etcetera and used to worry lest in a few years more she would have read everything and there would be nothing unread to read, she lived continuously with the english language. She read a tremendous amount of history, she often laughs and says she is one of the few people of her generation that has read every line of Carlyle's Frederick the Great and Lecky's Constitutional History of England besides Charles Grandison and Wordsworth's longer poems. In fact she was as she still is always reading. She reads anything and everything and even now hates to be disturbed and above all however often she has read a book and however foolish the book may be no one must make fun of it or tell her how it goes on. It is still as it always was real to her.*

The greatest fear of the habitual reader is to run out of things to read or to be stuck in a place where all reading material is an unknown language. *The reading question has turned into a problem for me,* Mabel Haynes lamented, housebound in Graz during the war, her daughter Enid too busy or too disobliging to procure enough books from the library, or when those sent by May Bookstaver from New York failed to arrive.

Few occasions do not provide an opportunity to peruse a newspaper, a paperback, a hardback, a folio, a magazine, a journal. There is solitary and companionable reading, side-by-side on a bench or on either side of a fireplace, or side-by-side in bed. Gertrude and Leo Stein were not companionable readers*: my brother and I were always together. He learned to read first and I earned to read after, but reading was something we never did together. I always did completely alone.*

Gertrude Stein read while her brother Leo was in the same room or on the same tram; but each was reading alone: *really being alone with reading is more intense than hearing anything, anybody can really know that and anybody when they are very young really can know that, Duncan's little boy did and liked it that he did, I always like it that nothing is so intense as being alone with a book.*

How intense the pleasure of reading alone is depends on the sort of book one is reading alone. Mabel Haynes' daughter Gabrielle only ever read romantic novels; she could though quite loose herself in light fiction written for women who only read such books. Mabel Haynes could not abide sloppily written romances. May Bookstaver, Mabel Haynes, Emma Lootz Erving, Alice B. Toklas, and many of their friends, loved to read Henry James; Gertrude Stein pretended she hadn't read him. They would write to each other about the books they read and what a great time they had reading such wonders as the latest Henry James.

The writing of books is a lonely task and the reading of books an intense form of being alone but talking about what has been read is a pleasure shared.

Gertrude Stein liked reading writing. She wrote in two modes, one being dictated by 'Mammon' and the necessity of selling books that are easy to read and full of gossip, the other the 'real writing', in which she pleased herself and her immediate inclination. If she thinks of a reader, it may be in a teasing or provocative manner, to teach her how to read attentively, differently, viscerally, as a feminist, such as Harriet Chessman, one of her attentive readers, took it, who described this technique as *reading as conversation*. Some, for instance Eric Neele, have risen to the challenge of reading the more opaque works of Gertrude Stein's as a form of musical improvisation, others by applying poststructuralist or psychosexual perspectives (notably Lisa Ruddick). Ulla Dydo recommends entering into the spirit of *taking language apart*. There are critics who tell the reader of *Ways of Not Reading Gertrude Stein*. I find one can never just read Gertrude Stein; she seems to foist on her reader a taking of a stance, to be with her or against her; to read her like a linguistic detective or a lover of abstraction; as a woman or a man; ideally aware of one's habits of reading; slowly or quickly, skimming or diving.

Gertrude Stein professed to read nothing but English, something that had puzzled Alice B. Toklas when they first knew each other: *But do you never read french, I as well as many other people asked her. No, she replied, you see I feel with my eyes and it does not make any difference to me what language I hear, I don't hear a language, I hear tones of voice and rhythms, but with my eyes I see words and sentences and there is for me only one language and that is english. One of the things that I have liked all these years is to be surrounded by people who know no english. It has left me more intensely alone with my eyes and my english. I do not know if it would have been possible to have english be so all in all to me otherwise. And they none of them could read a word I wrote, most of them did not even know that I did write. No, I like living with so very many people and being all alone with english and myself.*

Only she was not being alone with English and herself because she had her brother Leo Stein live with her at first, and then Alice B. Toklas. She had plenty of English around her but she preferred to believe or to make people believe that her ability to write in English was fed by her only reading English. Alice B. Toklas was the first reader of anything Gertrude Stein wrote, after she had joined the Stein household in 1910. She not only read the scraps of paper or the pages of the French exercise books that Gertrude Stein preferred for her writing, she also typed the handwritten texts and then proof-read the proofs: *you cannot tell what a book is until you type it or proof-read it. It then does something to you that only reading never can do. A good many years later Jane Heap said that she had never appreciated the quality of Gertrude Stein's work until she proof-read it.* Once it had been proof read, more or less perfunctory, the books could be printed and sold and read, some of them by many, some of them by very few.

There was also the matter of writing and delivering lectures; something Gertrude Stein first did in 1926, when she read 'Composition as Explanation' at Oxford and Cambridge: *Once the lecture was written the next trouble was the reading of it. Everybody gave her advice. She read it to anybody who came to the house and some of them read it to her. Prichard happened to be in Paris just then and he and Emily Chadbourne between them gave advice and were an audience. Prichard showed her how to read it in the english manner but Emily Chadbourne was all for the american manner and Gertrude Stein was too worried to have any manner.*

She read it in her own manner and it went off very well, as Harold Acton remembered: *Nobody was prepared for what followed, a placid reading of Composition as Explanation and several word portraits, including one of Edith Sitwell, who sat so near that the portrait could be compared with the original. The litany of an Aztec priestess, I thought, uttered in a friendly American voice that made everybody feel at home until they pondered the subject matter. What a contrast between manner and matter, between voice and written page!*

The experience of these English lectures made it easier for Gertrude Stein to eventually accept the invitation to lecture in America. Here too, she spoke in her well-modulated voice and held her audience enthralled. One of the lectures began like this: *I am going to read what I have written to read, because in a general way it is easier even if it is not better and in a general way it is better even if it is not easier to read what has been written than to say what has not been written. Any way that is one way to feel about it.*

She was talking about *The Making of Americans* and she read some excerpts. She would have been delighted to know that in 1974 the Paula Cooper Gallery in New York organised a marathon public reading of the whole thousand-page book in some 48 hours, read by many different people non-stop. A Second and Third Annual Marathon Reading took place through Triple Canopy in 2012 and 2014. Some of those present at these sessions may have agreed with Gertrude Stein: *reading what others have written, makes every one know is the nature of human being knowing this then in every one at each period in them is to some as I was saying astonishing and gratifying.*

Romance

There is some relation between romance and the human mind but no relation between human nature and romantic anything because human nature is not interesting but romance is.

That man Rochester so intrigued me, but then I always have had a hang for the romantic and still have.

When the anthropologist Robert Lowie wrote that *romance is nothing more than fiction* he did not make a point about literature but about erotic infatuation, often caused by reading too many romances in the first place. Romantic love, so Lowie and other ethnographers would say, was unknown in illiterate societies, or at least in societies where there was no romantic literature. Gertrude Stein, having read quantities of novels and romances from an early age, was thus well primed for romance and adventure. She did ponder the implications: *So those who create things do not need adventure but they do need romance they need that something that is not for them stays where it is and that they can know it is there where it is.* When Gertrude Stein wrote these lines, in 1936, more than three decades after her romance with May Bookstaver, she could say that *romance is having what is where it is, which is not where you are, stay where it is.* And she acknowledges that such a realization is necessary for those, like her, who create. It was important for her to have had the experience that *something that is not for them stays where it is and that they can know it is there where it is.* It stays where it is because the romance has been made into novellas and novels that make something of the particular experience of one loving another one who is one loving another.

She wrote one story, 'The Good Anna' – partly based on Anna Lebender, the cook/housekeeper Leo and Gertrude Stein employed when they lived in 215 Biddle Street, and made her into a romantic and tragic figure because of her fraught romance: *Mrs Lehntman was the only romance Anna ever knew. A certain magnetic brilliancy in person and in manner made Mrs Lehntman a woman another women loved.* Their relationship was too fraught to last: *Romance is the ideal in one's life and it is a very lonely living with it lost.* Having lost *the ideal of one's life* and *very lonely living with it lost*, Gertrude Stein wrote of her own romance and of those of others, that of members of her family, of the governesses and servants, of people who been the subject of gossip she had heard. She put them all into the thousand pages of *The Making of Americans*. Here she made her attempt to map the mechanics of resisting and attacking, being dependent and independent in the ways of loving. This was, at times, dispiriting work, when she came back again and again to the romance at the bottom of it: *Sometimes I am almost despairing. Yes it is very hard, almost impossible I am feeling now in my despairing feeling to have completely a realising of the being in any one, when they are telling it when they are not telling it, it is so very hard to know it completely in one the being in one.... I know the being in each one of these three of them and I am almost despairing for I am doubting if I am knowing it poignantly enough to be really knowing it, to be really knowing the being in any one of them. Always now I am despairing. It is a very melancholy feeling I have in me now I am despairing about really knowing the complete being of any one of each one of these three.* Her unhappy romances were all but forgotten when Alice B. Toklas consented to share her life: *Romance is the only way to be there there where they are.*

Mabel Haynes, part of the three of them, an avid reader of novels and romances, with a weakness for dangerous and sexy heroes such Rochester and Heathcliff, went on to find adventure and romance in Habsburg Austria. She succeeded in having a life full of drama and grief, falling for doomed heroes, while raising a large family. She had made *the distant approach nearer,* but her failure not make something that would not for her *stay where it is,* could be taken as evidence that she was incurably romantic and not one making things up.

In the same year that Mabel Haynes gave birth to her first child, in 1908, the year Gertrude Stein finished writing *The Making of Americans,* their mutual friend from Baltimore days, Emma Lootz Erving, writes to Gertrude Stein about meeting up with May Bookstaver, who had married Charles E. Knoblauch, former Rough Rider and dashing Wall Street broker: *During other excitements I lunched with May Knoblauch and a while later she and her husband turned up here in Washington. They seemed charmed with themselves, with each other, and with life and May has invested the past with a romantic mist of contemplation, which is edifying. She looks exceedingly well.*

Rooms

Mabel Neathe's room fully met the habit of many hours of unaggressive lounging. She had command of an exceptional talent for atmosphere. The room with its very good shape, dark walls but mediocre furnishings and decoration was more than successfully unobtrusive, it had perfect quality. It had always just the amount of light necessary to make mutual observation pleasant and yet to leave the decorations in obscurity or rather to inspire a faith in their being good.

It is true of rooms as of human beings that they are bound to have one good feature as a Frenchwoman dresses to that feature that the observer must see that and notice nothing else, so Mabel Neathe had arranged her room so that one enjoyed one's companions and observed consciously only the pleasant fire place.

But the important element in the success of the room as atmosphere consisted in Mabel's personality. The average guest expressed it in the simply comment that she was a perfect hostess, but the more sympathetic observers put it that it was not she had the manners of a perfect hostess but the more unobtrusive good manners of a gentleman.

The room that Gertrude Stein here describes in *Q.E.D.* as belonging to Mabel Neathe, the fictional counterpart to the real Mabel Haynes, was but a rented room in Baltimore, albeit one conducive to solitary as much as sociable *lounging*. Gertrude Stein's characterization conflates the room and the person who had arranged the room in a manner that was common among later 19th century writers, especially women writers, such as Constance Fenimore Woolson or Edith Wharton, who had written a book on interior decoration before becoming a novelist and who knew how to set her heroines in congenial parlours or have them suffer in uncongenial ugliness. Mabel Neathe's personality and the atmosphere of her room are of one piece – she provides a background for enjoyable conviviality by being politely unobtrusive amongst her unobtrusive but indubitably choice furnishings. Though exhibiting *the good manners of a gentleman,* she was, though this is not said, a gentlewoman. Mabel Haynes certainly saw herself as such, with her Puritan, New England ancestry and finely tuned sensibility. She had a gift of finding good houses and furnishing them well, to suit her habits, and to indulge her taste for good antiques and comfortable chairs.

At the same time as writing *Q.E.D.,* in 1903, Gertrude Stein had already begun to work on what was to become *The Making of Americans,* first conceived as a history of her own family of German-Jewish immigrants. In the following excerpt from the beginning of the book, Gertrude Stein not only describes the home that Julia Dehning had grown up in and the very different home she was to create for herself once she had married, but also gives expression to her own views on interior design: *It was good solid riches in the Dehning house, a parlour full of ornate marbles placed on yellow onyx stands, chairs gold and white of various sizes and shape, a delicate blue silk brocaded covering on the wall and a ceiling painted with angels and cupids all about, a dining room all dark and gold, a living room all rich and gold and red with built-in couches, glass-covered book-cases and paintings of well-washed peasants of the German school, and large and dressed up bedrooms all light and blue and white. (All this was twenty years ago in the dark age, you know, before the passion for the simple line and the toned burlap on the wall and wooden panelling all classic and severe).*

Gertrude Stein was averse to the taste of a college woman that she associated with *toned burlap.* For her a college woman's room lacked the authenticity and warmth that even a tasteless and ostentatious bourgeois one supplied. In keeping with the novelistic tradition of the 19th century, Julia Dehning's marriage, conducted in such a house, a modern house she had aspired to, could not be a success.

Gertrude Stein always disliked the cheerlessness of modern interiors, as did her brother Michael. When in the 1920's Michael Stein commissioned Le Corbusier to design the villa he was to share with Gabrielle de Monzie at Garches, he insisted on filling the modernist *machine-à-habiter* with Renaissance antiques and bric-à-brac, much to the displeasure of the architect.

There are no descriptions of the rooms Gertrude Stein inhabited in Baltimore, first with her brother Leo, then with Emma Lootz, though the latter remembered that Gertrude's room *was arranged to her liking* and that thanks to their housekeeper their *brass rails were polished till they glittered.*

When Leo Stein decided to settle in Paris early in 1903, he chose a studio near the Luxembourg Gardens, in 27, rue de Fleurus, consisting of a two-storey pavilion with a four-room apartment, a kitchen and bathroom, built next to a high-ceilinged studio with northern light. Gertrude Stein joined her brother, and they lived a bohemian existence, with Leo Stein painting in the studio, and Gertrude Stein writing. By 1911 Leo Stein had moved out, taking his Japanese prints and his share of the paintings with him, and Alice B. Toklas established herself as the woman of the house. Gertrude Stein describes the room, as it would have appeared to Alice B. Toklas, when she first saw it: *Against the walls were several pieces of large italian renaissance furniture and in the middle of the room was a big renaissance table, on it a lovely inkstand, and at one end of it note-books neatly arranged, the kind of note-books french children use, with pictures of earthquakes and explorations on the outside of them. And on the walls right up to the ceiling were the pictures. At one end of the room was a big cast iron stove that Hélène came in and filled with a rattle, and in one corner of the room was a large table on which were horseshoe nails and pebbles and little pipe cigarette holders which one looked at curiously but did not touch, but which turned out later to be accumulations from the pockets of Picasso and Gertrude Stein. But to return to the pictures. The pictures were so strange that one quite instinctively looked at anything rather than at them just at first.*

Decades later, long after Gertrude Stein had died, Alice B. Toklas wrote her own memoir, *What is Remembered* (1963), but when she tries to recollect the first impression of Gertrude Stein in her studio-room the present, with its lack of things and the lack of Gertrude Stein's presence, intrudes on her thoughts: *The studio walls were covered from cimaise to ceiling with pictures. The furniture and objects fascinated me. The big Tuscan table opposite me as I sit here now, and the rare octagonal Tuscan table with three heavy clawed legs is in the dining room, as well as the double-decked Henry IV buffet with its three carved eagles on the top. It was only after wiping these and other pieces of furniture that I fully appreciated their beauty, their details, their proportions, In the room here at rue Christine there are only a few objects remaining that were then at rue de Fleurus, seventeenth-century terra-cotta pieces of Italian pottery.*

This tactile remembrance of a room inhabited for many years privileges objects that can be handled, cared for, dusted – only Alice B. Toklas was allowed to dust the more fragile things and hence only she ever broke them - while most visitors remembered the pictures, the sheer quantity of pictures that covered the walls. As the writer Paul Bowles, interviewed in the 1950's, puts it: *Oh, I can remember it, yes. There was the door that would lead into the courtyard. And that was the entrance, the front door to the flat. And in front of it there was a staircase that went up to the next floor. I never went up there. That was apparently, that was probably the bedroom and bathroom and so on. I don't know, but it must have been. And there was a big room full of furniture and paintings, many paintings on the walls. Most of the paintings were by Picasso, not very big. She bought them directly from him over a period of a year or two, I don't know. They were very cheap. She told me, I think, she paid 1,000 francs a piece for a paintings…The room was absolutely full of paintings, almost every inch on the wall was covered. And off that room was smaller room which was the dining room, but I didn't see it, I never went in to it. It's hard to describe the apartment. It had big pieces of furniture in it. I don't know much about furniture; I think it was old. I know she was very incensed with Ezra Pound, because whenever he came to the apartment he broke something.*

Male visitors, like Ezra Pound, could be boorish and clumsy when it came to rooms inhabited by women who had rooms of their own.

The intimate connection between women, especially virtuous, spirited and unusually well-educated woman, and interiors, has a long pedigree. Gertrude Stein's favourite 18th century novel, Samuel Richardson's *Clarissa*, abounds in scenes in which the heroine all but despairs of the various locks and contraptions she devises in her attempts to keep the intemperate Lovelace from entering her closet and breaking down her last defences. Gertrude Stein, with or without having Clarissa's plight in mind, wrote that *if expression has emotion and emotion has a medium and a medium is adaptation and adaptation is not being used when anything is coming then all who the room that they they had when they were what they were saying was what saying is if it is producing and it is producing, all had the room where they put what they put as they made what they made and felt what they felt and followed what they lead led where they went.*

In her book *Tender Buttons,* Gertrude Stein included a text called "Rooms" that is markedly different from the other sections, "Objects" and "Food", and which seems to have been written some two years earlier, in 1911. Each paragraph suggests a different mood or view-point and it reads rather like the Portraits Gertrude Stein was writing at the time, with their many and varied associations triggered by impressions or by the act of writing itself. Some of these paragraphs do indeed have spatial references, but at times they read like a spoof of Mrs Wharton's design manual: *A little sign of an entrance is the one that made it alike. If it was smaller it was not alike and it was so much smaller that a table was bigger. A table was much bigger, very much bigger. Changing that made nothing bigger, it did not make anything bigger, it did not make anything bigger littler, it did not hinder wood from not being used as leather. And this was so charming. Harmony is so essential. Is there pleasure then there is a passage, there is when every room is open. Every room is open when there are not four, there were there and surely there were four, there were two together. There is no resemblance.*

The atmosphere of a room, not least, is a matter of size as much as size in relation to furnishings and size in relation to windows and doors, and size in relation to the number of people in a room. Mabel Haynes was used to living in large and spacious houses, in large and relatively sparsely furnished rooms. She was horrified to visit my father's flat in Weisskirchen and found that in order to accommodate his doctor's practice the family of four were all living and sleeping in one small room: *You can fancy what it means to have but one room for four people, and no bath.* Yet for me, a small child at the time, this crowded room with its rugs that covered walls, floors and beds, was filled with an aura of snug cosiness, of all of us being closely together, and the memory of it, with its *corners gathered together* was a comfort in later years when after my father's death we had moved into a much too large apartment in town.

Rudolf Franz Leick

(1882-1938)

Mabel Haynes' second husband, Rudolf Leick, was born on the 18th of December 1882 in Kaschau – present day Kosice in Slovakia - then within the Hungarian Kingdom of the Habsburg dual monarchy, the son of an officer, Franz Xaver Leick.

After four years at elementary school, Rudolf Leick entered the infantry cadet school in Vienna and entered the Royal and Imperial Austrian army on August 18th 1903, commanding a pioneer light infantry battalion and was promoted to the rank of lieutenant two years later.

The main source for the physical attributes, character, abilities and limitations for any Austro-Hungarian officer are the annual personal records known as *Qualifikationslisten*. They describe him as blond, blue-eyed, 1,76 m tall, speaking

German and Bohemian (only languages spoken in the Austrian empire were recorded in these lists. He also spoke English, French, and Italian). His personality was vivacious, with a barely controlled impetuousness, as his superiors remarked: *very temperamental* and *his spontaneous actions often are to the detriment his professional and private success (...) Generally very serviceable – his unfavourable temperament works very well in field duty and combat – but makes itself felt unfavourably in the treatment of inferiors.* He seems to have dedicated himself with more vigour to his duties and got promoted to *Oberleutnant* (senior lieutenant). It is possible that he made the acquaintance of Mabel Haynes, then married to the infantry officer Konrad Heissig in Linz, where the regiments of both were stationed in 1911. They were married in October 1913, not quite a year after Heissig's death, and due to an injury sustained during military exercises, he obtained a leave of absence. The couple went to Palermo, in Sicily, where in June 1914 their daughter Enid was born.

Austria-Hungary had declared war on Serbia on July 28th. On the 17th of August Rudolf Leick presented himself for active service and was transferred from the 4th Company to the Reserve and on March 1st 1915 to Second Regiment of the

Kaiserjäger (Tyrolian Riflemen). Promoted to Captain a few days later, he received 900 crowns towards buying a horse and a further 470 crowns for equipment. On July 14th the list notes the birth of a daughter, Gabrielle Seabury Elsa, in the barracks hospital of Brixen in South Tyrol (now Bressanone in Upper Italy).

Italy had declared war on Austria in the middle of June and the Italian General Cadorna hoped for a quick assault against the Austrian southern defences, relying on superior man-and-firepower. The first offensive was successfully repelled by the Austrian forces stationed in the mountainous limestone region of South Tyrol. The second battle, fought in the waterless karst in fierce heat, brought no territorial gains for Italy and resulted in 60, 000 Italian and 45, 000 Austro-Hungarian casualties, mainly from heavy artillery fire in rocky terrain where flying shrapnel and rocks caused horrific injuries. Rudolf Leick played his part in the defence of this frontier, *arriving from South Tyrol with the 10th marching battalion.* His commanding officer put in a request for a decoration and he received the Bronze Medal for Bravery with Two Swords. I was not able to find any of his medical records but he sustained a head wound that left something, a piece of rock most likely, lodged in his brain. He was sent to recuperate, first at the local army hospital, then to Vienna.

Rudolf Leick joined his regiment again for two more times, but his injuries proved too severe. He was retired on August 1st, 1916 and then, re-activated, served at the train station in Mürzzuschlag as military commander from October 1917 until August 1918. On November 11th, 1918 the last emperor, Charles, proclaimed the right of Austria to form whatever state she wished and he also released officials and officers from their oath of loyalty. The imperial and royal armed forces were disbanded. Rudolf Leick, aged thirty-nine, found himself without career or employment.

He had married Mabel Haynes, a fellow officer's American widow, eight years older than him, with her two children – perhaps to legitimize the child she was expecting. His charm, liveliness and sexual charisma were remembered long after his death. Mabel Haynes' old friend, Emma Lootz Erving, wrote to Gertrude Stein upon hearing about her new marriage, was not impressed: *I gasped at the thought of any one as comfortable and unencumbered as she deliberately involving herself again. And with a man eight years her junior, with a criminal cast of countenance. Mabel never will fail to get what is coming to her – and it will all come.*

Mabel Haynes had had bought a handsome small *chateau* in Graz, where they all lived, in some style – once she could access her money in America again when the war was over, - with the five children (her last son, Reginald was born in 1917), their governesses, a nursemaid, cook and servants. However, the head wounds that Rudolf Leick had sustained during his military career made him liable to fits and convulsions. His wife also later maintained that his character, always temperamental, became much more violent and unpredictable, especially towards the children. He was said to have ruled with such strictness, frequently resorting to beatings, that the children, especially the younger ones, suffered from stammering and bed-wetting, as well as difficulties at school.

In September 1924 Mabel Haynes sailed to New York with Rudolf Leick and she arranged for her eldest daughter to stay in Boston to attend college. The Leick children were sent to a boarding school in Hastings until Rudolf Leick insisted that they be sent to Catholic schools in Germany and Austria instead. By this time Mabel Haynes had begun divorce proceedings. It proved a protracted and expensive affair. Again, Emma Lootz Erving informs Gertrude Stein: *I wonder if you have been seeing Mabel Haynes, I am frightfully sorry for her – for while it may have been difficult to keep on living with Rudolf it may prove to be even more difficult to get decently away from him. Of course he needs money and freedom – We all do. But I hope the Haynes money won't grease his wheels too smoothly.*

The divorce was finally granted on March 3rd, 1927. Mabel Haynes wrote to Gertrude Stein to give her the news, picking up from when they had last met: *In the short three months since Paris many changes have come over my life – I have secured a divorce from my husband and custody of the children, so all is peaceful here after many years of torment.*

She was ordered to pay Rudolph Leick a monthly income and to accommodate him a flat in one of her houses in Graz. His children, who could come back from their boarding schools to live with their mother, were obliged to render regular visits. He made an effort to control his temper while they were with him. If he had hoped to obtain a greater share of Mabel Haynes' estate, this was thwarted by her father's testament that excluded divorced husbands of his heirs from benefitting. Rudolf Leick had inherited some money from his father's death and he bought a farmhouse in the country in Styria, not very far from Graz.

In the interwar period he was politically conservative, still a monarchist at heart. His state of health suddenly deteriorated, and he died on July 8th, 1938, a few months after the *Anschluss,* Austria's annexation to Germany.

Servants

There were then the servants living in the house with them, a governess and near them in the small houses around them poor, for them, queer people to make for them their daily living. They had foreign women as servants in the house with them when they could get them. Sometimes they could not get them (...) Mrs Hershland with them all had her important feeling, she had in getting them. In keeping them, and whenever she had to get rid of them. She has always in her with them an important feeling, sometimes she had an angry feeling with them, sometimes a resisting feeling, she never let any interfering come between her and her acting toward them, she was always of them and above them, she had all her feeling to herself from them.

Many women have a feeling of themselves inside them from the servants around them.

Servant girl being is the kind of being that many millions of many kinds of women have in them. Servant girl being in such of them is different from just servant beings in other kinds of men and women. Servant girl being that is something dirty or clean little girl being the scared little lying always in such a one when there is much in their living and there always is in such ones of them for they need it to keep them going, to keep them cleaning, to keep them washing and working, to keep them from lying, much directing from the mistress living in the house with them. Much teasing from children living in the house with them, much trouble with their living so that nobody stops them when they go to their loving, much sitting in the kitchen with their hands so grimy nothing can clean them.

Mabel Haynes, May Bookstaver and Gertrude Stein belonged to the class that was being served and they were served by Americans belonging to the servant class or by foreigners - immigrants from the Old World. Having servants and governesses living in the house with them and being able to exert some form of control over their lives, to be able to hire and fire them, gave Mrs Hershland (who represents Mrs Amelia Stein) *an important feeling.* Gertrude Stein was aware of how having servants had made her mother feel and she also remembered how she felt growing up in a house shared with people who *made for them their daily living.* In *The Making of Americans* she analyses not only how the mother was feeling towards the women who served her and her husband and the children – she never mentions any male servants – but also the feelings of some of those who served the family, as governesses mainly, or as house-keepers, and she probes their *bottom natures,* as resisting or attacking, dependent or independent. She saw that some women who were not domestic servants nevertheless had a *servant girl being* inside them, which destined them to be drudges regardless of their station in life. When she and her brother Leo Stein set up house together in Baltimore, they employed a German woman, Anna Lebender, as their housekeeper and cook. When she wrote *Three Lives,* inspired by her efforts at translating Flaubert's *Trois Contes,* she wrote two of the stories (The Good Anna and The Gentle Lena) about servants and servants she had known, as Flaubert had done in *Un Coeur Simple.* The third story, *Melanctha,* is the exception. Melanctha, though a poor mulatto woman, does not serve anybody, least of all those who profess to love her. That Gertrude Stein made two poor German servants the heroines of her first published writing endeared her to those who admired her awareness of the sad lives and deaths of those who spent their lives serving others. It is not known what May Bookstaver made of it, the Socialist and Suffragist. Perhaps the choice of such protagonists was some form of riposte to May Bookstaver, who was forever championing the cause of disadvantaged women, and perhaps their sad deaths say something about Gertrude Stein's disavowal of radical politics as espoused by some of her women friends.

Later, when she wrote about her own life, in *The Autobiography of Alice B. Toklas, Everybody's Autobiography, Wars I Have Seen,* she wrote about the various servants she employed in France, from the point of view of the one being served, one who was more or less content with the service received, being a *patronne*.

At first there was just one servant, the competent Helene, and in the voice of Alice B. Toklas, she draws Helene as an intrinsic part of the early years at 27, rue de Fleurus, one with her own, quite distinct, take on what was going on and who was around: *I must tell a little about Helene. Helene had already been two years with Gertrude Stein and her brother. She was one of those admirable bonnes in other words excellent maids of all work, good cooks thoroughly occupied with the welfare of their employers and of themselves, firmly convinced that purchasable was far too dear. Oh but it is dear, was her answer to any question. She wasted nothing and carried on the household at the regular rate of eight francs a day. She even wanted to include guests at that price, it was her pride, but of course that was difficult since she for the honour of her house as well as to satisfy her employers always had to give every one enough to eat. She was a most excellent cook and she made a very good soufflé (…) Helene stayed with the household until the end of 1913. Then her husband, by that time she had married and had a little boy, insisted that she work for others no longer. To her great regret she left and later she always said that life at home was never as amusing as it had been at the rue de Fleurus. Much later, only about three years ago, she came back for a year, she and her husband had fallen on bad times and her boy had died. She was as cheery as ever and enormously interested. She said isn't it extraordinary, all those people whom I knew when they were nobody are now always mentioned in the newspapers, and the other night over the radio they mentioned the name of Monsieur Picasso.*

Helene, we never get to know her by another other name – servants even in the Bohemian world were not addressed in any other way – was to do what many competent *bonnes* ended up doing, serving a husband and a child for no wages. When Gertrude Stein's financial situation improved through the sales of the *Autobiography of Alice B. Toklas,* she bought an eight-cylinder Ford car and *we gave up having one servant we had a couple, a man and a woman.* They were an Italian couple, Mario and Pia, and they were to help run the house in Bilignin, where Gertrude

Stein and Alice B. Toklas spent the warm half of the year. The servants found *the house too large for only two servants…they got sadder. They did not like lighting fires and he did not like cutting up kindling wood to light them so he sadly wandered and picked up what he could find. …. They were sad then, They had been deceived about everything.*

Never having seen them before they become your servants and live in the house and are just as intimate as if they were your parents or your children. It is funny that because there naturally is just is just as much need as possible of always having known everybody you know and they come in answer to an advertisement and you never saw them before and you live in the house with them. And they then go away and you never ever see them again.

It is indeed strange that living with servants creates an intimacy that starts and ends abruptly, either because the servant has had enough of serving in this particular household, as happened with the two Italian servants, and to the Alsatian man and his Portuguese wife with one kidney who cooked beautifully, who replaced the Italians. The Polish woman and her husband were sent away. The new ones arrived: *A very serious old pair came out of Grenoble, he was an old soldier and she was an old French cook and he was a valet de chamber and he did not care about the clothes we had and he wanted different ones, well he did not get them.*

And then another French couple came and there were always some struggles and so Gertrude Stein and Alice B. Toklas decided *to have an Indo-Chinaman* named Trac: *We love him and he loves us. When he is with use it is very pleasant for every one and in between he leans between the kitchen and dining-room against the door and goes on talking.*

So Trac was our first Indo-Chinaman, since then we have had so many that we cannot remember all of them but Trac was the first one, he went to the country with us and we all enjoyed eating the Chinese patty he made which is delicious for a picnic, and a Chinaman even a Indo-Chinaman is always pleasant to have with one and so we had Trac.

In *Wars I Have Seen* Gertrude Stein does not name those who came and went as servants while she lived in the country with Alice B. Toklas, they are simply referred to as the servants or the cook.

Alice B. Toklas had a more direct relationship with the servants than Gertrude Stein had as she took responsibility for the smooth running of the household. She herself delighted in being of service to Gertrude Stein and to serve Gertrude Stein's genius in a variety of capacities, apart from the title she preferred herself - Miss Stein's Secretary. She devoted a separate chapter 'Servants in France' in her Cook Book, illustrated with four rather grotesque heads by Francis Rose, beginning with these reservations: *Unfortunately there have been too many of them in my service. Unfortunately there have been too many unsatisfactory ones, and too many of the satisfactory ones did not stay long.*

The implication is that while there had been too many servants to be remembered, servants who were being paid for the services they rendered to the Stein-Toklas *ménage*, they were of no consequence and had to be put up with, though they could, at times be amusing or excellent cooks, like Jeanne, whose departure in order to get married she said she regretted for years. Several recipes in the book were Jeanne's recipes. She liked the Chinese food that Vietnamese cooks, Trac and Nguyen, were preparing, but not that of Agnes, the Polish-American woman who replaced Nguyen, though the Veal and Pork Meat Loaf found favour. Margit from Finland was deemed a perfect cook but she fled for the homeland as war threatened. For some of the war years, once they had to leave Bilignin and move to Culoz, the cook that came with the property was old and pessimistic and refused to cook with the meagre supplies at hand. Alice B. Toklas had to take over the cooking herself *while a great cook sat by indifferent, inert and too discouraged to pay attention when I tried to show her how to make A Restricted Veal Loaf.*

Alice B. Toklas was a hard taskmaster: *Her expectations were severe, and her means of dealing with her subordinates could be unkind. Friends were sometimes appalled at her impatience with servants; but she merely wafted away their objections by assuring them that replacements could be easily found.*

After Gertrude Stein's death she lived on with Gabrielle, a rather eccentric French woman, who had to go once she threatened to reveal the identity of a mysterious veiled lady who had apparently helped Bernard Faÿ to escape from prison. Later she was too poor to afford a live-in servant and took to spending months at a time in convents.

There are those who serve other people in order to make their living, there are those who serve others because that is what is expected of them at certain times in lives, as wives, mothers, carers for elderly relatives or for incapacitated offspring. It is often women who serve others in such a way and their reward is said to lie in the service itself. Service can be seen as a sort of sacrifice, necessary to sustain the family, and as such can be offered up to atone for the general sinfulness of the human condition. Emma Lootz Erving, who had studied with Gertrude Stein at Johns Hopkins, and who looked forward to serving a suffering mankind in a professional capacity, once she had married her fellow-student and had children, discovered the double burden born by professional women and she writes on May 28th 1910 to Gertrude Stein: *It looks like a heap long time since I wrote to you – but I am an overworked servant, with no horizon save babies and patients and no spirit to want anything else. My mainspring is rusted, somehow, and I get along better if I work continuously and wash dishes the rest of the time, I haven't even had a nurse girl for the last month, and domestic machineries are exigent and at the time of year highly tedious.*

Mabel Haynes, brought up in a house full of servants, and once married, employing nurse-maids, governesses and cooks, also had to do without them during the war: *Mabel was taking care of three children in a large and commodious schloss without a single modern convenience – and one maid and no money.* Mabel Haynes was getting a chance to do what she had been used to have done for her and she rose to it with her customary forbearance. When the war was over, and she could access her American funds once more, she modernized her house, engaged new staff and never set foot in the kitchen or scullery again. The letters she sent from America after 1946 showed her continuing affection and care for some of her former servants; that she sent them Care Packets, money and letters of encouragement and urged her children to pay them visits.

Not long before my mother's mother died, she confided something to me that she had always kept from my mother, who was only too painfully aware of her lack of social status. My mother's mother said that she had once answered an advertisement for a domestic servant at Dr Haynes-Leick's household. She did not get the position. It was the only time the two women met; she never thought that my mother had done the right thing in marrying Mabel Haynes's son.

Sex

The one she was actively living the nervous sexual asking to be object of all loving

Gertrude Stein, Mabel Haynes and May Bookstaver, like their educated contemporaries, used the word sex when referring to biological differences between male or female; they would never have spoken of having sex. As women who had studied enough science and biology to be aware of the reproductive system, they knew more about that than a great many of the women of their time who had to deal with the consequences of their ignorance by bearing too many children. May Bookstaver campaigned to make this knowledge much more widely available, a fight that was fiercely resisted by those who thought they knew best what was right for women to know, especially for poor and uneducated women. For May Bookstaver the fight for women's suffrage and the fight for women's knowledge about reproduction were closely linked.

The objections to the free dissemination of contraceptive knowledge are based on prejudice and the worn out formula: of fear and compulsion as a means of reforming humanity. They have not reformed for thousands of years, and they never will. Knowing how conception worked and what could be done to avoid or encourage it was the subject of Margaret Sanger's pamphlet *What Every Girl Should Know.*

There is a difference between knowing about conception and contraception and knowing about desire or love.

Gertrude Stein no doubt had as thorough an understanding about the former as someone enrolled at a medical school would have access to, but she was much less well versed in the latter. She had formed some ideas about the impact of education on women that she confidently shared with an audience of progressive Baltimore women, of 'The Value of a College Education for Women'. She argued that *as labor was done more and more away from the home and the woman did not follow it she began to pay for her keep in a new and unhealthy fashion that is by becoming herself oversexed and so adapting herself to the abnormal sex desire of the male.* She also thought that a higher education *does not tend to unsex but to rightly sex a woman.* She concluded her talk by saying that the value of education for women lay in the training of their minds, citing the dissection of crab brains on a picnic as an example.

If the affairs of some of her female fellow students with their male colleagues distressed her, she was equally ill at ease with the idea of women falling for women. When she fell for May Bookstaver she was ill prepared for her own response. All her early fiction, especially *Q.E.D.* and the short story *Melanctha* in *Three Lives*, concern a sexually naïve person's initiation into 'knowledge'. At first 'Adele', the character based on Gertrude Stein in *Q.E.D.* is confounded by her inability to know the other: she confesses to 'Helen' that she does not know *whether you are wicked or not*, she certainly does not know about the nature of Helen's relationship to Mabel; when kissed *intensely on the lips* she *felt vaguely that she was apathetically unresponsive*. Eventually, however something happens: *Then for the first time in Adele's consciousness something happened in which she had no definite consciousness of beginnings. She found herself at the end of a passionate embrace.* Adele is repulsed by her feelings. She learns to overcome *the completeness of revulsion* only to be tormented by not knowing what Mabel knows and whether her knowing would make any difference. Adele does not end up winning the struggle, but something has been demonstrated, something has been proven to be the case, as the title of the story makes clear, but whether she knows quite what she knows is left unsaid.

In *Melanctha*, the main character (cast as a bi-racial *yellow* woman from a poor black neighbourhood) is only interested in gaining wisdom; she is *wandering after wisdom*, gaining sexual knowledge by having casual encounters with all kinds of men; she also acquired knowledge from other women *who had wisdom*:

It was now no longer, even in the daylight, the rougher men that these two learned to know in their wanderings, and for Melanctha the better classes were now a little higher. It was no longer express agents and clerks that she learned to know, but men in business, commercial travellers, and even men above these, and Jane and she would talk and walk and laugh and escape from them all very often. It was still the same, the knowing of them and the always just escaping, only now for Melanctha somehow it was different, for though it was always the same thing that happened it had a different flavor, for now Melanctha was with a woman who had wisdom, and dimly she began to see what it was that she should understand. In this story the naïve, forever questioning and un-knowing character is male, a physician who is attracted to Melanctha though he remains too wary of her to be able to succeed in his efforts at loving her: *Jeff Campbell never could forget the sweetness in Melanctha*

Herbert, and he was always very friendly to her, but they never any more came close to one another. More and more Jeff Campbell and Melanctha fell away from all knowing of each other, but Jeff never could forget Melanctha.

Gertrude Stein would not be able to forget May Bookstaver; she may have forgotten her *sweetness* while relishing the sweetness of another lover, but she could not forget that first shock of understanding the limits of her understanding herself. When she came to know Alice B. Toklas in 1907, she had spent some years analysing her experience by writing, and she was better prepared. Although, as she wrote in her notebook on Alice B. Toklas that she *is May, the elusive, finer purer flame of the prostitute,* she could see herself as the object of a desire as something she could finally allow herself to own. In the following years, confirmed in the rightness of such a vision, they could both revel in their ever-discrete passion and sensuality that is hinted at, encrypted, flashed, laid bare, and hidden in Gertrude Stein's writing of the time, which has been recognized and claimed for the canon of Lesbian literature. In order to satisfy a curiosity peculiar to our time as to how Gertrude Stein and Alice B. Toklas consummated and enjoyed their union, Gertrude Stein's poems, note-books and notes have been subjected to close scrutiny and much speculation as what bodily functions, secretions or positions certain words, such *Caesar* or *cows,* might refer to - exegeses that would have appalled and perhaps amused Gertrude Stein and Alice B. Toklas.

Gertrude Stein certainly seems to have greatly enjoyed writing sexy lyrics, as in *Lifting Belly,* in such a manner that made it perfectly transparent to the one she was referring to, to Pussy from her Hubby, while making it appear innocuous or simply impenetrable.

> *Lifting belly in here.*
> *Able to state whimsies.*

Can you recollect mistakes.

I hope not.

Lifting belly the best and only seat.

Lifting belly the reminder of present duties.

Lifting belly the charm.

Lifting belly is easy for me.

Lifting belly naturally.

Of course you lift belly naturally.

I lift belly you lift belly naturally.

I lift belly naturally together.

Lifting belly answers.

Can you think for me.

I can.

Lifting belly endears me.

Lifting belly cleanly. With a wood fire. With a good fire.

Say how do you to the lady. Which lady. The jew lady.

How do you do. She is my wife.

Gertrude Stein gathered various American young men around her after the Great War, who looked for guidance as much as stimulation while she looked at their literary efforts and amorous adventures with interest, as she later described in *The Autobiography of Alice B. Toklas.* A favourite for a while and then an enemy was Ernest Hemingway, whom she described as *extraordinarily good looking.* She once berated him for writing a story with an explicit sex scene, which she compared it to the sort of paintings that could not be exhibited because of their salacious content and she advised against such writing: *There is no point in it. It's wrong and silly.* He later wrote with some bitterness about her having been *such a bitch* while admitting to having found her sexually attractive, as he described in his characteristic crudeness: *I always wanted to fuck her and she knew it and it was a good healthy feeling and made more sense than some of the talk.*

Gertrude Stein had a jealous wife who demanded that all of Gertrude Stein's erotic attention be focused on her. Alice B. Toklas put an end to all temptations, as the polyamorous Mabel Dodge Luhan found out, when Alice B. Toklas had caught Gertrude Stein looking at her: *Such a strong look over the table that it seemed to cut across the air to me in a band of electrified steel - a smile travelling across it – powerful-Heavens! I remember it now so keenly!*. Alice B. Toklas was not only jealous of any potential actual rivals, male or female, but of those who many years before had been the object of Gertrude Stein's desire. It was her furious reaction upon the chance recovery of Gertrude Stein's early manuscript of *Q.E.D.* that made her destroy all mementoes and letters received from May Bookstaver and thus delete her from the archive and all memory, and even interfered with the actual text of *Q.E.D.* – demanding substitutions to the word '*may*': *every "may" is changed to "can"*. Some thirty years previously, Gertrude Stein had suffered pangs of jealousy over May Bookstaver's attachment to Mabel Haynes. In *Q.E.D.*, the story that so incensed Alice B. Toklas that it was only published after her death, Mabel Haynes, or rather her equivalent 'Mabel Neathe', is described as a New England woman, one of those American women whose *angular form of a spinster is possessed by a nature of the tropics* and *whose mouth is heavy with the drag of unidealized passion, continually sated and continually craving.* Mabel Neathe as the experienced, self-aware and manipulative possessor of the equally experienced though dependent 'Helen' is the foil to Adele's pure fool. Mabel Haynes freely admitted to her passionate nature and romantic disposition while she was equally conscious of her New England sense of propriety. Referring to a promiscuous friend of her daughter's she commented the *she offends my Puritan sense of decency. She has only sex in her noddle.*

She had met May Bookstaver while they were both at Miss Baldwin's Preparatory School at Bryn Mawr. They both attended Bryn Mawr College and graduated in 1898. Mabel Haynes always acknowledged May as *her dearest friend* and they remained close until May died in 1950 - *Thine always* reads the written dedication on a photograph May gave to Mabel; it is undated but likely to have been taken around 1900. Crushes or *smashings* among college students were common enough at Bryn Mawr. Bryn Mawr's first Dean and second President, M. Carey Thomas, lived with her companion and lover Mamie Gwinn and thought that intelligent, educated women would let the side down by giving in to unions with men; such were her sexual politics. It was not a matter of deviancy or immaturity, but a natural inclination allied to the conviction that a union between two women was on a higher level than the conventional one geared towards reproduction and female subordination. By the time May Bookstaver and Mabel Haynes were students at Bryn Mawr, in the later 1890s, Oscar Wilde had been put on trial for homosexuality, and M. Carey Thomas had begun to read books such as Max Nordau's *Degeneration* (1892) Samuel-Auguste Tissot's *Onanisme* (1776) and Richard von Krafft-Ebing's *Psychopathia Sexualis* (1886) to discover, as her biographer Helen Horowitz put it, *that passion was sex and that she was a lesbian* and although some medical, male authorities would categorize such inclinations and practices as deviant, she still believed that *love of a woman for a woman was better than any love for a man.* To what extent Mabel Haynes, May Bookstaver, and many other young women who exchanged *impassioned kisses,* thought of their feelings and intimacies as *sex* cannot be ascertained. Mabel Haynes and May Bookstaver felt themselves to be in the vanguard of female emancipation and if their mutual emotional support, solidarity and fondness, included the sort of caresses that satisfied their passionate nature this was all quite natural. To what extent there was some sort of bet, as Emma Lootz Erving hinted in one of her letters, to seduce the naïve and bolshy Gertrude Stein in order to take her down a peg or two, remains unclear. May Bookstaver was, by Emma Lootz' account, ever ready for mischief but she might also have responded warmly to the vivacious Californian's sex appeal. The ensuing love triangle made none of the parties happy. May Bookstaver did not commit herself to Gertrude Stein. She managed to salvage her friendship with Mabel Haynes but their intimacy came to an end. For a while Mabel Haynes took up with another Bryn Mawr graduate, Mary Miller Buckminster. Nothing is known of May Bookstaver's attachments until her marriage to Charles E. Knoblauch in 1906. Mabel Haynes by that time was engaged to the Austro-Hungarian officer Konrad Heissig whom she married in January 1907, with the determination to start a large family. These were successful marriages, and both women, by now in their thirties, appear to have found their athletic husbands physically attractive. To what extent Mabel Haynes and May Bookstaver remained susceptible to the charms of women thereafter is unknown; Mabel Haynes had several Austrian female friends who were devoted to her throughout her life, but I doubt that they were ever her lovers. She liked being pregnant and getting pregnant and she developed a taste for masculine bodies, not least those of her husbands. It could have been the sex-appeal of Rudolf Leick, or *der Zauber der Montur* (the magic of the uniform) that aroused her appetite and made her succumb to his seduction while Konrad Heissig was dying and that made her stick to him as long as she did, despite the abuse he meted out to her and their children during their marriage. The men she admitted to swooning over in her widowed middle and old age were Clark Gable, Rex Harrison, Charles Boyer and James Mason. She writes about her favourite stars to her daughter: *Don't ever miss "The Ghost and Mrs Muir" if it comes your way. I saw it <u>four</u> times and fell completely for that irresistible ghost (Rex Harrison) … Clark Gable will be here soon in "Command and Decision" – some war part and only men in it. There one will again see that gorgeous figure…. James Mason is superb in "The Upturned Glass". What a man!* Swooning to such enticing specimens of masculinity in a darkened cinema she once failed to notice a creeping hand on her lap until the owner of that hand made a proposition that outraged her, coming as it did to a woman of seventy-one, with Puritan sense of decency. When her daughter Gabrielle, whose scintillating personality always attracted the sexual interest of men as well as women, asked her old mother one day when this itch or longing she felt would stop, Mabel Haynes told that not to count on that as she had not experienced the cessation of at least some longing. She also reproved her daughter once who had expressed revulsion at the thought of making love to a woman by simply remarking that one should try everything. She may have had Puritan sensibilities but not a Puritan sensuality, as Gertrude Stein had found out long ago.

Shoes and Sandals

A lean on the shoe this means slips slips hers.

When we were children, we were taken to a shoe shop in spring to buy summer shoes. In order to ascertain that they would fit well enough to allow the feet to grow the shop assistant squeezed the toe part of the shoes before taking us to the x-ray machine. We were told to wriggle our toes and through a screen at the top of the contraption we saw our skeletal bones move. The summer shoes were round-toed sandals with a strap that ran through a T-shaped centre part and was fastened below the ankle. For the Austrian winter months, we needed sturdy lace-up leather boots. Tennis shoes were strictly for playing tennis. My father bought me Elvis Presley's *Blue Suede Shoes* for my fifth birthday, my first record, endlessly played. I had no idea that the song was about shoes.

When Gertrude Stein became famous people who never read her knew what she looked like and what she wore. What she chose to put on her feet mattered as much as what she put on her head. In her youth she would have worn ankle-high lace-up leather boots not unlike those made by our village cobbler. The shoes she later bought for herself were not the kind of shoes her relatives would have bought her. They were not dainty calfskin shoes as those worn by the wealthy women she had tea with. They were not shoes at all but sandals: *Leurs pieds nus sont chaussés de sandals delphiques, ils lèvent vers le ciel des fronts scientifiques.* Thus Apollinaire described Leo and Gertrude Stein who were both moving about Paris in the early 1900s in the footgear of classical antiquity. Another pair of siblings, their old neighbours from East Oakland, Raymond and Isadora Duncan, liked to sport Grecian robes and sandals. Raymond Duncan made these sandals himself and they were reconstructed on the basis of classic sculpture, whereas Gertrude and Leo Stein's looked more like the ones worn by peasants in Greece, with upturned toes. In the winter she wore thick socks or stockings with the sandals and in the summer, she walked *in bare feet and heavy, thonged sandals, one toe on each foot separated proudly from its fellows like a little pig who went to market.*

Touring Spain with Alice B Toklas *Gertrude Stein wore a brown corduroy suit, jacket and skirt, a small straw cap, always crocheted for her by a woman in Fiesole, sandals, and*

she often carried a cane. She admired Saint Teresa of Avila and Saint Ignatius of Loyola, who, like all friars and nuns, wore sandals. They were the footwear for people who walk a lot; the Roman soldiers had tramped the earth on such tough leathered sandals; nuns and monks would glide along them in their cloisters. Gertrude strode through the hills of Tuscany and the gardens of Luxembourg in hers. In her later years, certainly in the 1930s, she wore leather shoes known as 'Mary Janes'. They were round-toed, flat shoes with a single strap across the arch that fastened with a button rather than a buckle. She also liked big leather boots to wear in the country.

Gertrude Stein wrote short compositions about all sorts of objects in *Tender Buttons.* They can be enjoyed as collages with words that defy meaning, but they have also been read as encrypted, erotically charged evocations of her intimate life with Alice B Toklas:

Shoes
To be a wall with a damper a stream of pounding way and nearly enough choice makes a steady midnight. It is pus.
A shallow hole rose on red, a shallow hole in and in this makes ale less. It shows shine.

Lisa Ruddick suggested that *Alice's [ale less] is a red rose, which can be entered: one can go "in". So also the words "shoes" and "shows" punningly refer to Alice's chose, French slang for vagina.* From this perspective, from the end backwards, or from below upwards, the whole poem becomes suffused with *double entendres*, though the shoe itself resists fetishization.

Alice B. Toklas was fastidious in her manner of dressing and she liked to wear good shoes. She remembered the only luxury Michael Stein allowed her during her first Tuscan stay with the Steins, *boots beautifully made to order* in Florence:

I had explained to Mike, who was managing my economics, that they were smarter, more comfortable and cheaper than the ready-made ones would be in Paris.

Mabel Haynes was tall, but she had small, narrow feet. Such feet can easily be shod in elegant footwear. On the photographs of Mabel Haynes that show her feet she always wears the sort of shoes that were in fashion at the time, with straps or no straps, usually with a small heel and worn with silk stockings, as on this snapshot, standing tall and straight in her white and black shoes:

The children she bore during the First World War did their growing at a time when food was scarce and shoes hard to come by. They suffered greatly from having to squeeze into ill-fitting shoes. All their feet had some deformities, such as bunions, but despite this, my aunt Gabrielle was a self-declared 'shoe fetishist' by which she meant buying rather a lot of expensive Jourdain's two-toned patent shoes, which she would fling from her when she returned home.

Of Mary Bookstaver's taste in shoes nothing is known though I suspect, given her place in New York society, that she would have worn the sort of shoes women of her class wore at the time. Not sandals and not Mary Janes; *pas la même chose.*

Sleep

why is not sleeping a feat why is it not

This part of a line in 'Rooms' from *Tender Buttons* can be read in two ways; why sleeping is not considered a feat or why not sleeping be considered a feat. Gertrude Stein's sleight of hand in weighing up the feat of sleep or not sleep could also be seen as a response to I. G. Gurdjieff, the Greek-Armenian mystic who had set up his teaching centre at the Chateau de Prieuré at Fontainebleau. Her friend Jane Heap from *The Little Review* had become a follower of Gurdjieff's in the 1920s. She took Gertrude Stein and Alice B. Toklas to meet the man, an occasion on which they *circled around each other warily.* The point of the many and strenuous mental and physical exercises Gurdjieff set his followers to perform was to allow them to reach a state of consciousness that broke through the *mechanized state of being asleep while not being asleep* in order to achieve the 'waking state'. Gertrude Stein was wary of Gurdjieff, but she had been a student of William James', who had pursued the same argument in his 1906 lecture 'The Energies of Men' where he addresses the issue of how to achieve what he terms the 'vital equilibrium': *When I speak of human energizing in general, the reader must therefore understand that sum-total of activities, some outer and some inner, some muscular, some emotional, some moral, some spiritual, of whose waxing and waning in himself he is at all times so well aware. How to keep it at an appreciable maximum? How not to let the level lapse? That is the great problem.* Gertrude Stein's ability to maintain what William James called vital equilibrium, her intense aliveness and her creative energy, was obvious to anyone who came to know her. Her writing, especially *Tender Buttons*, but also *Stanzas in Meditation* and *Lucy Church Amiably* could be taken as first-hand reports of a consciousness that lives in the present and sees everything in all its separate and yet not disconnected being, or at least as evocations of such a state of being when reduced to putting words on a page. As far as her sleeping was concerned, she could work all night to write before going to bed in the early morning: *But often the birds and the dawn caught her and she stood in the court waiting to get used to it before she went to bed. She had the habit then of sleeping until noon and the beating of the rugs into the court, because everybody did that in those days, even her house-hold did, was one of her most poignant irritations.*

Later, when they lived every summer in Bilignin, Gertrude Stein had plenty of time to write and to meditate, which entailed reclining in a deckchair with a dog in her lap and thinking. She could write during the day and go to bed at night, but she always liked staying in bed late: *I never get up early I get up as late as possible I like not to get up in the morning and no one ever wakes me.* Gertrude Stein liked her matitudinal sleep. It took much persuasion and a particular point of it to get her to rise earlier, such as the 'sentimental journey' to be undertaken with the 'Kiddies' in 1934. Even then she declared firmly when told by Alice B. Toklas to be early: *Only of course I won't get up until eight. I wouldn't get up until eight no matter where I was going I wouldn't get up until eight.*

Alice B. Toklas went to bed earlier than Gertrude Stein and she rose earlier to busy herself in the household and to type what Gertrude Stein had written during the night. Sometimes Gertrude Stein would leave her a little note:

Baby precious Hubby worked and
Loved his wifey; sweet sleepy wifey,
Dear dainty wifey, baby precious sleep
Sweetly and long is hubby's song,
And all mine and sweet is hubby's
Treat and precious and true and all.

When Alice B. Toklas found such a message, 'hubby' would be the precious baby sleeping. Gertrude Stein and Alice B. Toklas watched over each other's sleep and such a sleep was not a feat.

That Alice B. Toklas was a sound sleeper, even when frightening things were happening, is recorded in the war chapter of *The Autobiography of Alice B. Toklas*: *There were Zeppelin alarms from time to time, but like everything else we had gotten used to them. When they came at dinner time we went on eating and when they came at night Gertrude Stein did not wake me, she said I might as well stay where I was if I was asleep because when asleep it took more than even the siren that they used then to give the signal, to wake me.*

During the Second World War, when things in the countryside had become ever more frightening, the two women coped by carrying on as best they could, and Gertrude Stein wrote in her memoir of this war: *I walked a great deal and I cut box hedges, and every night I read the book of prophecy and went promptly to sleep.*

Gertrude Stein had a strong constitution, the daily exercise kept her fit and she was 'never' ill; she slept soundly at a time when other people and certainly Alice B. Toklas had been up for hours. She was not the type of writer who rose, very early, before dawn, to write, as was the habit of Ernest Hemingway and Edith Wharton.

In my family, there those with a nervous disposition, who were said to have a 'hysterical sleep', which meant sleep frequently interrupted and hard to achieve.

My aunt Gabrielle was such a self-confessed hysterical sleeper, though this did not diminish her high spirits during the day, while her sister Enid, who prided herself on her non-neurotic sleep, had a habitually grumpy disposition. Their mother, Mabel Haynes, began having problems with going to sleep when her first husband and then her son became ill and died. Thereafter she could only sleep with sleeping pills.

When we were children, we shared a bedroom with my parents. I would often wake because of my father's snoring. The noise of his snoring was not disagreeable to me, as I lay there listening to the loud intake of breath – it was a sign that he was fast asleep and that I was awake and witness to his being asleep. It made me feel grown-up not to be asleep when he was sunk in sleep. Later, when lying next to the sleeping father of my child and hearing his quiet breathing and that of the baby next to us, I would be filled with content and happiness before drifting off to sleep again myself. Why is not sleeping a feat? Perhaps it should say a feast.

Talking and listening

I always as I admit seem to be talking but talking can be a way of listening that is if one has the profound need of hearing and seeing what every one is telling.   And I began very early in life to talk all the time and to listen all the time. At least that is the way I feel about it.

In the winter of 1902-03, Gertrude Stein consoled herself for her loneliness in a gloomy London winter by reading eighteenth-century novels of letters, and she later often referred to Samuel Richardson's *Clarissa* as her favourite novel. *Clarissa* is full of reported talking, overheard conversations that should not have been listened to, talking across closed doors, talking in whispers, in assumed accents, in elegant and pure as well coarse and vile language. Gertrude Stein's first written works are similarly filled with copied letters, remembered and mis-remembered conversations, talking, endless talking, at cross-purposes and not listened to.

Gertrude Stein was a great talker, a formidable talker, before she became a writer. In one of her American lecturers she gave a long and chronologically ordered account of her awakening consciousness as a writer through talking and listening, especially listening to people talking: *I cannot remember not talking all the time and all the same feeling that while I was talking while I was seeing that I was not only hearing but seeing while I was talking and that at the same time the relation between myself knowing I was talking and those to whom I was talking and incidentally to whom I was listening were coming to tell me and tell me in their way everything that made them.*

Those of you who have read The Making of Americans I think will very certainly understand. When I was young and I am talking of a period even before I went to college part of this talking consisted in a desire not only to hear what each one was saying in every way everybody has of saying it but also then of helping to change them and to help them change themselves.

I was very full of convictions in those days and I at that time thought that the passion I had for finding out by talking and listening just how everybody was always telling everything that was inside them that made them that one, that this passion for knowing the basis of existence in each one was in me to help them change themselves to become what they should become. The changing should of course be dependent upon my ideas and theirs theirs as much as mine at that time.

And so in those early days I wanted to know what was inside each one which made them that one and I was deeply convinced that I needed to help them change something.

Then I went to college and there for a while I was tremendously occupied with finding out what was inside myself to make me what I was, I think that does happen to one at that time. It had been happening before going to college but going to college made it more lively. And being so occupied with what made me myself inside me, made me perhaps not stop talking but for a while made me stop listening.

And being so occupied with what made me myself inside me, made me perhaps not stop talking but for a while it made me stop listening.

(....)Then that was over and I went to the medical school where I was bored and where once more myself and my experiences were more actively interesting me than the life inside of others. But then after that once more I began to listen, I had left the medical school and I had for the moment nothing to do but talk and look and listen, and I did this tremendously.

I then began again to think about the bottom nature in people, I began to get enormously interested in hearing how everybody said the same thing over and over again with infinite variations but over and over again until finally if you listened with great intensity you could hear it rise and fall and tell all that that there was inside them, not so much by the actual words they said or the thoughts they had but the movement of their thoughts and words endlessly the same and endlessly different.

At first Gertrude Stein found in listening to people talking and in listening to herself talking a clue to understand their inner being, their 'bottom nature', and *The Making of Americans* was her way of accounting for all the variations of any one. There was also, she says, an urge to make people change, so her talking would be remonstrative in the Jeff Campbell manner, who remonstrates with wandering Melanctha, who while listening to his voice, does not listen in the sense that he hopes she would. Gertrude Stein drew not least on her experience of talking to May Bookstaver – who was talking to Gertrude Stein *tremendously* without being able to hear what the other was trying to say. Gertrude Stein talked to her other friends about the futility of talking with May Bookstaver and she too wanted more to talk than listen to what they had to say. Talking and trying to listen without being able to hear is hardly satisfactory. Gertrude Stein's sequence, some thirty years later, corresponds to the way she differentiates her talking and listening in respect to her writing – that arose from such different ways of talking and listening. She sees her way of listening to the way people speak, the way they repeat and make slight variations in their repetition, in the *movement of their thoughts and words endlessly the same and endlessly different* as a breakthrough in her understanding of what talking means. This insight was to inform the way she wrote; on the one hand like a recording device catching words from any direction and re-arranging them into patterns on the page, and on the other hand as recording a particular talker; Alice B. Toklas, most convincingly, or Gertrude Stein, in the lectures or in *Wars I Have Seen.* The *Autobiography* owed more to listening and the lectures more to talking.

One way of talking *being a way of listening* is by listening to oneself speaking; a slight relay in a communication satellite for instance sometimes echoes the last words being said while one is still speaking. Talking in a foreign language one has not yet learned to speak with ease makes one listen more to one's own mistakes or infelicities in pronunciation while speaking and to listen to someone listening to their mistakes makes understanding them even harder. Listening to people talking in language one does not understand at all one can either take as a musical experience or a sound poem or it can make one feel lonely.

We talk and talk, the whole evening, while Herta knits. Mabel Haynes writes this in a letter to her Austrian daughter, the one with whom she talked in English. She also talked in English to her son, and Herta, my mother, who did not understand English and sat knitting while she listened, calmly or irritably, as they went on talking. Such a way of listening can become a refusal to listen to anything said in any language, as Mabel Haynes found with this Austrian daughter-in-law, who felt excluded by her American mother-in-law talking in English to her husband. It was not an arrangement that would last. *No use talking again about Herta but she will remain a disturbing element in our otherwise closely-knit family.* Mabel Haynes eventually realized that in this family she was the disturbing element and removed herself. When she came on visits she would comment on her grandchildren: *Andrea still doesn't do any more talking; Gwendy manages that for two.* Being a younger sister to a talkative child, my sister Andrea listened for the first few years without talking much herself. As we were most of the time of one mind, she saw little reason to talk herself when I could say what had to be said, so she said afterwards, when she had discovered that she wanted to talk about things in her way.

My mother was not a woman of many words and many people came to talk to her. Some of them were my father's patients, and he would say that she sometimes made them feel better by listening than he did with his medicine. Being a woman of few words, she often said, which is after all true, that everybody can only say so many words in a lifetime and that when all the words are used up one dies. She would at times, look at us and say, when she listened to us talking and talking, 'Save your words, don't waste them so rashly'. She must have been allocated a meagre hoard of words, as despite her preference for silence, she died long before she grew old.

Teaching

Hutchins said to me as he and I were walking, you did make them all talk more than we can make them and a number of them talked who never talked before and it was very nice of him to say it and he added and if you will come back `I will be glad to have you do some teaching and I said I would and he said he would let me know and then I said you see why they talk to me is that I am like them I do not know the answers, you you say you do not know but you do know if you did not know the answer you could not spend your life in teaching but I really do not know, I really do not, I do not even know if there is a question let alone having an answer for a question. To me when a thing is really interesting it is then when there is no question and no answer, if there is then already the subject is not interesting and it is so, that is the reason that anything for which there is a solution is not interesting, that is the trouble with governments and Utopias and teaching, the things not that can be learnt but that can be taught are not interesting.

Gertrude Stein did not exercise the profession of teaching, unlike Mabel Foot Weeks, her New York friend who taught English literature at Barnard College, or Georgiana King, the art historian at Bryn Mawr. During her lecture tour in America, Gertrude Stein was asked to speak at universities and colleges, and usually she gave one of her lectures that she had prepared beforehand. When she did take a seminar, as on the occasion described above, she enjoyed the fact that she had a greater success at getting students to respond and to talk, rather than just listen to her talking. She said that the reason for this greater participation was that she said that she knew that she did not know the answers. Such an approach to teaching was, she thought, only possible if you did not make teaching a profession. Knowing the answers means knowing the questions.

Gertrude Stein liked talking to Hutchins' students in Chicago and she liked to be told that she had drawn them out more than the professional tutors felt able to do. She could come at them from a position of being an outsider, one to whom they would not be obliged to give answers to and one who professed not to know the answers. She had little respect for the sort of knowledge that could be had from teachers or governesses. She certainly never entertained the wish to become one of them. Teachers represent authority and they teach respect and obedience, bending the savage spirit of the unformed mind to the rules and strictures it would have to bend to. Such teaching embodies the imperative injunction - "I will teach you!" – the threat that even with fingers in both ears the teaching will take effect.

Some teachers suppress their own resistance to having been taught and in a form of revenge teach everything to those who have to submit to their teaching. Such teaching leaves nothing but resistance.

Teachers who know that the things really worth knowing are not to be found within the official canon of knowledge teach in such a way as to make those they teach aware of this. They teach as if they were not teachers but were fellow explorers in territories unknown and in such a way that it becomes so form of loving and Gertrude Stein had some knowledge of that: *She being that one she was teaching, she being teaching she was telling something, she being telling something, she was telling that thing again, she telling that thing again was asking if any one telling that thing was not one teaching and if any one telling that thing was teaching was not being one teaching being a thing having the meaning that in doing anything one was meaning that in helping anything one was loving. In asking everything she was helping everything, in helping everything she was asking that she was telling that she was teaching and doing that thing. In being teaching she was asking if she was not loving. In loving she was asking if she was teaching everything. In teaching everything she was asking if any one needed any helping.*

The context is not at all one in which teaching takes place normally, but in the intimate exchange of doing things that women, her *many many women* engage in. Here 'teaching' follows long paragraphs that evoke, in incantatory cadences, what *many many women* do: remembering, forgetting, kissing, living, giving, being lonesome, paying, feeding, knowing, having children, working, marrying, needing, expressing an opinion, mentioning something, feeling, saying something, saying anything, saying everything, seeing, loving, taking something, being sad, liking children, waiting to be refusing to be waiting, not expecting anything, helping, hearing, continuing, deciding, needing having loving, being a tender one, being an honest one, being one succeeding, coming again, not coming again, coming and going, feeling and coming, being exciting, moving. No chalk dust clings to a teaching person who teaches some one (not someone) in these experiential processes: *That one being one teaching is one teaching some one everything. That one being one learning everything is being one being taught everything by the one that can teach that one everything.*

Everything is a nice Gertrude Stein hyperbole but then, unless one is willing to give everything (not every thing) one cannot even give something.

Tempers and temperament

It is hard living down the tempers we are born with. We all begin well, for in our youth there is nothing we are more intolerant of than our own sins writ large in others and we fight them fiercely in ourselves; but we grow old and we see that these our sins are of all sins the really harmless ones to own, nay that they give a charm to any character, and so our struggle with them dies away.

When Gertrude Stein wrote this observation in her thirties she was far from having a dispassionate distance from her own temperament.

270

However, a tolerance of her own sins writ large in others had been achieved by carefully describing and accounting for the 'bottom nature' of every one in 'The Making of Americans'. Her method was to calibrate *attacking and resisting, dependence and independence*, as the main binary opposites that in each person can be combined in different configurations (e.g.: *she was a resisting sensitive fairly of the resisting sensitive being, dependent as dependent independent ones have it to be dependent in them, not at all in bottom being an engulfing one.*

Gertrude Stein would have been familiar with the Four Types of Constitution, later known as Temperaments, which on the basis of body type and mental disposition contrasted dry and moist, cold and hot tempers and melancholic, sanguine, choleric, and phlegmatic temperaments. The ideal personality would have an even distribution of all these qualities or modalities without being dominated by any one. Gertrude Stein was not very interested in ideal types or medieval classification, but she did pay attention of the epistemology of such systems: *In the eighteenth century that age of manners and of formal morals, it was believed that the temper of a woman was determined by the turn of her features; later in the beginning nineteenth century, the period of inner spiritual illumination it was accepted that the features were moulded by the temper of the soul within; still later in the nineteenth century when the science of heredity had decided that everything proves something different, it was discovered that generalisations must be as complicated as the facts and the problem of interrelations was not so simply solved.*

The fact remains that people are different and similar in ways that are not easily reduced to any scheme and that such schemes may tell us more about ideas on human nature prevailing at one time. Gertrude Stein eventually tired of the system she had invented and came to see people less as types than individuals, which says something about her time and her being an American.

Then there are tempers. To temper etymologically means to even something out but to have a temper stirs things up and brings to the surface a generally hidden power: In *The Making of Americans,* the figure of Fanny Hershland (based on her own mother), *a sweet little gentle mother woman,* is said to have had *a fierce little temper. The sweet gentle little mother who had sometimes a fierce little temper in her that could be very stubborn when it rose strongly inside her...she had a little temper that could make her big husband pay attention to her.* Then, when the mother became ill, she could no longer assert herself in this way: *The little stubborn temper in her broke into weakness and helplessness inside her and they had in a way to be good to her.*

It is primarily in the early part of her novel that Gertrude Stein refers to her personages' temper. Julia Dehning, wishing to marry Alfred Hershland, gets her way eventually despite her *eager and impatient temper* that had to endure the long sermons of her father, though he *was cheerful in his temper.* Alfred Hershland, though *not an angry or sullen person,* had *a temper in him that is a common thing with those having resisting being tending to the engulfing kind.*

Gertrude Stein herself, in the self-parodying depiction of Miss Mathilda in *Three Lives,* is said to have a *cheerful and lazy temper,* one that contrasts with Gentle Lena's increasingly difficult and irritable one. Gertrude Stein seems to have had some of her father's irascibility in her and cultivating a comfort-seeking indolence may have been one way to temper it. But while she was genial and good-natured much of the time, she could call up more than a little temper: *'She's the greatest artist in the world', he said, but my dear, she has such a temper, such a temper! She has already had three violent quarrels with Picasso and I suppose ours is coming along.*

In *The Autobiography of Alice B. Toklas* quarrels, arguments and Gertrude Stein's *explosive temper,* act like a pinch of spice to make the dish the more piquant. Alice

B. Toklas, who cultivated a ladylike composure, could make the most impassioned scenes, especially if her jealousy was aroused. May Bookstaver's temperament can only be surmised from Gertrude Stein's fictionalised accounts – *a woman of passions, but not of emotions, capable of long sustained actions, incapable of regrets.* She is shown to be neither as phlegmatic and melancholic as her reluctant lover, nor as sanguine and phlegmatic as her beloved. She may have tempered her temperament in such a way as to inspire others to lose their temper and their heads over her.

Mabel Haynes freely admitted to her own *violent nature* – Gertrude Stein called it *a nature that could hate subtly and poison deftly.* She was, so her daughter admitted, malicious and enjoyed watching a drama being enacted for her benefit. Romantic but not sentimental, she could make decisions to follow her heart. She then paid for them dearly. Her friend Emma Lootz Erving, in a letter to Gertrude Stein, felt that on the whole Mabel Haynes *counts up to a very respectably proportioned human being.* Here Dr Erving sounds like her ancient colleagues.

Votes for Women

Thanks dear Susan B. Anthony, thanks we all know that whatever happens we all can depend upon you to do your best for any cause which is a cause, and any cause is a cause and because any cause is a cause therefore you will always do your best for any cause, and now you will be doing your best for this cause our cause the cause.

In 19th century America the worthy causes people fought for were many - temperance, abolition of slavery, prison reform, suffrage for negroes, education for women, suffrage for women, worker's rights, socialism. One of the women campaigners who campaigned her whole adult life (1820-1906), trying to convince other people of the worthiness of the causes she believed in supporting – temperance, the abolition of slavery, more equal rights for women, was Susan B. Anthony. She saw the XIVth and XVth Amendment to the constitution of the United States, one that enfranchised the freed Negroes of the South, as well as males with Civil War debts, but she did not live to see the XIXth Amendment, which secured the vote for women in all the states of the United States. Gertrude Stein's libretto for an opera about Susan B. Anthony, for which Virgil Thomson composed the music, has the title *The Mother of Us All.* She wrote this from October 1945 and completed it in 1946. Written in an ostensibly less hermetic style than her previous opera *Four Saints in Three Acts* the libretto presents the setbacks and successes of Susan B. Anthony's pursuit of her cause to win the vote for women in a pageant peopled with historical characters (Daniel Webster, Ulysses E. Grant, Anthony Comstock, Anne Shaw), personal friends (Constance Fletcher) and 'types' (Chris the Citizen, Jo the Loiterer). It ends with the posthumous inauguration of a statue of Susan B. Anthony who makes her last reflections from beyond the grave.

Anne alone in front of the statuary. The Vote. Women have the vote. They have it each and every one, it is glorious glorious glorious.

274

Susan B. Anthony behind the statue. Yes women have the vote, all my long life of strength and strife, all my long life, women have it, they can vote, every man and every woman has the vote, the word male is not there any more, that is to say, that is to say.

Gertrude Stein lived to see the success of Susan B. Anthony and she also lived to see the success of her own cause, the cause of serving her genius and being popular: *I always did want to be a popular author; that is one that anybody could read. I am one that am personally quoted by everybody, but not yet my books and I want that to(o).* While Gertrude Stein was never a suffragist and was wary of the idea that political activism could succeed in undoing patriarchy, she was, so some of her critics believe, working on language to free language from patriarchal discourse. From such a viewpoint, in her opera libretto, she *asserts a historical continuity between nineteenth-century suffragists' project to authorize a political voice for women and twentieth-century literary modernists' experiments with literary voice.*

The last words in Gertrude Stein's Opera are spoken by Susan B. Anthony while the chorus intones: *The vote we vote we note the vote* are interspersed with pauses (*a silence a long silence*) and there is no jubilation, no exultation, no rejoicing but a looking back at a long life full of strife: *We cannot retrace our steps, going forward may be the same as going backwards. (….) Life is strife, I was a martyr all my life not to what I won but to what was done.*

Gertrude Stein put Susan B. Anthony up as a symbol of one who had fought and won and she could speak through Susan B. Anthony's figure about her own misgivings about what that *life of strife* had achieved.

May Bookstaver was especially interested in politics. She studied Political Science and History at Bryn Mawr so as to have a firm intellectual footing for her pursuit of the cause for women's rights and woman's suffrage. When she met Gertrude Stein, who had also chosen medicine and was studying at Johns

Hopkins Medical School, May Bookstaver was active in the suffrage movement in Baltimore. She retained her interest in politics and the cause of women's suffrage after Gertrude Stein had lost interest in medicine and had moved to Paris. The entry in the *Woman's who's who in America, 1914-15* lists her interests and affiliations: *Writer of articles in several magazines. Favors woman suffrage; member executive, board Women's Political Union; captain 29th Dist. Woman Suffrage Party, College Franchise League, Equal Franchise Society, N.Y. State Suffrage Society.* May Bookstaver, like so many other women who were campaigning to secure woman's suffrage in all states of the United States, worked in various capacities - serving on committees, writing letters and articles, attending meetings, holding placards. Once she had married the stock-broker Charles E. Knoblauch, she participated in social functions that raised funds for the cause, *thés dansants,* dinners and theatrical evenings, all reported in the press. Unlike the suffragists in London, New York suffragists did not engage in acts of violence in order to publicize their cause, but preferred to stage well-ordered pageants and parades, which demonstrated women's ability to mobilise mass support without resorting to provocation. At least this was a tactic favoured by the Woman Suffrage Party, an organisation founded by Carrie Chapman in 1909, specifically for New York. The parades, which were held annually from 1912 to 1917, were effective in bringing together women of different social classes, ages and economic backgrounds and even women who would not march in public could watch the march from viewing platforms or from the pavements. Newspapers gave long descriptions of the parades and their best-known participants, remarking on the outfits the women wore and how the crowds responded to their appearance; some were openly hostile to the cause and reported more favourably on the activities of the anti-suffrage campaigners. May Bookstaver's moment of parade glory came about by accident rather than design, when she replaced a woman rider as the leader of the suffrage cavalry division in 1912. As this division led the whole march of some 10,000 women, she was at the head of the whole parade and most news reports picked this up, commenting on the style and the outfits worn as if it were yet another social event to show off one's finery:

New York Times, Sunday May 5th, 1912, p. 10:

Washington Square saw the chief preparations, for little knots of women assembled there early in the afternoon. There was much excitement when grooms from a riding academy swept down and around the arch, each man leading five of the horses that were to bear the horse women. These assembled just behind the arch, and with Ann Tinker Hill the task of leading them fell upon Mrs Charles E. Knoblauch, who can ride as well as her husband, and he was one of Co. Roosevelt's Roughriders. There was no uniformity among the horsewomen. Some wore the old style habits and derbies of black and sat side saddle. Some wore riding breeches of check cloth and rode astride. Some were in linen habits. The favourite hat among the horse-women was made of the black straw, with the cockade of the Women's Political Union.

Mrs Knoblauch may have cut a dashing figure on her mount in 1912, but most of her work for the cause was done where no reporters were present. The important political work, influencing legislators and politicians by lobbying, forming public opinion and producing information, was carried out behind the scenes. By November 1917, the efforts of the National Suffrage Party achieved suffrage for women in New York. This marked a decisive victory for the cause, and finally, on August 18th, 1920, the XIXth Amendment to the Constitution was signed and all women in the United States who were citizens and of age, could exercise their right to vote.

For Susan B. Anthony, the cause for the vote had become the most urgent of causes and she had argued that other causes for reform could only be achieved once the vote had been won. For other suffragists too, the vote was but the first necessary step towards woman's battle for recognition and emancipation from patriarchal constraints. May Bookstaver Knoblauch's activities after 1920 were no longer reported in the press, but it is unlikely that she would not have continued to support the cause of women's rights. She could and did exercise her vote and her right to participate in elections, but although Gertrude Stein and Mabel Haynes did have the same rights they could not vote as they lived as expatriates and legal provisions for overseas voting were not introduced until 1975. They would have voted for the Republican Party.

Walking

…walking is an alleviation, and yet this astonishes everybody the distance is so sprightly

It was this first hot tired they all had in them now just in its beginning, and they were all in their various ways trying to press themselves to go through it, and they were mostly very good about it and not impatient or complaining. They were now beginning with the dull tired senses of hot trudging when every step has its conscious meaning and all the movement is as if one were lifting each muscle and every part of the skin as a separate action. All the springiness had left them, it was a weary conscious moving the way it always is before one presses through it to the time of steady walking that comes when one does not any longer do it with a conscious sense with each movement, It is not until one has settled to it, the steady walk where one is not conscious of the movement, that you have become really strong to do it, and the whole family were now coming to it, they were just pressing through their first hot tired.

Early in her book *The Making of Americans* Gertrude Stein tells of story of her Jewish ancestors leaving Germany in order move to another life, loading their necessities and the smaller children onto a wagon, and walking beside it, a long and hard walking, the steady walking that had to pass through the pain and tiredness. Such walking was endured by those who were forced to get on the move and by those who decided to displace themselves, like the pioneering ancestors of the Americans.

It is not the sort of walking that is done for the enjoyment of walking itself. There are those who like walking in cities, happily turning down this ally or that, cross into squares, follow avenues, sauntering, picking up speed, slackening pace, resting in cafés. Mabel Haynes was a city walker; she walked about in Boston and Baltimore, in Paris, in Rome, in New York City, in Venice, in Florence, in Vienna, but she did not enjoy walking in the countryside. She preferred to drive about in the countryside. May Bookstaver was a New Yorker and New Yorkers are prodigious walkers. In the countryside she preferred to ride, to sail, to motor.

Gertrude Stein was a walker who liked to walk country lanes as much as city streets.

She had the enjoyment that habitual walkers have, of simply walking, one step after the other, on and on. She had acquired the habit in her early youth, tramping about in the Californian hills, in New England valleys, through the woods of Baltimore. She had a good stride and stamina enough to walk for hours. When she was sitting for her portrait that Picasso was painting, she acquired her habit of walking through Paris: *Practically every afternoon Gertrude Stein went to Montmartre, posed and then later wandered down the hill usually walking across Paris to the rue de Fleurus. She then formed the habit which has never left her of walking around Paris, now accompanied by the dog, in those days alone.*

In Italy, she made Alice B. Toklas walk with her: *It was a very hot Italian day and we started as usual about noon, that being Gertrude Stein's favourite walking hour, because it was hottest and beside presumably Saint Francis had walked it then the oftenest as he had walked it at all hours. We started from Perugia across the hot valley. I gradually undressed, in those days one wore many more clothes than one does now, I even, which was most unconventional in those days, took off my stockings, but even so I dropped a few tears before we arrived and we did arrive.* This was a test of her new friend's mettle, to see if she could have the endurance and the joy of walking with Gertrude Stein under the hot skies of Tuscany. Alice B. Toklas, not an enthusiastic walker, forced herself to keep up. Gertrude Stein could do nothing but yield to such devotion.

The habit of walking, alone, and with her dogs, stood Gertrude Stein in good stead during the Second World War: *I walked a great deal and I cut box hedges, and every night I read the book of prophecy and went promptly to sleep. And none of us talked about the war because there was nothing to say.* Although nobody starved in the Bugey countryside, where they lived, in order to find the better things that make eating pleasurable, such as butter, cream, cakes, she had to walk for miles. Gertrude Stein met other people walking across the Bugey countryside, like her in search of food, or of other supplies, and to pass on news. They would stop and talk to those they met on these walks, and Gertrude Stein liked talking to them all, and so they came to know her as a friendly and talkative woman, a foreigner and one who lived in a manor house, but walking the same roads as they did, daily, and exchanging greetings and news, and so the days of that grim war were made bearable.

Walking, so some people aver, stimulates the brain in a way that sitting down does not. The rhythm of the feet as they touch the ground is the scansion of the most elementary form of poetry. There is skipping and running and trampling and tip-toeing, and all these forms of locomotion have their measures and equivalents, but each person has a walk that's peculiar to hers; mine caused great hilarity when I was in Africa, where the rapid walk of a Londoner was thought quite ludicrous. Gertrude Stein's way of walking can be felt in the lines she wrote, unhurriedly, steadily filling page after page; and what she thought and saw and heard on her walks found its way into her writing – an alleviation.

Wars

Gertrude Stein's book *Wars I Have Seen* was written as a diary during the German occupation of France, but she also muses about the wars that the United States had been engaged in during her lifetime. She liked to ponder the question of these wars' modernity: *the Spanish-American War was the first to be modern war. Modern is like realism, modern is always modern to some one as realism is always real to some one, not to some one but to a great many at one time…what was modern then was seeing all the middle western men, young men, boys too many, going out to san Francisco, and catching everything and then going off in boats to the Philippines.* Young men also went to Cuba, as Charles E. Knoblauch did, who later married May Bookstaver. *The Spanish-*

American War was romance simple and realistic, so Gertrude Stein thought, and for those Rough Riders, like Charles E. Knoblauch, who had a triumphant homecoming, it had been romantic and simple. The twentieth century wars were not romantic. Gertrude Stein and Mabel Haynes experienced the wars of 1914-18 and 1939-45 in Europe. Unlike many of their compatriots, they did not return to their native country on either occasion.

When the Austrian crown prince and his wife were shot in Sarajevo, on June 28th, 1914, Mabel Haynes was living in Palermo with her Austro-Hungarian officer husband Rudolf Leick. She had given birth to her third child, a daughter, less than three weeks before that, on the 11th of June. Her husband had been granted a leave of absence but volunteered for active service and in August joined the 2nd Regiment of Tyrolian Riflemen stationed in South Tyrol. The newspapers suggested that this was going to be a short war, quickly decided; and the Austrians, allied with the much better equipped Germans, were confident that victory would soon be on their side. Mabel Haynes moved her family to Brixen (now Bressanone) in order to be near her husband, and she was delivered of another daughter there on the 14th of July 1915, during a brief lull in the fighting on the Italian front that was close enough for her to hear artillery fire. Thousands of soldiers lost their lives in the battles that were fought in the mountains and Karst plateaus. Rudolf Leick was hit by a piece of rock or some shrapnel, it was never clear exactly what was lodged in his head, and he was declared unfit for combat. Mabel Haynes left the South Tyrol where the fighting was to continue right until the war was over and settled in the Austrian city of Graz. Emma Lootz Erving informs Gertrude Stein in a letter from December 10th 1915 how Mabel Haynes fared: *Her second husband, having some trouble with his head as a result of a fractured skull, is not wanted at the front, and he was in a reserve corps in Fulnek, Moravia, but he was so hellbent on fighting that he was going to the front anyhow to see if they would send him back. Meanwhile Mabel was taking care of three children in a large and commodious schloss without a single modern convenience – and one maid and no money. She is still interested in what is going to happen.*

The civilian population, especially in urban areas, suffered as the war continued. Rationing was introduced in 1915, though the State was not able to meet even these reduced requirements. Mabel Haynes' son Oswald had been ill before, but the poor nutrition caused his state of health to decline rapidly and he died in 1917. She was pregnant with her last child at the time and her second son was born in September the same year. In December the United States declared war on Austro-Hungary and this meant that Mabel Haynes became an enemy alien in Austria and was unable to receive her income from her estate in America. Emma Lootz Erving wrote to Gertrude Stein in 1918: *Mabel Haynes has lost her son from starvation and has been standing in the breadline. Lord help the Austrians – and all the rest of us too.* When the war ended, the fighting ended but the deprivation in the cities continued and in fact worsened. Food sent by America helped to prevent more widespread starvation in the cities, but America was still at war with Austria until 1921, three years after Austro-Hungary had ceased to exist.

May Bookstaver, by then Mrs Charles E. Knoblauch and living in New York, would have heard what happened to Mabel Haynes through letters and she would have read the newspaper reports about the war in the American press. Nothing much is known about her activities between 1914 and 1918 other than the court case fought in 1915 against a law prescribing all dogs to be muzzled in public places and that she visited Cuba with her husband in 1917.

Gertrude Stein's experiences of the Great War were mediated by herself, not least in her books, such as *The Autobiography of Alice B. Toklas*, *Everybody's Autobiography* and *Wars I have seen*, which were all written quite a long time afterwards and they were instrumental in creating an impression of herself not so much as a witness but as a protagonist, a thinking, combative participant who met historical contingency with courage and determination.

When the Austrian Archduke was assassinated Gertrude Stein and Alice B. Toklas were in England. After Germany had invaded Belgium in August 1914, the *casus belli* for Great Britain and France to declare war - Gertrude Stein and Alice B. Toklas were guests of the philosopher Alfred Whitehead and his wife at their country house in Wiltshire. Gertrude Stein and Alice B. Toklas spent the first war winter in Paris, in 27 rue de Fleurus, their first winter alone without Leo Stein who had moved to Italy in April 1914. It was a winter gloomy with frequent blackouts and the threat of Zeppelins and the German army coming ever nearer. Gertrude Stein felt she needed to make money and hoped to do so by having the work that she had done over the last ten years published. This did not happen, and she had to sell Matisse's *La Femme au Chapeau* to her brother Michael. In March 1915, the Zeppelin raids became frequent and frightening and the two women left Paris for Palma de Mallorca, where they stayed until the summer of 1916, when news of the French victory at Verdun encouraged their return. It is a curious coincidence that both Mabel Haynes and Gertrude Stein lived by the Mediterranean during part of the war, though not simultaneously; both with their new spouses and both enraptured by erotic bliss, before the reality of the war put an end to these idyllic intervals.

When Gertrude Stein and Alice B. Toklas returned to Paris, many of their expatriate women friends and acquaintances had begun to engage themselves in the war effort. Gertrude Stein was very taken with the idea of driving a motor vehicle for the American Fund for the French War Wounded. She asked her relatives in the States to collect enough money to send over a Ford van for the purpose. It arrived early in 1917, and Alice B. Toklas and Gertrude Stein reported for duty at the organization's headquarters. They were sent south to distribute parcels ('comfort bags') in the Perpignan area and Nîmes region. They invented their own outfits for the task: *they both wore helmet-shaped hats and belted, big-pocketed coats approximating uniforms; and Gertrude continued to wear sandals and the knitted vest and shirtwaist with gathered sleeves that had already become her trade-mark.* It was physically demanding work, as the van was tough to handle, and they were not seated in a cab but in the open while their supplies were in the covered part of the vehicle. They had to brave the elements, first snow and sleet, then rain and then the fierce southern sun. The reward lay in the human contact: *Driving day and night down the lonely roads they gave lifts to any soldier they saw and, in this way, made 'military godsons'. (…) She liked these French godsons of the first war and the men in the hospitals to whom she and Alice Toklas personally presented the American 'comfort bags', but when the Americans arrived she loved the doughboys best of all. And the soldiers, in spite of Miss Stein's appearance being very odd, specially to the eyes of a Frenchman, loved her.*

Gertrude Stein understood that war work also meant writing about the war and trying to influence American public opinion to support the Allies. When American magazine *Vanity Fair* published a poem that Gertrude Stein had written, 'The Great American Army', which praised the success of the American intervention in the war in France, the author was introduced to the magazine readers not as an intellectual but as an intrepid relief worker: *Gertrude Stein has, since the outbreak of the war, been living in France and working in war relief as an ambulance driver. Few American women have taken a more active part in the conflict than she.* The Armistice came, and Gertrude Stein and Alice B. Toklas were sent to the Alsace region where they saw devastated battle fields and where they distributed clothing and blankets to the civilian population of shelled cities and burnt out villages. They stayed there until May 1919. The French government awarded Gertrude Stein and Alice B. Toklas with *Medailles de la Reconnaissance Française* for their service. Mabel Haynes' husband was awarded a medal for exceptional bravery before the enemy.

Gertrude Stein was in her country house in Bilignin on September the Third 1939, when she heard the news that France, following Britain by a few hours, had declared war on Germany over the invasion of Poland: *We were spending the afternoon with our friends, Madame Pierlot and the d'Aiguys, in September '39 when France declared war on Germany. England had done it first. They all were upset but hopeful, but I was terribly frightened; I had been so sure there was not going to be war and here it was, it was war, and I made quite a scene. I said, 'They shouldn't! They shouldn't!' and they were very sweet, and I apologized and said I was sorry, but it was awful, and they comforted me they, the French, who had so much at stake, and I had nothing at stake comparatively.* When she says that she had nothing at stake, *comparatively,* she, as an American, felt that she had nothing at stake, nor did she have sons or a husband of an age to be called up to arms. She reacted more strongly than her French neighbours by admitting to feeling *terribly frightened.*

Gertrude Stein was sixty-five and Alice B. Toklas sixty-three. They were understandably frightened at the prospect of having to face another war. Yet this time they were not caught out as last time in another country. They thought they would have a better chance of making it through the war away from the capital, and after retrieving their winter clothes and settling their affairs, they locked their flat in rue Christine, having taken a few of the small pictures from their collection from the walls, and drove back to Bilignin: *Those few hours in Paris made us realize that the country is a better place in war than a city. They grow the things to eat right where you are, so there is no privation, as taking it away is difficult, particularly in the mountains, so there was plenty of meat and potatoes and bread and honey and we had some sugar and we even had all the oranges and lemons we needed and dates; a little short of gasoline for the car, but we learned to do what we wanted with that little, so we settled down to a comfortable and pleasantly exciting winter.* This strategy worked out as they managed to have enough fuel and enough food throughout the war. Gertrude Stein's long acquired habit of taking long walks paid off as it helped her to obtain butter and fresh fish, even cakes: *well anyway to-day when I walked my fourteen kilometres to get the cakes a nice country baker makes us and they are mighty good layer cakes, he made a nice one for each of our birthdays, with congratulations written on it in sugar.* Alice B. Toklas's Cookbook (written in 1954) includes a chapter entitled 'Food in the Bugey during Occupation', which strikes a tone made perhaps more cheerful by hindsight. She vaunts their ingenuity in bartering so that they could have lunch parties featuring crawfish and brioche.

In 1943, when the outlook was bleak, and France was divided, Gertrude Stein began to write what was later entitled *Wars I Have Seen*, that chronicles the day to day survival of Gertrude Stein, Alice B. Toklas, and their friends and neighbours in the Bugey. She wrote this in such a simple and straightforward manner (in what she called her *audience writing*) and she puts in the voices of her neighbours, their fears, worries and occasional triumphs, not just as disembodied snippets to be collaged into an abstract pastoral as she had done in *Lucy Church Amiably*. Her talking to everybody about everything could be seen, so Dana Cairns Watson has suggested, as a sort of resistance to the occupation, in the way that such conversations could be a useful passing on of what one had seen or heard. She struck a different tone in the other wartime book, *Mrs Reynolds,* written in her *real writing* style, although the dread of the unfolding war is conveyed vividly enough in it. In both books she also writes of finding solace, as many others did, in reading about the predictions of St. Odile, the Carolingian saint of the Alsace.

From 1941 to 1943, Gertrude Stein was also kept busy by translating the collected speeches of Marshal Pétain into English in order to make the Marshal's ideas better known in the States; she thought of his acquiescence to German occupation of half of France as an act that saved the country from greater evil: *And so we in France having seen France governed, having seen everybody pretty well fed having seen everybody slowly regain their health and strength, felt every one gradually recovering their liberty and their activity, and having seen every time that all being lost actually everything was being held together, I must say little by little the most critical and the most violent of us have come gradually to do what the Maréchal asks all French people to do, to have faith in him and in the fact that France will live.* The endeavour to endear the *Maréchal* to Americans, endeared Gertrude Stein even more to her friend Bernard Faÿ, who had gained a prominent position as head of the National Library of Paris. He had always been an admirer of Gertrude Stein the writer, he had become an intimate friend of hers and Alice B. Toklas, and whatever protection he could affect for his friends was not to be discounted.

The matter of Gertrude Stein's attitude towards Vichy and the Resistance, and how to account for her and Alice B. Toklas' survival as Jewish lesbians in Nazi occupied France, has been much discussed in the last twenty years. In 2003, Janet Malcolm wrote a long article for *the New Yorker,* having consulted the most eminent Stein scholars she could muster – Ulla Dydo, Bill Rice and Edward Burns - to examine what Gertrude Stein had done and what she had written during the war, letters as well as books. She found if not exactly innocence, naivety; by concentrating on getting by, neither Gertrude Stein nor Alice B. Toklas allowed themselves to be conscious of the implications of their friendship with Bernard Faÿ (who had been responsible for many deaths, mainly Freemasons) or to what extent her *liking fascists* had been a mistake. When the deportations of Jews began to be carried out in earnest, reaching the more isolated parts of France in the course of 1942, it was up to the local officials to supply information about any Jews living in there, and there were some *who simply omitted information when it was demanded of them.* The two women were well known and generally well liked around Belley, but there was no knowing for sure that they would, as it turned out, simply not be added to the list. Although Gertrude Stein never directly addressed the fate of Jews in *Wars I Have Seen* her nervousness and fear is palpable. The greater is her relief when the long-promised landing of US troops finally takes place and the Germans begin to retreat: *And now they have just announced on the radio that the Americans are at Grenoble and that is only eighty kilometres away and no opposition in between, oh if they would only come by here. We must see them…. Glory hallelujah Paris is free, imagine it's less than three months since the landing and Paris is free. All these days I did not dare to mention the prediction of Saint Odile, she said Paris would not be burned the devotion of her people would save Paris and it has vive la France. I can't tell you how excited we all are and now if I can only see the Americans come to Culoz I think all this about war will be finished yes I do.*

The war being over, she could tell Eric Sevareid, the war correspondent, that the past five years *had been the happiest years of my life.* In June 1945, together with Alice B. Toklas, she was taken to visit various U.S. Army bases in Germany and they were photographed on the terrace of Hitler's Berchtesgaden retreat, raising their arms in a Hitler salute. The war years had taken its toll on Gertrude Stein's state of health. She never regained the portly indestructibility she had been enjoyed before and was plagued instead by gastric complaints that were eventually diagnosed as stomach cancer. She died on July 27th, 1946.

Mabel Haynes, the American who had divorced her Austrian husband Rudolf Leick in 1927, spent the summer of 1939 in Italy. She had wished to visit Florence again- *I can refresh old memories there* – and hoped to go to the United States from Trieste after a stay in Venice. She needed to raise $1000 and produce an affidavit in order to take her daughter and son-in-law with her. Some difficulty arose, and she had returned to Graz when England and France declared war on Germany. She would not, so she later always insisted, have been able to bear the separation from her children during the war. Mabel Haynes wrote about the fractious situation at her daughter Enid's with her difficult marriage and difficult temper; about young friends that had died on the various fronts and her anxiety about her youngest son Reginald: *I can't sleep any more without medicine but that doesn't matter – that won't be better until Reggie is out of the firing line.* Graz suffered fifty-seven bombing raids and some two thousand civilians died as a result.

In 1945, in the last intensive weeks of fighting and during the worst air raids, Mabel Haynes stayed just outside the city with friends. When Germany surrendered, and the war was over, the Russians occupied Graz until July 24th 1945, when the British took over. Had Mabel Haynes still lived in Linz, she would have been in the American sector and she would have seen the G.I.s that so delighted Gertrude Stein. Mabel Haynes had survived the war, so had her family. Given her fragile state, it was decided that Mabel Haynes better not try to withstand the post-war food shortage for longer than necessary, and at the beginning of October 1946, she boarded an airplane for New York and went on to install herself in a rented flat in Boston. In New York she met May Bookstaver, who had lived through the war years in her apartment on Seventh Street, a widow and in straightened financial circumstances. Gertrude Stein quotes a friend who had lived through the war in the States as having suffered even more: *you do not know about the real hardships of war, over there you were in it you were busy every minute in the midst of it but over here we had the real nervousness and anxiety of war we were not in it we could only suffer about it.*

May Bookstaver might also have suffered the *real nervousness and anxiety of war* while not in it; she would certainly have been glad to see her friend safely back, if in a shocking state. They would have seen the obituary notices about Gertrude Stein and they may have read her book *Wars I have seen.*

Wives

> *An incredibly sweet wife loved by an incredibly loving husband*

Much of the 18th century English literature that Gertrude Stein enjoyed reading concerns young women scheming to become the wives of men that were not only their social superiors but to whom they could bear to be married. The tension between marriage and romantic love continued to be the subject of novels, and among the favourite short words Gertrude Stein liked using, were 'wives', 'marriage' and 'love'.

Educated women of her class and time thought being taken as wives by men as betraying their ideals for *the highest kind of life,* a life free from personal subjection. Especially women engaged in the suffrage movement would *rather live and die an old maid,* as Susan B. Anthony said, who believed that only women who did not *have the special call for special work* should think of marrying men. May Bookstaver was an unlikely person to become a wife in the conventional sense but she must have thought of her husband Charles Knoblauch as an able person willing not to interfere with her 'special work'. She led a professional life by editing the *Birth Control Review,* writing articles, organising political protests, charity events, finding publishers for Gertrude Stein's work, attending salons and running one herself in her fashionable apartment in Seventh Street. Being the wife of a high-flying, flamboyant banker gave her radical political activity a certain cachet not unhelpful to the cause. She was his wife until he died in 1936 and remained his widow as long as she lived. May Bookstaver showed that the New Women of the 20th century did not have to die an old maid, or spend her life with a woman in order to fulfil her aspirations for a useful and interesting life.

Emma Lootz, who had studied with Gertrude Stein and Mabel Haynes at Johns Hopkins Medical School, got married to her fellow student, William Erving, in 1903, a year after they graduated. Theirs was a modern marriage among equals, both working as doctors, and with her having to work in the practice as well as in the household. This double burden was the fate of the modern wife that she bewailed so in her letters to Gertrude Stein.

Mabel Haynes had a generous allowance, an excellent education and an impeccable New England pedigree. She worked as a doctor in Boston for some years while trying to recover from the fall-out of Gertrude Stein's romance with May Bookstaver. She did not seem to relish becoming the wife of a suitable Bostonian. Instead she chose an Austrian officer, and her father paid the commission that the Austrian Crown charged for the privilege. Widowed after six years of marriage, she became the wife of another Austrian officer. Being the wife of a wounded and retired Austrian after the war was very tiresome and it cost her a lot of time, effort and money not to be his wife anymore.

If Gertrude Stein had really hit it off with Leon Solomons, with whom she worked on various psychological experiments at Harvard, and if she had not gone to Baltimore and met May Bookstaver, and if Leon Solomon had not been ill and died, she could have become the wife of the brilliant Leon Solomons and they might have carried on researching together and she might made a name for herself as Gertrude Solomons. It would have pleased her relatives and especially her sister-in-law Sarah Stein, wife of her older brother Michael, who urged her *dear and beloved sister-in-law go and get married – for there is nothing in the whole world like babies.* Gertrude Stein, beloved sister-in-law, sister and niece of her anxious relatives, did not get married in the sense they had envisaged, and she did not produce the sort of babies they had wished her to bear. Gertrude Stein did not become a wife. When she proposed to Alice B. Toklas on a hot day out in the Tuscan countryside in 1908, she was to be the husband in their marriage and that is how she always understood her role, to be *incredibly loving husband* to her *incredibly loving wife.* Being the incredibly loving wife meant doing everything a dutiful and loving wife in a patriarchal family would do, having full responsibility for the smooth running of the household, the provisioning and preparation of meals, the supervision of servants, as well as secretarial work (typing Gertrude Stein's handwritten notes was a daily task), making arrangements for social contacts (by telegram or letters or telephone) and, at such social gatherings, to shield Gertrude Stein from those who might not amuse her, meant sitting with the wives of the interesting men Gertrude Stein found pleasure in talking to.

While Charles E. Knoblauch seems to have given Mrs Charles E. Knoblauch plenty of encouragement and scope to do the things that she was interested in, Gertrude Stein was as egoistical a husband as any patriarch, but she saw it as the prerogative of being a genius rather than a husband. Being an incredibly loving husband entailed a different sort of work than that of the incredibly loving wife and Gertrude Stein wrote about the work of intimacy in a great many texts and the metaphor she uses most is that of giving the wife a cow. There has been much speculation of the meaning of giving the wife a cow, but from a cow is full of potential for sustenance, life itself. By all accounts of their marriage Alice B. Toklas was a wife that had a cow.

Citations

Alcohol
I have seen so many people drunk EA 52
No one in the family EA 120

Alice Babette Toklas
Trembling was all living 'Ada' GAP 16
she did not like it all 'Ada' GAP 16
dynamic magnetism cited in Simon, *Biography of ABT,* 15-21
A liar of the most sordid Leon Katz, 'The First Making of the Making of Americans: A Study Based on Gertrude Stein's Notebooks and Early Versions of her Novel (1902-8); cited in Malcolm, *Two Lives,* 148
Day after day she wept letter by Harriet Levy, cited in Souhami, *Gertrude and Alice,* 135
I got a Gertrude Stein technique Toklas WIR 59
She was slight and dark Dodge Luhan, Intimate *Memories,* 324
Lifting belly LB 3
Baby boy BPAS 158
it does not bother me cited in Souhami, *Gertrude and Alice,* 259
When Alice B. Toklas read the novel Simon, *Biography of ABT* 144
Alice in her widowhood Simon, *Biography of ABT* 211
conversion came over me letter by ABT cited in Souhami, *Gertrude and Alice* 371
The walls were bare letter by ABT cited in Souhami, *Gertrude and Alice,* 376

Analysis
it is so rudimentary to be analysed 'A Box' TB 249
Metaphysics Mary R.S. Creese, *Ladies in the Laboratory? American and British Women in Science, 1800-1900. A Survey to their Contributions to Research.* The Scarecow Press (Lanham, Maryland and London) 1998, 259
Freudian notions Ruddick, *Body, Text, Gnosis,* 54-136
there is no demarcation in Dydo, *The Language that Rises,* 435
Leo Stein on psychoanalysis: Fuller, *Journey Into the Self,* 91-95

Analysis is a womanly word GS, from 'Sentences and Paragraphs', GSR 457

Appetite

And now then as to appetite 'American Biography and why waste it' SWGS 269

Pale yellow complexion FQED 55

 with the collection impounded, James R. Mellow, 'The Stein Salon was the First Museum

of Modern Art", The New York Times December 1st 1968,

https://www.nytimes.com/books/98/05/03/specials/stein-salon.html

Arguments

Quarrelling to me MOA 665

What matters Mellow, *Charmed Circle* 456-6

Mostly everyone MOA 666

Aristocracy

In the American woman QED 59

With us, the manners Mrs M.E.W. Sherwood, *Etiquette. The American Code of Manners. A Study of the Usages, Laws, and Observances Which Govern Intercourse in the Best Circles of American Society.* George Routledge and Sons (New York) 1884, v

the original and beautiful: Mrs John Sherwood 'American Girls in Europe', *The North American Review* 150 (No 43) (June 1890), 688ₛₑₚ

in this American version QED 54

 on Saturday evenings AABT 94-5

We did give a great many parties AABT 247

pardon the fretful aristocrat 'A Long Gay Book', MPGS 100

Aunts

those cheerful pleasant little people AABT 73

She was the quintessence MOA 13

after Gertrude Stein's aunt AABT 172

I was very fond; you could keep everybody EA 131

It is best support Allan 'Patriarchal Poetry', in Dydo, *Language that Rises,* 136

Automobiles and airplanes
Europe and America' WIHS 15
just one day To Do 15
she was enthusiastic' AABT 168
she would regard corners Rogers, http://www.ellensplace.net/gstein4.html
would pull out a pencil Maria Popova, http://www.brainpickings.org/tag/gertrude-stein
everything in America; mostly words of one syllable EA 226, 227
just now are great many are getting killed' EA 255

Baby
Babiest preciousest BPAS 131
Baby Gertrude So GS's aunt, Rachel Kayser, in Wineapple, *Sister Brother*, 15
If two little ones had not died EA 115, 133
Baltimore, Maryland
Baltimore is famous EA 52
the good rich living a standard phrase employed in MOA when Mrs Hershland, the
fictionalised person of Amelia Stein, is mentioned
cheerful life AABT 75
not at all well brought up Sprigge, *GS* 38
legally domiciled in Baltimore cited by Kostelanetz, GSR xviii
This can be Baltimore UK 67
Business in Baltimore need never be finished UK 75
and yes and yes UK 23-24

Bilignin
Lucy Church rented a valuable house LCA 130-1
enjoying using the furniture AABT 223
The landscape at Bilignin 'Lectures in America' GSW 262-3
a one-street, four-or-five house Rogers, *When this you see.* 86

Books
Book was there TB 261
I like book people Emma Lootz Erving letter to GS, December 12th 1909

We bought Jules Verne EA 125

We had by that time EA 120

She reads books AABT 84

I am still like that EA 124

Her library Donald Gallup, 'The Gertrude Stein Collection', *The Yale University Library Gazette.* Vol.22, No.2 (October 1947), 30

A book 'Descriptions of Literature' AGSR 471-4

We will have your book set AABT 245

It was easy AABT 243

Boston marriages

There were, in my parent's circle Helen Howe, *The Gentle Americans, 1864-1960: Biography of a Breed.* Harper & Row (New York) 1965, 83

those friendships F.O. Matthiessen & Kenneth B. Murdock (ed.) *The Notebooks Henry James.* Oxford University Press (New York) 1947, 47

I share with her thoughts Florence Converse, *Diana Victrix: a novel.* Houghton, Mifflin and Company (Boston and New York) 1897, 214 SEP

Bryn Mawr

Is there any place in the world Georgiana Goddard King, 'Free Among the Dead', in Margaretta Morris & Louise Buffum Congdon (eds), *A Book of Bryn Mawr Stories.* Annotated edition, The Bi-Co Press (New York City) 2011, 72-3

which are made to harmonize Mary Patterson McPherson, 'A Century of Building at Bryn Mawr', *Proceedings of the American Philosophical Society* Vol.142, No.3 (Sept. 1989), 400 *if the Bryn Mawr woman* M. Carey Thomas, 'Notes for the Opening address at Bryn Mawr College 1899', reprinted in Barbara M. Cross (ed.), *The Educated Woman in America.* Columbia University (New York) 1965, 139

they even had the photographs EA 158

Busts

as an exceedingly attractive www.the crimson.com/article/1959/2/18/Gertrude-stein-at-radcliffe-most-brilliant/

was very short and buxom Leo and Gertrude Stein's art collection, March 2 2010
https:/julienimitz.wordpress.com/1-stein-corporation
like and like and likely 'Lipchitz' AGSR 491
like a goddess of pregnancy
www.thecjm.or/storage/images/text_pages/presskit/Gertrude
Stein_CompleteWallText.pdf
she looked now a shrivelled Raphael Rubinstein, 'Imperturbable Buddha? Not likely. Why
Gertrude Stein didn't like this likeness, or likenesses, for that matter.' July 25,
2007*Poetry Foundation.* www.poetryfoundation.org/article/179961

Cancer
She was lost among them MOA 113-4
Several times as many people http://demography.cpc.unc.edu/2014/06/16/mortality-
and-cause-of-death-1900-v-2010/; also http://www.businessinsider.com/leading-
causes-of-death-in-1900-and-today-2014-6?IR=T
after the anaesthetic was administered Rogers, *When this you see*, 247

Catholicism
Avec Gertrude Bernard Faÿ , in Will, *Unlikely Collaboration*, 205
Catholic to be turned 'Rooms' TB 299
It had been made liveable AABT 54
Lucy Church heard LCA 97
A saint a real saint 'France' GAP 33-4
by recasting traditional Linda Watts, "Can Women Have Wishes": Gender and Spiritual
Narrative in Gertrude Stein's "Lend a Hand or Four Religions" *Journal of Feminist
Studies in Religion*, Vol.10, Nr. 2 (fall 1994),54
When Toklas later Maurice Grosser, "Visiting Gertrude Stein," *New York Review of Books*
33:17 (Nov.6, 1986), 36

Character
Then there will be realised 'The gradual Making of The Making of Americans' SWGS 231
The differences between Leo Stein, 'Last notes a few days before Leo Stein's death on July
29th 1947, in Fuller, *Journey Into the Self*, 298

While I was at college The gradual Making of The Making of Americans' SWGS 271 *TYPE II., CASE I* "Cultivated Motor Automatism: A Study of Character in Its Relation to Attention." Motor Automatism. 1898. New York: The Phoenix Book Shop, 1969, 27-37

She always says she dislikes AABT 83

so little of my past EA xxiv

the idea of describing The gradual Making of The Making of Americans' SWGS 276

Then there will be realised MOA 226

Gertrude's whole interest Leon Katz, 'Weininger and the Making of Americans', *Twentieth Century Literature,* Vol. 24, No.1, Gertrude Stein Issue (Spring 1978), 18, 21

had successfully integrated quoted in Fuller, *Journey Into the Self,* viii

Charles E. Knoblauch

where he had the reputation From biographical note on his brother Edward Knoblock, http://fantastic-writers-and-the-great- war.com/the-writers/edward-knoblock/ꞮSEP

Nothing is known C. E. Knoblauch, 64, Rough Rider, Dies' *New York Times* Friday, October 12, 1934;

http://timesmachine.nytimes.com/timesmachine/1934/10/121185

Knoblauch [is] a giant Edward Marshall, *The Story of the Rough Riders,* 45

https://archive.org/stream/storyrough00marsrich#page/n325/mode/2upp.IX-X

Childhood

About an unhappy childhood EA 59

I led in my childhood said by 'Alice B. Toklas' in AABT 4

I am the youngest EA 3

When I was young EA 3

I am a little girl 'The World is Round' GSW 538

Cigars and cigarettes

Left open 'A Box' TB 250

Fellow students Kathleen Waters Sander, 'The Unknown Gertrude', *Johns Hopkins Medical News,* Spring/Summer 2002;

http://www.hopkinsmedicine.org/hmn/S02/annals.html

the pleasures of conversation Constance Fenimore Woolson, "Miss Grief" (1880) in Jan Myers Weimer, *Women Artists, Women Exiles. "Miss Grief: and Other Stories. Constance Fenimore Woolson.* Rutgers University Press (New Brunswick and London) 1988, 268
the cigarette became a symbol Amanda Amos, Margaretha Haglund, 'From social taboo to "torch of freedom"; the marketing of cigarettes to women.' *Tobacco Control,* Vol.9, No.1 (March 2000), 4

Clothes
There was nothing to distinguish QED 117
A LONG DRESS 'Objects' TB 252
refused to be bound from the Radcliffe Quarterly 1946, cited in Simon, *GS Remembered,* 13
What she wears becomes Mitranto, *Woman Without Qualities,* 53
That is one of the nice things EA 140
Pierre Balmain so in the film *When this You See Remember Me* by Perry Miller Adato (1970)

Clubs
Our Modern celebrated Clubs so Joseph Addison, *The Spectator,* IX, Mar. IO, I7IO/II, cited by David S. Shields, 'Anglo-American Clubs: Their Wit, Their Heterodoxy, Their Sedition', *The William and Mary Quarterly,* Vol. 51, No.2 (April 1994), 267
Mr. Haynes was never a club man from 'John Cummings Haynes' *Biographical History of Massachusetts. Biographies and Autobiographies of the Leading Men of the State.* New York, 1909
http://www.archive.org/stream/biographicalhistmass01elio/biographicalhistmass01el io_djvu.txt*B*

Communism and fascism
Do away with money; passion to be enslaved cited by Will, *Unlikely Collaboration,* 95
Roosevelt tries to spend EA 3
For Gertrude Stein and to the other artists http://www.writing.upenn.edu/~afilreis/88/stein-per-gold.html
Writers only think from *Partisan Review,* cited by Renate Stendhal, 'Why the Witch-Hunt against Gertrude Stein?' June 4th 2012; http://www.tikkun.org/nextgen/why-the-

witch-hunt-against-gertrude-stein
It could be a puzzle PF 65

Cooking
Alas, alas the pull 'Milk' TB 276
I do inevitably AABT 41
Corsets
the corset is Veblen, *The Theory of the Leisure Class,* 113-114
Gertie flopping around in Sprigge, *GS,* 36
Because of the heat Toklas, WIR 53

Countenance
If can in countenance 'New' YGS 154

Dance
Dance a clean dream 'Rooms' TB 299
And the minuet EA 89
Dancing excites me tremendously AABT 136
Susie Asado GAP 13
extraordinary melody GSW 306-7
This one is one being dancing 'Orta or One Dancing' GSR 121-36

Depressions and the Great Depression
They believed the depression EA 86
There is evidence Holland Clotter 'Modern is Modern is..' *New York Times.* June 2nd
2011
From a clinical perspective Three Lives annotated by Jack Coulehan, July 5yh 1998:
http://medhum.med.nyu.edu/view/1340
All this time EA 49-50
When the success began article in *Vanity Fair,* cited in Mellow, *Charmed Circle,* 358-9
I wish I could tell you
https://archive.org/stream/brynmawralumnaeb11bryn/brynmawralumnaeb11bryn_d
jvu.txt

because he is removing Lansing Warren, 'Gertrude Stein Views Life and Politics', *New York Times,* May 6th 1934, 9

Doctors

knowing what such an honorary degree in Dydo, *GS: The Language that Rises,* 611, note 18

There was great excitement AABT 82-3

They had some troubles MOA 129

Then, however, the surgeons Toklas, WIR 186

Dogs

Qu'est ce que c'est HTW 9

Gertrude Stein always AABT 210

I am I because my little dog much used sentence throughout the 1930s; see 'Geographical History of America' GSW 401

Kuroki is the devoted subject El Paso Morning Times, Vol.35, Thursday July 29 1915

that the Board of Health 'Court Rules Dogs Must be Muzzeld', *New York Times* February 25 1915

However further the case El Paso Morning Times, Vol.35, Thursday July 29 1915

In December 1911 Dorothy Norman, *Alfred Stieglitz, An American Seer.* Random House (New York) 1970, 112

one man in this country Rachel Cohen, *A Chance Meeting. Intertwined Lives of American Artists and Writers 1854-1967.* Jonathan Cape (London) 2004, Chapter 14

we had a dog AABT 164-5

We now had our country house AABT 247

the French men and women; Basket liked it EA 76

have no sense of home EA 49

"Le roi est mort" in Brinnin, Third Rose, 364

(…) it was absolutely unbelievable WIHS 215

took him down WIHS 238

We called him Byron; Basket was happy EA 36

I always write about dogs EA 176

Dreams

A novel is what you dream 'The Superstitions of Fred Anneday, Annday, Anday' TGSR 84-85

using a mode of narration Cynthia Secor, 'Ida, a Great American Novel', *Twentieth Century Literature*, Vol.24, No.1, Gertrude Stein Issue (Spring 1978), 103

When she shuts her eyes 'What Does She See When She Shuts Her Eyes' GSW 491

Eating

Eating is a subject AABT 147

vigorous egotistic sensual natures MOA 463

a very hearty eater so Michael Stein, letter to Meyer Stein, cited by Wineapple, *Sister Brother*, 26

There are many ways MOA 120

Gertrude Stein never likes her food hot AABT 114

The only way Toklas, *Cookbook* 37

contain any of the ingredients Watson, GS, 62

It was a shame 'Food' TB 285

Emma Lootz Erving

Emma was not that one 'A Long Gay Book' GMP 95

Fathers and daughters

There is too much fathering AABT 113

was very proud of his children; ending with the angry word MOA 45

free herself Ruddick, *Reading GS,* 113

Then one morning EA 120

Life without a father; we had our time EA 121

drew a very unpleasant QED 74

Films

My life has been troublous Mabel Haynes, letter to Gabrielle Bett, April 28th 1944

Well however we went to tea EA xxiv-v

Charlie Chaplin was like that AABT 162

Not really Bennet Cerf, 'Notable New Yorkers' 1967, Session 6, see
http://www.columbia.edu/cu/lweb/digital/collections/nny/cerfb/transcripts/cerfb_
1_6_284.html; also http://allanellenberger.com/tag/gertrude-stein/
Of course I did not think of it GSW 293-295
it gave me a funny feeling EA 243
Goes home 'Portraits and Repetions' GSR 434
it was William Cook AABT 162
Deux soeurs qui ne sont pas soeurs 'Film' GSR 436-7
her theories are ideally Beth Hutchinson, 'Gertrude Stein's Film Scenarios.' *Literature/Film
Quarterly*, Vol.17, No.1 (1989), 37

Friendship
Sometimes in Paris EA 100
In friendship TL 49

Grace Constant Lounsbery
a valiant little thing Gertrude Atherton, *Adventures of a Novelist.* Liveright (New York)
1932, 326
she was born in New York A.A.G. Bennett, 'A Short Biography of Miss Grace Constant
Lounsbery', in *Maha Bodhi*, Vol,.73/3-4 (January-February 1965), 83
I find her so solidly clever cited in Emily Wortis-Leider, *California's Daughter. Gertrude
Atherton and Her Times.* Stanford University Press (Stanford California) 1991, 192
the fateful twenty-ninth year MOA 473
She is becoming more Emma Lootz Erving, letter to GS, May 4th 1906
a striking figure cited in Joel Sachs, *Henry Cowell: A Man made of Music.* Oxford University
Press (Oxford) 2012, 122
Grace Lounsbery, an early acquaintance Toklas, WIR 69-70

Hair
A package and a filter 'Rooms' TB 293
her lovely, thick Ernest Hemingway, *A Moveable Feast.* Vintage Books (London) 2000
(1936), 13
That night Gertrude said Toklas WIR 148-9

Handbags
A purse was not green 'Objects' TB 254
Androgynous Ruddick, *Reading GS*, 205
the promiscuity alenier.blogspot.co.uk/2012/01/steppingon-tender-buttons-frightful.htlml

Handwriting
writing automatically Dodge Luhan, *Intimate Memories,* 328
a little handwriting 'A Sonatine Followed By Another', TYGS, 287
They asked the children AABT 75-6

Hats
Having gone to the opening AABT 40
She liked hats AABT 14
Gertrude Stein used to comment Simon, *GS Remembered*, 96
Colored hats are necessary 'Objects' TB 258
Gertrude says cartoon by Alan Dunn, *The New Yorker,* October 27th 1934
 http://www.nytimes.com/books/98/05/03/specials/stein-arrives.html
The hat was a Stein hat in *New York Times,* October 25th 1934
It's just a hat Rogers, *When This You See,* 126

Itha Heissig Pielsticker-Karminski
Mabel Haynes Leick's daughter Bryn Mawr Alumnae Bulletin, 1927, Class notes by Mary M. Campbell'
https://archive.org/stream/brynmawralumnaeb07bryn/brynmawralumnaeb07bryn_djvu.txt

Jealousy
In loving some MOA 486
I was a sad resisting MOA 609
Baby preciousest BPAS 131
she was just jealous Ernest Hemingway, *The Green Hills of Africa.* Scribner's (New York) 1935, 65

She destroyed quoting Ulla E. Dydo, in Janet Malcolm, 'Gertrude Stein's War', *The New Yorker*, June 2nd 2003; http://www.newyorker.com/magazine/2003/06/02/gertrude-steins-war

Throughout the stanzas Dydo, *The Language that Rises*, 490

Jewellery

Please be, 'Preciosilla' GSSW 489

says that I am to say in Fuller, *Journey into the Self*, 18

thus *forming the only ostensibly "feminine"* Vincent Giroud, 'Picasso and Gertrude Stein', *Metropolitan Museum of Modern Art Bulletin*. New Series, Vol. 64, NO. 3 (Winter 2007), 23

thought that her voice Toklas WIR 26

Nancy H. Rummage, *Gertrude Stein's Brooches,* Metropolitan Museum Journal, Vol. 45 (2010), 225

Manet for the impecunious AABT 50

Alice wore straight dresses Dodge Luhan, *Intimate Memories*, 324

Jews

Can a Jew be wild 'Have the Attacked Mary. He Giggled' GSSW 472

Nobody in Krumpendorf Mabel Haynes, letter to Gabrielle Horner, August 5th 1936

The Jew shall marry cited by Malcolm, *Gertrude and Alice,* 190

Adele was aroused from it QED 102

while the reaction is about the physical touch; This representation Concetta Principe, 'The Trauma of *The Making of Americans: Stein and Protestant America'*, *Interdisciplinary Literary Studies*, Vol. 15, No. 2 (2013), 254-5

filled dozens of manuscript books; they persistently and consciously educated themselves Amy Feinstein, 'Gertrude Stein, Alice B. Toklas and Albert Barnes. Looking like Jew in the Autobiography of Alice B. Toklas', *Shofar*, Vol. 25, No. 3 (Spring 2007), 51; 52-3

Konrad Heissig

The army severely István Deák, *Beyond Nationalism. A Social & Political History of the Habsburg Officer Corps 1848-1918.* Oxford University Press (Oxford) 1990, 19-20

Laughter

Go red go red 'Objects' TB 260

people roaring with laughter; upset by them all AABT 35

Laugh if you like Robert Bartlett Hass, 'Gertrude Stein Talking – A Transatlantic Interview', in Karen Leick, *GS and the Making of an American Celebrity*, 53

charmed by the lightness Mellow, *Charmed Circle*, 14

deep, rich, contralto; she had an exceptional, a rare laugh film clip (Mytelene Films) formerly available on YouTube

Gertrude rocking happily Steward, *Dear Sammy*, 9

fine large laugh Toklas, *Cookbook*, 259

She walked heavily up and down cited in Simon, *Gertrude and Alice*, 103

had a hard-forced laughter TL 83

He sang when he was happy TL 100

full on the earth TL 191

euphoria and brilliant storms Toklas, *Cookbook* 259

Place the laughter where the smile is 'A Long Gay Book' GMP 97

Stein knew that a laughing life Sara Crangle, *Prosaic Deserts: Modernism, Knowledge, Boredom, Laughter and Anticipation.* Edinburgh University Press (Edinburgh) 2010, 135

Letters

like roundelays of sprightliness Norman Holes Pearson, 'The Gertrude Stein Collection', *The Yale University Library Gazette*, Vol.16, Nr.3 (1942), 47

Some men and women are *inquisitive* MOA 556-7

a first close-up Simon, *Biography of ABT*, 49

Sometimes one reads a letter MOA 441

Mrs. Redfern arose QED 46-7

I am not satisfied AFAM 163

Mabel Foote Weeks

and the allure of seeing May Wagner-Martin, *Favored Strangers,* 113

The Portrait I am very glad to own in Gallup, *The Flowers of Friendship,* 67-68

will endure long after in Fuller, *Journey Into the Self,* IX

It is in the variety Mabel Foote Weeks, 'The True Measure of Success' *The American Scholar*, Vol. 19, No. 2 (Spring 1950), 233

Marion Walker Williams

I have been in Baltimore, in Wagner-Martin, *Favored Strangers,* 113

There was great excitement AABT 82

It was good to see you Gallup, *Flowers of Friendship,* 223

Marriage is an admirable institution you Gallup, *Flowers of Friendship,* 23-4

Money

It is a very difficult thing MOA 487

There is no doubt about it EA 81

Before one is successful EA 27

I had never made any money before EA 28

Every now and then EA 28

money who likes money Geographical History of America' GSW 454

I know a lot about money EA 28

It did not frighten Vanity Fair. September 1934;

http://www.vanityfair.com/culture/1934/09/gertrude-stein-my-success-essay

There is not enough money see Bryce Conrad, 'Gertrude Stein in the American Marketplace', *Journal of Modern Literature* Vol.19, No. 2 (Autumn 1995), 215-33

If you write the way What is English Literature' GSW 223

Music

A cup is readily 'Food' TB 278

I came not to care Brinnin *Third Rose,* 21

Music she only cared for AABT 75

a charming dinner guest AABT 169

she delighted in listening AABT 229

He frosts his music Watson, *Prepare for Saints,* 42

to improvise on a piano EA 15

Just as we were sitting down WIHS 246

I had received a parchment Toklas WIR 14

For what he said about Bach Sprigge *GS* 158

Negroes

"Negro" is a fine word W.E.B DuBois, *The Crisis* (March 1928), 96

I am afraid that I can never write GS letter to Mabel Weeks, in Souhami, *Gertrude and Alice,* 93

I was brought up EA 225

Spear contended John Buescher, 'Charles Spear', *Dictionary of Unitarian and Universalist Biography; http://uudb.org/articles/charlesspear.html*

Originally associated Atkins, *Biographical History of Massachusetts,* 159; https://archive.org/stream/biographicalhistmass01elio/biographicalhistmass01elio_djvu.txt

Of all the crimes Knoblauch, Mary. Letters to Angelina Weld Grimke. 4th and 13th October 1920. Angelina Weld Grimke Papers. Box 38-1, Folder 10.

She had youth TL 99

This brings me to fact in Fuller, *Journey into the Self,* 137

"No, I ain't no common nigger" TL 78

disparagingly or approvingly James Smethurst,*The African American Roots of Modernism. From Reconstruction to the Harlem Renaissance.* The University of North Carolina Press (Chapel Hill) 2011, 179

The story of the Three 'Among Negroes' UK 60

the encounter between James Donald, *Some of the Days: Black Stars, Jazz Aesthetics, and Modernist Culture.* Oxford University Press (New York) 2015, 24-25

Carl Van Vechten sent us quantities AABT 237

I thought she had nothing to offer Claude McKay, *A Long Way from Home.* Edited and with an introduction by Gene Andrew Jarrett. Rutgers University Press (New Brunswick, New Jersey, and London) 1975, 204

delighted delighted Burns, *The Letters of GS and Carl van Vechten,* 131

there were school houses EA 249

New Orleans Negroes EA 222

he does not get the same justice EA 238

the man who played Porgy EA 242

The whites always kind of resisted Watson, *Prepare for Saints,* 251 *as if she had herded her thoughts* Ben Burns, *Nitty Gritty, A White Editor in Black Journalism.* University Press of Mississippi (Jackson) 1996, p. 77-80

Nerves

Some have all their living MOA 622

not Great Britain George M. Beard, 'Neurasthenia, or Nervous Exhaustion', *Boston Medical and Surgical Journal* 3 (1869), 217-18

even a tiny excess Barbara Sicherman, 'The Uses of Diagnosis: Doctors, Patients, and Neurasthenia', *Journal of the History of Medicine and Allied Sciences.* Vol. 32, No. 1 (January 1977) 34

engage in vigorous physical activity Anne Stiles, 'Go rest, young man'. *Monitor on Psychology* (January 2012) Vol.43, No.1, 32. http://www.apa.org/monitor/2012/01/go-rest.aspx

whether my attempts to teach her in Steven Meyer, *Gertrude Stein and the Correlations,* 79

Some of them have in them MOA 194

I am all unhappy MOA 348

Then also beside the curtain LOP xxx

New York was coming nearer EA 144

Miss Stein gets up every morning Janet Flanner, James Thurber, and Harold Ross, 'The Talk of the Town. Tender Buttons', *The New Yorker* October 12, 1934, http://www.newyorker.com/magazine/1934/10/13/tender-buttons

Pens and pencils

My dear Carl Burns, *The Letters of GS and Carl van* Vechten, 185

Peeled pencil 'Objects' TB 262

She refused to accept Leonard Lyons, 'The Lyons Den', *Pittsburgh Gazette* September 3rd 1946, 19

I am writing all this 'Geographical History of America' GSW 455

one may hear Ruddick, *Reading GS,* 211

In "Peeled Pencil" Ruddick, *Reading GS* 212

Perfume

Of course to have a lesson AABT 26

What is a sentence HTW 170

What is a cook 'G.M.P' GMP 275

Fania has discovered Burns, *The Letters of GS and Carl van* Vechten, 217

Photographs

A regret a single regret 'What Happened' GAP 209

It was one of the little AABT 197-8

At any rate AABT 140

Act III 'Photograph' ASR 346

Photographs are small 'Photograph' ASR 344

Reading

She read anything AABT 74

I do like reading writing 'What is English Literature' GSW 213

All our family Mabel Haynes letter to Gabrielle Bett, February 2nd 1951

It was funny that AABT 237

From her eighth year AABT 74

my brother and I EA 55

really being alone EA 221

reading as conversation Chessman, *The Public is invited to Dance*, 8

taking language apart Introduction ASR 9

Ways of Not Reading Natalia Cecire, 'Ways of Not Reading Gertrude Stein', *ELH*, Vol. 82, No. 1 (Spring 2105), 281-312

But do you never read French AABT

you cannot tell what a book is AABT 70

Once the lecture written AABT 233

Nobody was prepared Brinnin, *Third Rose*, 283

I am going to read 'The Gradual Making of The Making of Americans' SWGS 208

and reading what others MOA 389

Romance

There is some relation 'Geographical History of America' GSW 435

That man Rochester Mabel Haynes, letter to Gabrielle Horner, March 22nd 1948 *romance is nothing more* Robert Lowie, *Social Organization.* Rinehart & Co (New York) 1948, 220

So those who create from 'America and France' in Winnet, *Writing back,* 207

Mrs Lehntman was the romance TL 47

Romance is the ideal TL 50

Sometimes I am almost MOA 458

Romance is the only 'Geographical History of America' GSW 443

Rooms

Mabel Neathe's room QED 70

It was good solid riches MOA 28

their *brass rails were polished* Sprigge, *GS,* 39

Against the walls AABT 9

The studio walls Toklas, WIR 27

Oh, I can remember Florian Vetch, "Desultory Correspondence. An Interview with Paul Bowles'", in *Sporadische Korrespondenz: Ein Interview mit Paul Bowles über Gertrude Stein.* 1995 http://www.paulbowles.org/vetsch.html

if expression has emotion 'G.M.P' GMP 214

A little sign of an entrance 'Rooms' TB 290

corners gathered together 'Rooms' TB 297

Rudolf Franz Leick

very temperamental Qualifikationsliste 1907, 1912; War Archive Vienna

arriving from South Tyrol Anton Graf Bossi-Fedrigotti, *Kaiserjäger Ruhm und Ehre. Nach dem Kriegstagebuch des Oberst v. Cordier.* Leopold Stocker Verlag (Graz, Stuttgart) 1977, 134

Servants

There were then the servants MOA 168

Servant girl being MOA 172

I must tell a little AABT 7

we gave up having one servant EA 34

the house too large EA 37-8

A very serious old pair EA 48

We love him EA 102

Unfortunately there have been too many Toklas, *Cookbook,* 167

while a great cook sat by Toklas, *Cookbook,* 210

Her expectations were severe Simon, *Biography of ABT,* 204-5

Mabel was taking care letter to GS dated December 10th 1915

Sex

The one she was actively MOA 591

The objections to the free dissemination Mary Knoblauch, Editorial Comment, *Birth Control Review.* Vol. III, November 1919 (New York), 3

As labor was done more and more 'The Value of College Education for Women', The Baltimore Museum of Art Library and Archives, Claribel and Etta Cone Paper, p. 10; http://cdm15264.contentdm.oclc.org/cdm/ref/collection/p15264dc/id/454

intensely on the lips; Then for the first time QED 66

It was now no longer TL 94

Jeff Campbell never could forget TL 189

is May, the elusive, Ruddick, *Reading GS,* 107

Caesar or *cows* eg: Chessman, *The Public in Invited to Dance;* Stimpson, 'Gertrude Stein and the Transposition of Gender', in Miller, *The Poetics of Gender;* Dydo, *Gertrude Stein;* Cope, *Passionate Collaborations*

Lifting belly in here LB 43-44

There is no point in it Mellow, *Charmed Circle,* 263

I always wanted letter to W.G.Rogers, July 29 1948, cited in Stant Trybulski, The Hemingway Attack (Part iii) http://stantrybulski.com/2014/07/la-generation-merdue-hemingway-gertrude-stein/

Such a strong look Dodge Luhan, *Intimate Memories,* 332

every "may" Dydo, *The Language that Rises,* 502

whose *angular form* QED 491-501

she offends my Puritan sense MH letter to Gabrielle Horner, June 5th 1951

that passion was sex Horowitz, *Power and Passions,* 286-291

Shoes, sandals

A lean on the shoe 'Suzie Asado' GSSW 482

Leurs pieds nus cited by Willard Bohn, 'Apolinnaire chez le Stein', *Que Vlo Ve?* Serie 4 No 8 octobre- decembre 1999, 151

in bare feet Samuel Barlow in Simon, *GS Remembered,* 67

Gertrude Stein wore AABT 116

Shoes 'Objects' TB 260

Alice's [ale less] Ruddick, *Reading GS,* 226

boots beautifully made Toklas, WIR 57

Sleep

why is not sleeping 'Rooms' TB 291

circled around each other warily reported by Edward Field, *The Man who would marry Susan Sontag: and other intimate literary portraits of the Bohemian Era.* The University of Wisconsin Press (Madison, Wisconsin) 2005, 189-90

mechanized state G. I. Gurdieff, *Belzebub's Tales to His Grandson.* All and Everything. First Series, http://www.holybooks.com/wp-content/uploads/Beelzebubs-Tales-to-His-Grandson-by-G-I-Gurdjieff.pdf, p. 432; see also Colin Wilson, *G. I. Gurdjieff, The War Against Sleep.* The Aquarian Press (Wellingborough, Northamptonshire) 1986, 45

When I speak of human energizing
https://archive.org/stream/energiesofmen00jameuoft/energiesofmen00jameuoft_djvu.txt

But often the birds AABT 41

I never get up early EA xxii

Only of course Rogers, *When this you see,* 158

Baby precious BPAS 8

There were Zeppelin alarms AABT 41

I walked a great deal 'A Picture of Occupied France', GSSW 549

Talking and Listening

I always as I admit 'The Making of the Making of the Americans' GSW 270

I cannot remember not talking 'The Making of the Making of the Americans' GSW 270-1

Teaching

and Hutchins said to me EA 183-4

She being that one; That one being one teaching 'Many Many Women' GMPGS 165

Tempers and Temperament

It is hard living down; she was a resisting sensitive MOA 569

In the eighteenth century cited by Steven Meyer in MOA xxvi

the sweet gentle little mother MOA 24, 26, 53

The little stubborn temper MOA 53

not an angry or sullen person MOA 24

Votes for Women

Thanks dear Susan B 'The Mother of Us All' GSW 810

Anne alone 'The Mother of Us All', GSW 814

I always did want letter to Virgil Thompson, LGSVT 269

asserts a historical continuity Mary Chapman, *Making Noise, Making News: Suffrage Print Culture and U.S. Modernism.* Oxford University Press (New York) 2014, 207

Writer of articles John William Leonard (ed.) *Womens' Who's Who of America.* The American Commonwealth Company (New York) 1914, 464

Walking

walking is an alleviation 'Rooms' TB 294

It was this first hot MOA 40

Practically every afternoon AABT 49

It was a very hot italian day AABT 89

I walked a great deal 'A Picture of Occupied France' SWGS 549

Wars

Spanish-American War WIHS 39-40

They both wore helmet-shaped hats Brinnin, *Third Rose,* 221

Driving day and night Sprigge, GS 122-23

Gertrude Stein has cited in Wagner-Martin, *Favored Strangers,* 141

We were spending the afternoon; Those few hours in Paris 'A Picture of Occupied France',
GSSW 543-4

well anyway WIHS 178

And so we in France cited in Will, *Unlikely Collaboration,* 143

who simply omitted information so Edward R. Burns, 'Gertrude Stein: a complex itinerary
1940-1944' in Charles Bernstein, 'Gertrude Stein's War Years: Setting the Record
Straight' *Jacket* 2017; http://jacket2.org/article/gertrude-stein-complex-itinerary-
1940%E2%80%931944

And now they have just announced WIHS 237

had been the happiest years cited in Mellow, *Charmed Circle,* 456

you do not know WIHS 212

Wives

An incredibly sweet BPAS 49

dear and beloved sister-in-law cited in Wineapple, *Sister Brother,* 115

Note: Unreferenced, unpublished letters are either from the Gertrude Stein and Alice
B. Toklas Papers at the Yale Collection of American Literature or from the private
collection of Gwendolyn Leick

Works by Gertrude Stein

AABT *The Autobiography of Alice B. Toklas.* Vintage Books (New York) 1990 (1933)

AFAM *As Fine as "Melanctha"(1914-1930).* Books for Libraries Press (Freeport, New
York) 1954

EA *Everybody's Autobiography.* Virago Press (London) 1985 (1937)

GEP in *Geography and Plays.* Dover Publications, Inc. (Moneola, New York) 1999
(1922)

GAP, *Geography and Plays.* Dover Publications (Mineolo, New York) 1999

GMP *Matisse Picasso and Gertrude Stein with two shorter stories.* Something Else Press
(Barton, Berlin, Millerton) 1972

HTW *How to Write.* Sun and Moon Press (Los Angeles) 1995 (1931)

Ida, *Ida. A Novel.* Vintage Books (New York) 1968 (1941)

LB *Lifting Belly.* Edited by Rebecca Mark. Naiad Press (Tallahassee, Florida) 1989 (1953)

LCA *Lucy Church Amiably.* Something Else Press (New York) 1969 (1930)

MOA *The Making of Americans.* Dalkey Archive Press (Normal, Illinois) 1995 (1926)

PAP *Portraits and Prayers.* Random House (New York) 1934

PF *Paris, France.* Personal Recollections. Peter Owen (London) 1995 (1940)

QED *Fernhurst, Q.E.D., and other early writings.* Peter Owen (London) 1972

SIM *Stanzas in Meditation.* Part II.i Sun and Moon Press (Los Angeles) 1994 (1956)

TL *Three Lives.* Penguin Books (London) 1997 (1907)

TB *Three Lives & Tender Buttons.* Edited by Diana Souhami, Signet Classic (New York) 2003 (1914)

To Do: A Book of Alphabets and Birthdays. Green Integer (Copenhagen and Los Angeles) 2001 (1957)

UK *Useful Knowledge.* Station Hill Press (Barrytown, New York) 1988 (1928)

WIHS *Wars I have Seen.* Brilliance Books. Plain Edition (London) 1984 (1945)

Collected Editions

AAB *Gertrude Stein, Alphabets and Birthdays.* Vol. 7 of Vol. 7 of The Yale Edition of the Unpublished Writings of Gertrude Stein. Books for Libraries (Freeport)1957

ASR Dydo, Ulla E. (ed) *A Stein Reader. Gertrude Stein.* Southwestern University Press (Evanston, Illinois) 1993

BPAS Turner, Kay (ed.) *Baby Precious Always Shines. Selected Love Notes between Gertrude Stein and Alice B. Toklas.* St. Martin's Press (New York) 1999

GSR Kostelanetz, Richard (ed.), *The Gertrude Stein Reader.* Cooper Square Press (New York) 2002

GSS Retallack, Joan (ed.), *Gertrude Stein, Selections.* University of California Press (Berkeley, Los Angeles, London), 2008

GSW Stimpson, Catharine and Harriet Chessman (eds), *Gertrude Stein. Writings 1932-1946.* The Library of America (New York) 1998

LOP Van Vechten, Carl (ed.), *Last Operas and Plays.* With an Introduction by Bonnie Marranca. Johns Hopkins University Press (Baltimore and London) 1995

OAP Mellow, James R. (ed.) *Operas and Plays. Gertrude Stein.* Station Hill Press (Barrytown, New York) 1987

SWGS Van Vechten, Carl (ed.), *Selected Writings of Gertrude Stein.* Random House (New York) 1946

YGS Kostelanetz, Richard (ed.) *The Yale Gertrude Stein. Selections.* Yale University Press (New Haven and London) 1980

Works by Alice B. Toklas

Cookbook *The Alice B. Toklas Cookbook.* Serif (London) 1994 (1954)

WIR *What is Remembered. An Autobiography.* Cardinal (London) 1989 (1963)

Letters

Burns, Edward (ed.) *Staying on Alone. Letters of Alice B. Toklas.* Vintage Books (New York) 1975 (1973)

-------------------*The Letters of Gertrude Sten and Carl van Vechten. 1913-1946.* Columbia University Press (New York) 1986

Dilworth, Thomas and Susan Holbrook (eds), *The Letters of Gertrude Stein and Virgil Thomson.* Oxford University Press (Oxford) 2010

Everett, Patricia (ed.), *A History of Having a Great Many Times not continued to be Friends. The Correspondence between Mabel Dodge and Gertrude Stein.* 1911-1934. University of New Mexico Press (Albuquerque) 1999

Gallup, Donald (ed,) *The Flowers of Friendship. Letters written to Gertrude Stein.* Alfred A. Knopf (New York) 1953

Madeline, Laurence (ed.) *Pablo Picasso. Gertrude Stein. Correspondence.* Translated by Scott-Fox Seagull Books (London, New York, Calcutta) 2008

Steward, Samuel M. (ed.) *Dear Sammy: Letters from Gertrude Stein and Alice B. Toklas.* St. Martin's Press (New York) 1984 (1977)

Other works

Benstock, Shari, *Women of the Left Bank. Paris, 1900-1940*. Virago (London) 1986

Boyd, Janet and Sharon J. Kirsch (ed.) *Primary Stein. Returning to the Writing of Gertrude Stein*. Lexington Books (Lanham, Maryland) 2014

Brinnin, John Malcolm, *The Third Rose, Gertrude Stein and Her World*. Weidenfeld & Nicolson (London) 1960

Chessman, Harriet, *Representation, the Body, and Dialogue in Gertrude Stein*. University of California Press (Berkeley) 1982

------------------------, *The Public is invited to Dance: Representation, the Body and Dialogue in Gertrude Stein*. Stanford University Press (Stanford) 1989

Cohen, Rachel *A Chance Meeting. Intertwined Lives of American Artists and Writers 1854-1967*. Jonathan Cape (London) 2004

Cope, Karin, *Passionate Collaborations. Learning to Live with Gertrude Stein*. ELS Editions (Victoria, British Columbia) 2005

Crangle, Sara, *Prosaic Desires: Modernist Knowledge, Boredom, Laughter and Anticipation* Edinburgh University Press 2010

Daniel, Lucy, *Gertrude Stein*. Reaktion Books (London) 2009

Dodge Luhan, Mabel, *Intimate Memoirs. Vol. Two: European Experiences*. Sunstone Press (Santa Fee) 2014 [1933]

Dydo, Ulla E., *Gertrude Stein: The Language That Rises: 1923-1934*. Northwestern University Press (Evanston, Illinois) 2003

Franken, Claudia *Gertrude Stein, Writer and Thinker*. (Hallenser Studien zur Anglistik und Amerikanistik; 7) LIT Verlag (Münster, Hamburg, London) 2000

Fuller, Edmund (ed.), *Journey Into the Self being the letters, papers and journals of Leo Stein*. Crown Publishers (New York) 1950

Hollister, Susannah and Emily Setina (eds.), Gertrude Stein, *Stanzas in Meditation. The Corrected Edition*. Yale University Press (New Haven and London) 2012

Horowitz, Helen Lefkowitz, *The Power and Passion of M. Carey Thomas*. Alfred A. Knopf (New York) 1994

Jaffe, Aaaron and Jonathan E. Goldmann (eds.) *Modernist Star Maps: Celebrity, Modernity, Culture*. Ashgate Publishing (Farnham) 2010

Katz, Leon, 'The First Making of the Making of Americans: A Study Based on Gertrude Stein's Notebooks and Early Versions of her Novel (1902-8) Ph.D. Columbia University, 1963

Leick, Karen, *Gertrude Stein and the Making of an American Celebrity*. Routledge (London), 2013

Linzie, Anna, *The True Story of Alice B. Toklas. A Study of Three Autobiographies*. University of Iowa Press (Iowa City) 2006

Malcolm, Janet, *Two Lives. Gertrude and Alice*. Yale University Press (New Haven and London) 2007

Meyer, Steven, *Gertrude Stein and the Correlations of Writing and Science*. Stanford University Press (Stanford, California) 2001

Nancy K. Miller (ed.) *The Poetics of Gender*. Columbia University Press (New York) 1986

Mitranto, *Gertrude Stein. Woman Without Qualities*. Ashgate (Aldershot and Burlington) 2005

Rogers, W.G., *When this you see remember me. Gertrude Stein in person*. Rinehart & Company (New York and London) 1942

Ruddick, Lisa, *Gertrude Stein, Body, Text, Gnosis*. Cornell University Press (Ithaca and London) 1990

Neuman, Shirley and Ira B. Nadel (eds.), *Gertrude Stein and the making of Literature*. Macmillan Press (Houndsmill) 1988

Showalter, Elaine *A jury of her Peers. American Women Writers from Anne Bradsteet to Annie Proulx*. Virago (London) 2009

Simon, Linda (ed.), *Gertrude Stein Remembered*. University of Nebraska Press (Lincoln and London) 1995, p.172-3

Souhami, Diana, *Gertrude and Alice*. Pandora (London) 1991

Sprigge, Elizabeth, *Gertrude Stein. Her Life and Work*. Hamish Hamilton (London) 1957

Stein, Leo, *Appreciation: Painting, Poetry and Prose*. University of Nebraska Press (London and New York) 1995

Stone, Sarah 'The Plain Edition. Gertrude Stein and modernist Book History', *Jacket 2*. 2017; https://jacket2.org/article/plain-edition

Wagner-Martin, Linda, *"Favored Strangers': Gertrude Stein and her Family*. Rutgers University Press (Brunswick, New Jersey) 1995

Watson, Steven, *Prepare for Saints. Gertrude Stein, Virgil Thomson and the Mainstreaming of American Modernism.* University of California Press (Berkeley) 2000ß

Watson, Dana Cairns, *Gertrude Stein and the Essence of What Happens.* Vanderbilt University Press (Nashville) 2005

Weininger, Otto, *Sex and Character. An Investigation of Fundamental Principles.* Translated from German (*Geschlecht und Charakter*) by Ladislaus Löb. Indiana University Press (Bloomington and Indianapolis) 2005 (1906)

Weiss, M. Lynn ,'Among Negroes: Gertrude Stein and African America', in Heather Hathaway, Josef Jarab, Jeffrey Melnar (eds.) *Race and the Modern Artist.* Oxford University Press (Oxford, New York) 2003

Will, Barbara, *Gertrude Stein, Modernism, and the Problem of 'genius'.* Edinburgh University Press (Edinburgh) 2000

------------*Unlikely Collaboration: Gertrude Stein, Bernard Faÿ, and the Vichy Dilemma.* Columbia University Press (New York) 2011

Wineapple, Brenda, *Sister Brother. Gertrude and Leo Stein.* G.P.Putnam & Sons (New York) 1996

Photo credits

Acknowledgments

I am grateful for the permission given by the Trustees of the Gertrude Stein Estate for the use of archive photographs, the Yale Collection of American Literature, Beinecke Rare Book and Manuscript Library for the material of the Gertrude Stein and Alice B. Toklas Papers, the National Portrait Gallery, Smithsonian for May Ray photographs, for Valloton: Baltimore Museum of Art; The Cone Collection, formed by Dr. Claribel Cone and Miss Etta Cone of Baltimore, Maryland.